Lorraine Hansberry

Twayne's United States Authors Series

Warren French, Editor
Indiana University, Indianapolis

TUSAS 430

LORRAINE HANSBERRY
(1930–1965)
Photograph by Gin Briggs,
courtesy of Robert Nemiroff

Lorraine Hansberry

By Anne Cheney

Virginia Polytechnic Institute and State University

Twayne Publishers • *Boston*

Lorraine Hansberry

Anne Cheney

Copyright © 1984 by G. K. Hall & Company
All Rights Reserved
Published by Twayne Publishers
A Division of G. K. Hall & Company
70 Lincoln Street
Boston, Massachusetts 02111

Book production by Marne B. Sultz

Book design by Barbara Anderson

Printed on permanent/durable acid-free
paper and bound in the United States of
America

**Library of Congress Cataloging in
Publication Data**

Cheney, Anne, 1944-
   Lorraine Hansberry.

   (Twayne's United States authors series; TUSAS 430)
   Bibliography: p. 163
   Includes index.
   1. Hansberry, Lorraine, 1930–1965—
Criticism and interpretation.
I. Title. II. Series.
PS3515.A515Z6   1984   812'.54   84-10946
ISBN 0-8057-7365-7

This book is dedicated to

Warren R. Kark, University Architect, VPI & SU
Wilson Currin Snipes, Head of the English Department, VPI & SU (1966–76)
Juanita Krentzman Snipes, Chairman of Montgomery County Democrats
(1975–81)

Contents

About the Author

Anne Cheney was born in Birmingham, Alabama, on November 1, 1944. She was educated at Birmingham-Southern College, where she studied music and English (B.A., 1966), and Florida State University (M.A., 1968, and Ph.D., 1971). Since 1968, she has taught at Virginia Polytechnic Institute and State University. She has chaired several programs on Southern literature for the Modern Language Association and has published essays in *Context,* the *Village Voice,* and the *Mississippi Quarterly.* Her first book was *Millay in Greenwich Village* (University of Alabama Press, 1975). She has three cats, Edna, Edith, and Edward. Her husband, Warren, is an architect.

Preface

Bethel Cemetery in Croton-on-Hudson, New York, lay quiet and humid the June 1978 morning I stood before the grave of Lorraine Hansberry. To the left loomed a stark white contemporary library. Just beyond the grave on a small hill rose a long-haired marble girl holding a cross with a powerful oak towering above her. Nearby were sounds of schoolchildren at play and men trimming grass. Lorraine Hansberry's monument was different. Softened by shrubs on either side, the polished black marble ascended to a crescent top. Inscribed at the top was the distinctive signature of Lorraine Hansberry; just below were the dates 1930 to 1965; further below were simple block letters, Lorraine Hansberry Nemiroff.

Superimposed on the black stone was a facade of gray marble, fashioned as an open book. Printed on these pages was a passage from *The Sign in Sidney Brustein's Window,* selected by Robert Nemiroff, her husband:

> I care. I care about it
> all. It takes too much
> energy not to care.
> . . . The *why* of why
> we are here is an
> intrigue for adolescents;
> the *how* is what must com-
> mand the living. Which is
> why I have lately become
> an insurgent again.
>
> —Lorraine Hansberry

In *Brustein* Hansberry sought to correct one of the most serious problems of her generation—the lack of commitment. Like the Wastelanders, they had become a people led by ailing Fisher Kings, searching for water and meaning, content to let the Wheel of Fortune take its course with their lives.

The lack of commitment, the search for meaning, and modern man's and woman's spirals on the Wheel of Fortune have not been unusual themes of twentieth-century American writers. Modern readers have, however, come to expect such issues in the works of white Episcopal writers, such as T.S. Eliot or Joan Didion, or lapsed Catholics, such as F. Scott Fitzgerald and Ernest Hemingway. Historically, the spiritual, social, and emotional center of black life has been the Protestant church—a truth witnessed by Frederick Douglass and Booker T. Washington, implied by Langston Hughes and Maya Angelou, satirized by James Baldwin. Granddaughter of a Tennessee bishop, Lorraine Hansberry would have seemed more within the mainstream of black American writers had she found meaning and commitment within organized religion. But Lorraine Hansberry was different. She was an outsider.

The black marble tombstone, in the midst of gray and white monuments, is the mark of an outsider. Standing in Westchester County—the haunt of the creative and the affluent—the tombstone also suggests something of the duality of Lorraine Hansberry's life and works. She was a member of the upper middle class: her parents gave her a white fur coat in the middle of the Depression; her first story dealt with football, a white middle-class sport; she studied art in Mexico. Except for a period in New York, she lived in privileged circumstances all her life. Money from her parents, her husband, and later her own work freed her from the writer's usual necessity of earning a nonliterary living. Artistic success came to her early.

Simultaneously, Lorraine Hansberry was a member of a proud, ancient race. Her remarkable father, Carl Hansberry, Sr., sought to reform racist institutions by integrating restaurants, taking a case to the Supreme Court, owning and managing real estate. His death at fifty-one was arguably caused by the strains of racism. Friends of the family—W. E. B. DuBois, Paul Robeson, Langston Hughes—provided exemplary models of the black artist to young Lorraine Hansberry.

Lorraine Hansberry never fully resolved the duality of her life and works—upper-middle-class affluence and black heritage and revolution. Not surprisingly, two of her plays deal with essentially white intellectual issues, and three of her plays treat black challenges—of increasing violence—to white society or rule. She remained an outsider in the white upper middle class because of her blackness; she was an outsider in the black community because of her affluence and education. Fortunately for American drama, she was an outsider in American society. All artists, of necessity, must distance themselves from their worlds: they observe the status quo, reject the dross, and create new, valuable works of art. *A Raisin in the Sun* (1959) was such a work, and it made Lorraine Hansberry America's greatest black playwright.

Less than a mile east of the Hudson River, Bethel Cemetery is the fitting resting place for Lorraine Hansberry. Here in Croton, she had written prolifically in the house that *Raisin* bought. Many other writers have flourished in the friendly seclusion of Westchester County—with its narrow roads, small shops, Tudor architecture.

The warm humidity of that June morning carried me back to a cold, damp evening in Tallahassee, Florida, when Lorraine Hansberry became a part of my life early in 1971. As a graduate student at Florida State University, I wrote play reviews for a local newspaper which sent me to Florida A&M University to cover a "touring company from New York." As *To Be Young, Gifted and Black* unfolded, I was enchanted by Tina Sattin's portrayal of Lorraine Hansberry, mesmerized by the kaleidoscope of black experiences, electrified by the audience's response. Only my first reading of Eliot's *The Waste Land* and Conrad's *Lord Jim* rivaled this initiation. I could not write the review: Lorraine Hansberry was too cosmic for two typewritten pages. The editor did not understand and fired me.

Two months later, on March 8, 1971, Dr. Fred Standley introduced a guest speaker at Florida State: Dr. Darwin T. Turner would present an overview of black writers. He spoke of Frederick Douglass, Sojourner Truth, Jean Toomer, Langston Hughes, Angelina Grimké, but the last name especially intrigued me—Lorraine Hansberry. Drs. Fred and Nancy Standley had invited me to a reception afterwards at their home, where I cornered the guest of honor for an hour. I thank Dr. Turner for asserting that someone must write a book on Hansberry and regret that we met only briefly after that night.

When I returned to Blacksburg, Virginia, in the fall of 1971, Lorraine Hansberry became a permanent part of my life when my good friend Jeff Clare tracked down the address of Robert Nemiroff. Later, Nemiroff loaned me uncollected and unpublished works; he introduced me to the Schomburg Collection; he arranged my meeting with Mamie Hansberry Mitchell; he booked me tickets for the Washington tryout of the musical *Raisin,* which won the Tony on Broadway in 1973. The ideas and interpretations in this final manuscript, however, are appropriately mine alone. One evening in Croton, Robert Nemiroff was weary after a long day in Manhattan. I asked him why he had included a passage in *Young, Gifted and Black.* He replied: "I am trying to keep Lorraine's work alive." On a smaller scale, I have tried to do the same.

This book is the first full-length study of Lorraine Hansberry, which chronicles her childhood in Chicago, her youth in Wisconsin, her maturity in New York. To understand her life more fully, I interviewed Robert Nemiroff many times from our first meeting on June 15, 1972, until our last on June 15, 1978, and corresponded with him frequently during this six-year period. I also spent a week in 1975 in Marina del Rey, California, with Mamie Hansberry Mitchell, who provided more biographical data from the perspective of a loving sister. To understand her works more thoroughly, I immersed myself in the major figures of the Harlem Renaissance before I analyzed Hansberry's six plays. In *The Crisis of the Negro Intellectual,* Harold Cruse cites several of Hansberry's *Freedom* articles. I went to the Schomburg Collection in the Harlem Branch of the New York Public Library to read Hansberry's extant *Freedom* articles. The final original feature of this study is that I have included the substance of all these articles in this book.

Ideally, this book will spark a revival of Hansberry scholarship as well as renewed interest in her work. Dr. Margaret B. Wilkerson is now writing an in-depth critical biography with full access to the Hansberry papers. Robert Nemiroff plans to publish her short stories, unfinished plays, novel, and other miscellaneous pieces. Other work, however, remains. A scholar in the Chicago area could easily investigate her formative period (1930–1950), clarifying her years at the three grammar schools and Englewood High School. Mr. Carl Hansberry, Sr., would yield a fascinating study of black politics and finance. Harold Issac's fine initial research on Hansberry's African heritage (*Phylon,* 1961) could be pursued. A scholar of her mature period (1950–1965) should interview Ossie Davis, Ruby Dee, Dorothy Secules (who lived at 112 Waverly Place in 1965), Gin Briggs, Alice Childress, James Baldwin, her college housemate Edythe, Shelley Winters, Nina Simone, Lloyd Richards, Shauneille Perry, and Perry Hansberry, Sr. (who refused to talk with me). American literature may then unveil a finished portrait of the artist as a young woman.

Anne Cheney

Virginia Polytechnic Institute
and State University

Acknowledgments

My Blacksburg, Virginia, friends and colleagues have made substantial contributions to this study. I especially wish to thank Mrs. Hazel Hubbard and Mrs. Anita Malebranche of the Newman Library; Dr. Thomas C. Howard for his advice on African History, Dr. J. Dean O'Donnell, Jr., and Dr. G. G. Williamson, Jr., all of the Department of History. My leave of absence was made possible by the administrative support of Provost John D. Wilson, Assistant Provost Ronald Nurse, Dean Max H. Kele (now of Bradley University), and Dean Laura Jane Harper. I am also indebted to Ms. Sandy Graham, an exemplary work/study student; Mrs. Jeane Yongue, director of Upward Bound; Mr. Jeff Clare of Prodesign. The Department of English is always challenging and supportive. I appreciate the leadership of Dr. Wilson C. Snipes and Dr. Hilbert H. Campbell and the professional help of Dr. David D. Britt, Dr. Christopher Clausen, H.R.H. Nancy Clausen, Dr. Ali Isani, Dr. Charles E. Modlin, Dr. Edward Tucker, and Ms. Renée Walsh.

Several writers and scholars have made important contributions: Dr. Virginia Spencer Carr and Ms. Maxine Brown; Mr. and Mrs. Jesse Hill Ford; Dr. Fred Standley and Dr. Claude Flory of Florida State University; Dr. J. Lee Greene of the University of North Carolina; and Dr. Frank C. Weightman of Memphis State University. I am indebted to Warren French for editing this book and to Bill Riley for his copy editing. On a more personal level, I wish to thank Dr. Mary Ann Brown and Ms. Ann Rutledge; Mr. Hubert A. Grissom, Birmingham attorney and writer; my parents, Billie and Alan Cheney of Allgood, Alabama; my sisters and brothers and their families, Celia, Lydia, Rebecca, Alan, John, Edith, and Lewis; and particularly, Warren R. Kark, AIA.

I wish to thank Hansberry friends and experts, including Mr. Robert Nemiroff and Dr. Jewell Gresham and the endlessly charming Mrs. Mamie Hansberry Mitchell. I also appreciate the help of Mrs. Pulliam, librarian of the Lorraine Hansberry Child/Parent Center in Chicago; Mrs. B. Franklin, records clerk of Englewood High School in Chicago; Dr. Carol H. Tarr of the University of Wisconsin; Dr. Forrest L. Ingram, head of English and Communications at Roosevelt University; Mr. Paul Robeson,

Jr.; Mrs. Jean Blackwell Hutson, past director of the Schomburg Collection.

Robert Nemiroff has granted permission to quote certain materials and has stipulated that they be cited as follows:

Acknowledgments

"No More Hiroshimas" by Lorraine Hansberry, copyright 1955 by Freedom Associates, Inc. All rights reserved.

"Playwrighting: Creative Constructiveness" by Lorraine Hansberry, © 1963 by the American Academy of Psychotherapists. All rights reserved.

"Thoughts on Genet, Mailer and the New Paternalism," © 1961 by Robert Nemiroff as Executor of the Estate of Lorraine Hansberry. All rights reserved.

All previously unpublished quotes of Lorraine Hansberry and Robert Nemiroff © 1984 by Robert Nemiroff. All rights reserved.

Chronology

1930   Lorraine Vivian Hansberry, second daughter of Nannie Perry Hansberry and Carl Augustus Hansberry, born in Chicago, May 19. Older brothers, Carl, Jr., and Perry. Older sister, Mamie.

1935   Parents give her white fur coat for Christmas present in middle of the depression. Is beaten up by classmates at school.

1938   Hansberrys buy home in white neighborhood. Hostile neighbors gather and throw brick, which barely misses Lorraine, through window. Black family friends help guard Hansberry house (genesis of *A Raisin in the Sun*). Family is evicted by Illinois courts. Carl Hansberry, Sr., and NAACP lawyers appeal case in federal courts.

1940   Mother and Mamie begin to find letters written to public officials in untidy room. Reads poetry of Langston Hughes. Father wins Supreme Court decision which prohibits racial restrictive covenants.

1944   Enters Englewood High School. Excels in English and history. Writes story about football and wins school prize. Sees *Dark of the Moon*.

1946   Carl Hansberry, Sr., dies of cerebral hemorrhage in Mexico.

1946–1948   Elected president of high school debating society. Impressed by poorer black students' resistance to racial discrimination. Sees *The Tempest* and *Othello* (starring Paul Robeson at pinnacle of his popularity). Prof. William Leo Hansberry (uncle), Langston Hughes, Dr. W. E. B. DuBois, Duke Ellington, Paul Robeson, and other luminaries visit Hansberry home.

1948–1949   Graduates from Englewood High School, January of 1948. Enters University of Wisconsin, February. Studies art, geology, stage design, and English. Sees *Juno and the Paycock*. Active in Henry Wallace campaign. Becomes chairman of

Young Progressives of America. In summer of 1949, attends University of Guadalajara art workshop in Ajijic, Mexico.

1950   Leaves University of Wisconsin permanently, February. In fall, moves to New York. Writes for Young Progressives of America magazine. Attends classes at the New School for Social Research. First learns about Marcus Garvey. Hansberry Enterprises (family business) continues to have problems with Richard Daley and Chicago machine.

1951   Begins to work full time for *Freedom* magazine. Meets Robert Nemiroff on picket line at New York University, where he is a student. In spring, flies with delegation of women to Jackson, Mississippi, to try to stop execution of young black man, Willie McGee. In summer, covers Communist trials in Foley Square. In fall, travels to Washington, D.C., for Sojourners for Truth Conference. In December, writes pageant on history of Negro newspapers for 1,500 Harlemites.

1952   Becomes associate editor of *Freedom*. Teaches classes at Frederick Douglass School. Flies to Montevideo, Uruguay, to deliver speech to banned peace congress for Paul Robeson, whose passport is revoked, in March. Her passport is revoked.

1953   Marries Robert Nemiroff on June 20, 1953, in Chicago. Quits job at *Freedom* but continues to contribute shorter articles. Studies African history under Dr. DuBois. Teaches black literature at Jefferson School of Social Science. Hansberry and Nemiroff live in apartment at 337 Bleecker Street in Greenwich Village.

1953–1956   Works full-time at sequence of various jobs. Writes dramatic script for second Harlem rally, "Pulse of the Peoples: A Cultural Salute to Paul Robeson," in May 1954. Nemiroff works part-time for Avon Books.

1956   Begins *A Raisin in the Sun*. In August, Nemiroff's song, "Cindy, Oh, Cindy," released and becomes a hit. Hansberry now free to write full time.

1957   Reads first draft of *Raisin* to Philip Rose.

1959   January and February, *Raisin* tryouts in New Haven, Philadelphia, and Chicago. On March 11, play opens to popular and critical acclaim on Broadway. Wins New York Drama Critics' Circle Award over plays by Williams, O'Neill, and MacLeish. Meets James Baldwin. Buys and moves to 112 Waverly Place, a brownstone in Greenwich Village. Commissioned by NBC to write *The Drinking Gourd*. First draft of screenplay of *Raisin*.

1960   Completes *Raisin* screenplay and *Drinking Gourd*. Begins *Les Blancs*, *The Sign in Sidney Brustein's Window* (originally entitled *The Sign in Jenny Reed's Window*), and several other works, never completed. Hansberry family moves from Chicago to Los Angeles.

1961   Movie version of *Raisin* wins Cannes Film Festival award. Hansberry/Mailer exchange in Village Voice during May and June. Conceives idea for *What Use Are Flowers?* in December.

1962   Completes *Flowers* (never produced). Increasingly involved in SNCC and support activities for Southern freedom movement. In August, Hansberry and Nemiroff move to Croton-on-Hudson.

1963   Becomes ill in April. May 24, challenges Attorney General Robert Kennedy on civil rights. In June, operation reveals cancer of the duodenum. In August, second operation in Boston. Meets Malcom X.

1964   March 10, Hansberry and Nemiroff obtain Mexican divorce, but continue collaboration. Writes *The Movement: Documentary of a Struggle for Equality*. September 28, names Nemiroff her literary executor in will. *The Sign in Sidney Brustein's Window* opens on Broadway, October 15.

1965   Dies on January 12. Funeral in Harlem on January 15.

1966   Mrs. Hansberry dies.

1967   "Lorraine Hansberry in Her Own Words," a WBAI radio tribute broadcast in New York, Los Angeles, San Francisco.

1969   *To Be Young, Gifted and Black* opens at Cherry Lane Theater, New York.

1970   *Les Blancs*, completed by Nemiroff, opens on Broadway.

1970–1972   National tour of *To Be Young, Gifted and Black*.

1972   Nemiroff edits and publishes *Les Blancs: The Collected Last Plays of Lorraine Hansberry* (also includes *The Drinking Gourd* and *What Use Are Flowers?*).

1973   Nemiroff produces *Raisin,* based on *Raisin in the Sun,* which wins Tony for best Broadway musical.

1976   *Lorraine Hansberry* (documentary film) written and produced by Ralph J. Tangney.

1979   *Lorraine Hansberry: Art of Thunder, Vision of Light,* a "special retrospective issue," published by magazine, *Freedomways.*

Chapter One

White Fur and Football in the Depression

Leaves were turning brown and gold and the air was crisp outside the Hansberry home at 5936 South Park Way (now Martin Luther King Drive) in Chicago. A young man walked up the sidewalk, rang the doorbell, and was greeted by a pudgy, serious fourteen-year-old girl, who led him into the living room. Her ever popular, pretty older sister Mamie would be ready for her date in a few minutes. Everyone knew that being on time for a date in 1944 was gauche. In the thirty minutes' wait, Lorraine Hansberry asked questions and listened to her sister's beau. He, like most middle-class young men in autumn, was fascinated by football.

A few hours later, Lorraine Hansberry went to her room, and began to write. She had never seen a football game; she did not even particularly care for sports. But the vibrant colors of football pennants, sounds of the cheering crowds, smells of fresh popcorn and spilled drinks, whistles and mechanical hands and arms of the referees, and the fluid runs and passes of the football players seemed to flow onto her writing pad. On Monday morning, she shyly gave the story to her English teacher. A month later at Englewood High School, the principal announced that Lorraine Hansberry's football story had won an award. Her classmates were astounded. This fat, bookish, rich girl—this outsider—had captured a coveted prize.[1] For the first of many times, her imagination had seized the raw clay of an idea and sculpted it into a work of art.

Chicago Childhood

Lorraine Vivian Hansberry was born on May 19, 1930, to Nannie Perry Hansberry and Carl Augustus Hansberry in Provident Hospital at 16 W. 36th Street in Chicago. On Lorraine's birth certificate, Mr. Hansberry listed his occupation as U.S. deputy marshall and Mrs. Hansberry as ward committeeman of the Republican party.[2]

Natives of the South, Carl and Nannie Hansberry had been reared in educated, cultured homes. Carl Hansberry was born in Gloster, Mississippi, to two teachers, who occupied respectable and comfortable positions in the black community. The Reverend Mr. Perry had risen to the position of bishop[3] and sent his daughter Nannie, born in Columbia, to nearby Tennessee State University at a time when education was not commonly valued for women of any race. Shortly after Carl Hansberry moved north to Chicago, he became an accountant for Binga National Bank, the first black bank in Chicago. He then founded a bank of his own and married Nannie Perry, who worked as a teller at his Lake Street Bank.[4] Throughout his life, Carl Hansberry displayed talents for finance, law, invention, and social and political action—gifts he bequeathed variously to his four children.

At first the young Hansberry couple could only afford to live in one room, but they began to prosper when he put his considerable financial talents to use. His shrewd real-estate investments, especially in Chicago's lakeside property, further enhanced their material well-being. His experience with a one-room apartment taught him how to make existing properties more valuable, as his daughter Mamie Hansberry Mitchell explained:

He [Carl Hansberry] struck upon the idea of the kitchenette. When he got an opportunity to buy a piece of property, he put little stoves and sinks into each one or two bedrooms, and this is a kitchenette. . . . He made quite a fortune during the depression because the white landlord simply couldn't collect the rent, and he could.

Things just grew from there. Most people were going broke. He was making quite a lot of money and set up our business. We had a maintenance crew and housekeepers, and his half-sister came as a secretary and my mother's niece was secretary and his half-brother was collector. He'd have to go collect from all the buildings from the housekeepers, and the housekeepers would collect the rest . . . [from the tenants]. That grew and grew and things got better and better.[5]

By the time Lorraine was born, at the beginning of the depression, their neighbors considered the Hansberrys wealthy and benevolent.

The Hansberrys took the new baby home to 5330 Calumet Avenue on Chicago's South Side. The older children—Carl, Jr., Perry, and Mamie—were at first fascinated by their new sister, but seven years separated Lorraine from the youngest of her siblings, and after two or three years they began to regard Lorraine as a nuisance. As an adult, Lorraine recalled, "By the time you are five you are a pest that has to be attended to in the washroom, taken to the movies and 'sat with' at night."[6] Even as a kindergarten student, Lorraine had become an outsider who listened and observed care-fully—traits that would later benefit her as a writer. On a few steamy sum-mer nights in Chicago, the Hansberrys piled their children into their car, drove to the park, and spread blankets on the moist grass. Drawing on his southern heritage, Mr. Hansberry would tell stories of his childhood and muse about the distant stars until the family fell asleep.[7]

Carl and Nannie Hansberry had a pride and dignity in their bearing that made a lifelong impression on their children. At the same time, they were a loving, passionate people, as Mamie explained:

[Mother] was a very erect person and spoke with authority in a soft manner. I tended to think in terms of her as tall. She was always dressed; she was not a casual type person and always in her high heels the first thing in the morning and dressed as if she were going shopping. She just gave you the feeling—Dad did too, be-cause he was an average height, he wasn't a tall man—so they both gave you the feeling of being tall and stately.

Daddy . . . called mother honey, it came out like honey dew. . . . He was a gentle, came off as a gentle, mild-mannered person, very gentlemanly. He never used profane language in our presence. The best Mother ever could get out was when something burned her finger . . . was "dammit to hell." Then you knew she was really mad. They lived a very good life.[8]

On her fifth Christmas morning, Lorraine tore open the largest package, from her adoring parents, removed the white tissue paper, and discovered a gift which stunned, then outraged her. Her parents had given her a white ermine coat in the middle of the Depression. The grown-ups sighed, fon-dled the soft fur, and insisted that Lorraine try it on over her pajamas. Decked out in pajamas, fur coat, muff, and small hat, she paraded for the adults and walked to the hall mirror. She looked like one of those huge stupid rabbits in her coloring book.

Lorraine Hansberry was sent to school several mornings later in her new coat. Her classmates—who ate bologna sandwiches on white bread, whose mothers worked twelve hours daily or lay ill on a mattress on the floor, whose homes were bare, rugless, poorly lighted—assailed her with fists, curses, and inkwells. For weeks afterward, she could expect a crowd of children, ready to spring on her with sharp blows and open hands, flinging insults and the upstart child to the sidewalk. Even as a five-year-old, Lor-raine Hansberry somehow understood their hostility to shows of wealth, their rejection of her as an outsider. She respected their courage, their fight. The white coat was ruined, but Lorraine gained an admiration for these rebels, for Carmen Smith, who refused to be embarrassed, who refused to apologize for her poverty.[9]

During her years at Betsy Ross Grammar School, Lorraine made her strongest alliances with the very children who had destroyed her white fur coat. She especially admired the independent and determined Carmen Smith, who had her own key to her family's apartment with no curtains or carpets, and who came and went as she wished. Although the school building was relatively well designed and modern, classrooms were overcrowded and teachers were pressed to find time for individual students. (Lorraine later observed similar conditions in Harlem schools when she wrote for *Freedom* in the 1950s.) Consequently, Lorraine could not compute the simplest arithmetic even as an adult, but she could read at a college level by the sixth grade.[10] The Hansberrys had a fine family library, replete with world classics, works of black writers, and an encyclopedia. By the time she was ten, Lorraine Hansberry had chosen Toussaint L'Ouverture and Hannibal as her "heroes" and Pearl Buck as her favorite writer.

By 1938, the Hansberrys were becoming cramped in their home. According to Robert Nemiroff, the Hansberrys lived in at least three different apartments after they left Calumet Avenue. In the last apartment, otherwise all white, trouble with the landlord and neighbors culminated in yellow paint being poured all over their car. Carl Hansberry then decided "to go the whole hog," to buy a house.[11] After examining real estate in many areas of the city, Mr. Hansberry finally settled on a house in a predominantly white community. Later, Lorraine Hansberry described this area as "to put it mildly, a very hostile neighborhood."[12] The following incident could have provided the germ of *A Raisin in the Sun*. One day Mamie and Lorraine were sitting on the porch, swinging their legs, when a mob gathered. When the girls went inside to the living room, a brick came crashing through the window with such impact that it implanted itself in the wall.[13] Narrowly missing eight-year-old Lorraine Hansberry, the brick could well have killed her.[14] Published sources do not clarify whether or not this mob represented the entire neighborhood or a few racists.[15]

One summer in the late 1930s, when Mrs. Hansberry drove her children to their grandmother Perry's home in Tennessee, Lorraine was surprised that her grandmother was no longer the great beauty everyone remembered but a wrinkled, nearsighted old lady rocking in her caneback chair. Still the child relished the old lady's cornbread cupcakes as much as the older woman delighted in riding in the family's new car. She listened to her mother and grandmother speak of earlier times in the rolling hills. She heard how her grandfather Perry had run away and hidden from his master in these very hills. His mother had wandered into the moonlight and left food for him in hidden places. One question continued to haunt young Lorraine: what might a "master" be?[16] Many years later, she was to answer this question in *The Drinking Gourd*. During the 1930s, Mr. Hansberry began to plan a campaign for Congress.[17] Raising contributions in the community, adding his own personal funds, walking and talking door to door, Carl Hansberry passed out fliers, cards, and leaflets. He was a staunch Republican who totally embraced the free enterprise system. But Chicago was, and still is, a heavily Democratic city. He was trounced by his opponent in the November 1940 election.

Lorraine Hansberry left Betsy Ross and looked forward to her freshman year at Englewood High School with a love of literature and a historical and philosophical curiosity beyond her years. By the time she was fourteen, she had an enduring set of attitudes molded from her parents' values. The Hansberry children were expected to attend college. Self-respecting people did not indulge in aimless self-discovery: they worked or they went to school. While in elementary school, Lorraine had decided she would study at Howard University, which Mamie attended, or at the University of Wisconsin.[18] She was a descendant of a proud race, and she must never betray the race or the family. Life was not difficult, and one succeeded as a matter of course. And the only sinful people were—*dull* people.[19]

Lorraine Hansberry sensed that she had inherited the natural drive and talent of her remarkable family. Her parents, her sister Mamie, the children of the poor—all knew that Lorraine Hansberry was young, gifted, and black.

Englewood Adolescence

Entering Englewood High School in the fall of 1944, Lorraine Hansberry found herself surrounded by unfamiliar faces—black, white, East Indian[20]—yet longed for the intimacy of her classmates at Betsy Ross and her family. She would soon know the "strange and bewigged teacher . . . Pale Hecate,"[21] whose adoration for Shakespeare and disdain for underachievers greatly amused her students. Lorraine Hansberry would write her football story. No longer the "adorable" child dressed in white fur, she had become an overweight adolescent. Her sister Mamie was kind enough not to point out that she expanded three dress sizes.[22] Brighter than most, she would sometimes slight those subjects that bored her, but she embraced English and history. At times, she felt lonely, clumsy—an outsider.

As the younger sister of glamorous Mamie, Lorraine Hansberry became less and less gregarious, often retiring to her room to read, to write free-verse poems about winter landscapes, industrial skylines of Chicago, elevated trains. But her poetry also meandered into fanciful dreams of clouds, existence, and love.[23] Just as these poems came to young Lorraine, fresh-faced young men began to call at South Park Way—for the younger sister. Chaperoned by parents, Lorraine and her dates usually went to school dances or games.

One winter night, Lorraine Hansberry and her date were riding to the theater. For the first time, she would see a real play, Howard Richardson and William Berney's "folk musical," *Dark of the Moon*. When the curtain rose and the lights faded in on the backdrops of the Smoky Mountains, she became entranced by John, the witchboy, and his ill-fated love for Barbara Allen, whom he met and loved in the dark of the moon.[24] The evening was full of magic: Conjureman and Conjurewoman, low clouds and hoot-owls, dark witches, the witchboy and Barbara's dark baby with arms curled like a bear, astrology, mountain folk, their love and religion. There was music and dancing, lighting and sets, and actors and actresses. The theater had cast its spell.

Other dates to plays were soon to follow. She marveled at the majesty of Othello, the noble Moor, who "loved not wisely but too well." Enchanted by Ariel's songs in *The Tempest* she still suffered with the enslaved Caliban, prisoner in the brave new world.[25] She went on at her friends about mountain folk, Desdemona dying, Miranda playing chess with her love. "Theatricality,"[26] she called it.

Family Friends

Just as *Dark of the Moon* had roused Lorraine Hansberry from her adolescent ennui, the visitors at South Park Way excited her young creative imagination. The Hansberry home had long been a mecca for black leaders in the arts, society, and politics.[27] One of the most distinguished visitors was Dr. W. E. B. DuBois; his classic *The Souls of Black Folk* (1903), one of the books in the Hansberry library, rejected Booker T. Washington's theory that blacks should placate whites by learning trades rather than history or philosophy.[28] Lorraine found DuBois fascinating; he believed the superior "talented tenth"[29] should lead the black working class. Dr. DuBois, Mamie Hansberry Mitchell explains, "was a great favorite of my father."[30] At times the two men would disappear for hours into the library, oblivious to food, gaiety, and the other guests.

Warm, amber-skinned, and unpretentious, Langston Hughes was another frequent guest at the Hansberry home.[31] Here he was always pleased to see his old friend DuBois, who as editor of the NAACP's *Crisis* magazine had published his first poem in the 1920s.[32] While he respected DuBois's analytical, political mind, Hughes himself was more the intuitive artist, the chronicler of the "common man."[33] As a young man in Harlem, he had captured the spirit of the Jazz Age in his poems about flappers, jazz musicians, brass spittoons. Now forty-two, he wrote poems of dreams deferred, drying up like "a raisin in the Sun," of the "ancient, dusky rivers" of Africa. Lorraine would slip into the library to read more— a mother telling her son to keep on climbing even if "life . . . ain't been no crystal stair."[34] He made the most ordinary people—matter.

In the fall of 1944, Paul Robeson, was touring America, starring in the Broadway production of *Othello.*[35] At forty-six, this internationally famous actor and singer had the humility of the great and the gentleness of many large men (he had lettered in football at Rutgers University). Famous for his exceptional, rich baritone, Robeson sang Negro spirituals, arias, roles in *Show Boat* and other musicals, solos from *The Emperor Jones* and other movies. Her parents told her that his *Othello* had been on Broadway longer than any Shakespearean play before. (Mamie Hansberry Mitchell said that Robeson visited the Hansberry home, but Robert Nemiroff and Perry Hansberry do not recall the decade—1940s or 1950s.)[36]

Over the years, Robeson's reputation as artist had become fused with his role as the defender of the oppressed. He shared DuBois's and Hughes's vendetta against American racism, but he also supported various Jewish and left-wing causes. In England he had met Jomo Kenyatta and Kwame Nkrumah, and from them learned details of black Africa's struggle for freedom from European rule. During his frequent travels to the Soviet Union, he began to admire the people, language, and government.[37] Robeson's enchantment with socialism sometimes troubled Carl Hansberry, Sr., who still believed racism could be cured within the free-enterprise system. Robeson's problems, however, with the House Committee on Un-American Activities and at Peekskill, New York, were yet to come. In 1944, he had reached the pinnacle of his career and popularity.

Few young people are able to appreciate the opportunity of such distinguished company in their homes. Despite her shyness, Lorraine Hansberry could not resist the magnetic power of these artists and leaders. Developing a lifelong respect for Langston Hughes and his poetry, she began to hear the rhythms and melodies of the common man, his dissonance with white society, his basic harmony with the family. "Mother to Son," especially, was a theme to which she would add her own variations years later in *A Raisin in the Sun*. Also at this early age, Lorraine Hansberry first witnessed in Paul Robeson the possible union of politics and art. For the time being, these men were familiar presences, friends of the family. Later on, they became something more—intellectual influences on a writer who was having difficulty reconciling the fact of her blackness with the equally plain fact of her privileged upbringing.

Death of a Father

As spring came to Chicago in 1945, Lorraine Hansberry had gained confidence in her studies and renewed zest for life. She even thought she might like to write a play some day. At the same time, the family was becoming excited about a trip to Mexico. Over the years, her parents had become friends with an influential general and manufacturer who had visited them in Chicago.[38] This dignitary and his wife were pleased when the Hansberrys finally bought a home in Polanco, a suburb of Mexico City, where they planned to retire.[39] The family hoped that the climate would lower Mr. Hansberry's blood pressure and generally improve his failing health. Mexico was special for an even more important reason. As Mamie explains, "Even though he would win his scrimmages and restaurants were opening up. . . . there was still a great deal more that he could see [of racism]. He was becoming discouraged. . . . Daddy . . . loved Mexico. . . . He said for the first time in his life he felt very free. He felt like a full man."[40]

After her parents were in Mexico, Lorraine Hansberry was glad to see her father relaxed and healthy. She began to understand fully what a truly remarkable man he was. He had absorbed Illinois law and written lucid abstracts in little booklets. He had invented pumps and railroad devices. He was a self-tutored expert on American history. He had won a Supreme Court decision concerning "restrictive covenants." He was rightfully a proud man with an "educated soul."[41]

One warm day shortly before her sixteenth birthday, Lorraine Hansberry was thrust back into the insecurities of adolescence. Writing and painting suddenly became unimportant. At the age of fifty-one, Carl Hansberry dropped dead of a cerebral hemorrhage.[42]

The full impact of a father's death on a fifteen-year-old girl cannot be measured. Later, however, Lorraine asserted that "American racism helped kill him,"[43] a sentiment shared by Mamie.[44] As the years wore on, she certainly grew to question the Republican party, the free-enterprise system, American justice, the possibility of democracy. Those things that he cherished, she perhaps thought, did not rescue him in the end.

After Mrs. Hansberry moved back to Chicago, Lorraine Hansberry gradually began to reexamine her views of family members. In an unpublished memoir, she described her mother as a "vain and intensely feminine person . . . that . . . the Southland alone can thrust upon the world." Mrs. Hansberry believed the family should go to church (recalling her Southern sense of ritual), but she did not allow God to "intrude" in everyday life. Describing her as a "product of robust semi-feudal backwardness," Lorraine still conceded that her mother's great gift was her incapacity for "slighting true improvement."[45] With time, Lorraine Hansberry's image of her mother mellowed.

As her final year at Englewood High School began, Lorraine Hansberry saw her Uncle Leo as a more fascinating man than she had in years before. As a professor of African studies at Howard University, William Leo Hansberry had not always lived up to Carl Hansberry's notion of a practical, aggressive man. Now her uncle's references to Ghana, Mali, and Songhay intrigued Lorraine.[46] Well-respected in his field, Leo Hansberry did not shrink from controversial ideas; he believed that the Nordic race was descended from "more or less Negroid stock." Years before pride in African heritage recaptured the popular fancy (this feeling diminished after the Harlem Renaissance), Uncle Leo insisted on the existence of prehistoric man in Africa. Far from being the "Dark Continent," Africa was the "Continent of Light," bejeweled with diamonds, gold, cobalt, and uranium, glowing with the patina of an ancient, complex civilization.[47] Uncle Leo made Lorraine wonder about these men Kwame Nkrumah and Jomo Kenyatta. What did Africa mean to a young woman in Chicago? Years later, she would not be surprised when the University of Nigeria named a college after her uncle.

Graduation day finally arrived in January 1948. Lorraine Hansberry knew that Mamie would be over that afternoon, checking her hair, her hemline, her smile. Her brothers and their families would try to come tonight. Mrs. Hansberry smiled quietly over her "baby's" success, although she had not distinguished herself in every subject. Lorraine felt as though she were preparing for a long trip—excited over new sights and sounds, yet already nostalgic for people and places left behind.

The time had come for Lorraine Hansberry to move beyond adolescence. Much thinner than she had been, she desperately missed her father but was becoming more tolerant of her beautiful mother. In the past four years, she had reveled in plays, Langston Hughes, the blues, the first kiss. Despite

Pale Hecate, she had learned to love Shakespeare. She had been the center of some groups—president of forum and secretary of her gym class[48]—but usually she had been on the periphery, absorbing impressions and preparing for a future that was gaining definition. A month after graduation from Englewood, she began the first stage of her adult life.

Wisconsin Awakening

As Perry and Mamie drove her the hundred miles from Chicago to Madison, Wisconsin, Lorraine Hansberry let her eyes and thoughts wander across the level winter land. In *Young, Gifted and Black,* Hansberry stresses that snow was beautiful, so clean and soft it blanketed minor flaws, yet so pristine it highlighted black trees, straight pines, and major imperfections. Catching the lilt of Mamie's chatter, Lorraine recalled her sister's understanding about Howard: she simply could not fit the social pattern cut by her older sister. Wisconsin was a prominent national university. A white university, but a Hansberry would not shrink from *that.* Still, she wished there had been a room in the dormitory.[49] Unfortunately, university administrators could not provide on-campus housing for black students at that time—in 1948—on most campuses. From that point on, Lorraine remained overwhelmed by the bigness of the campus.

Hours later when her brother and sister drove away from Langdon Manor, Lorraine Hansberry walked back into the large, two-story residence. There were Midwestern farm girls, New York girls, two Oriental girls, even one from Australia.[50] She went back to her room, hoping to read, write, or sketch a bit before bedtime. Classes began in the morning. She searched through her closet, trying to remember what Mamie had told her to wear. Drifting off to sleep, she felt happy and hopeful about her professors, her classes. No longer the "kid sister," she was a young woman about to discover new ideas, new worlds.

The next few months of the Wisconsin awakening passed quickly for Lorraine Hansberry outside the classroom. She and her best friend, Edythe, enjoyed discussion late into the night, their rooms bluing with smoke, filling with talk of politics, fascism, the meaning of life, God, boys.[51] She continued her painting and sketched a line drawing of herself on the want-ad page of the newspaper.[52] She drew a stark, yet slightly blurred, portrait of a man lynched;[53] she began to experiment with sculpture.[54] Required freshman courses left little time for writing.

Just before her eighteenth birthday, she wandered into the university theater one afternoon, never suspecting that the next three hours, during which she saw a production of Sean O'Casey's *Juno and the Paycock,* would eventually change her life. "The Irish wail" somehow recalled the pains of her own people. Later Lorraine Hansberry wrote, "It [*Juno*] entered my consciousness and stayed there. . . ."[55]

After a restful summer at home in Chicago, Lorraine Hansberry returned to the frenzy that marks all fall college terms. This fall, however, was marked by a concern larger than university life—Republican Thomas E. Dewey was challenging Democrat Harry S. Truman for the presidency of the United States. Lorraine Hansberry, however, decided to support the third-party candidate—Henry Wallace of the Progressive party. She was elected campus chairman of the Young Progressives of America. After Wallace's loss in November 1948, however, her interest in political parties waned.[56] Perhaps, she thought, this was the system that enjoyed her father's loyalty, that betrayed him. Her casual friendships with young radicals at Wisconsin probably extinguished the sparks of the reformer while fanning the slow fire of the young revolutionary.

As her freshman year drew to a close, Lorraine Hansberry had found little of the enlightenment she had expected in the classroom. She particularly disliked physical geography, a course that included a laboratory four hours a week, or "knocking on rocks with a little metal hammer. . . ." (Not surprisingly, she failed the class.) Life Drawing 101 and Fine Arts 3 were much more tolerable, but mathematics and sciences had always been difficult for her. Her courses in literature, history, and philosophy were exciting.[57] When A's and F's were tallied, however, her grades were just good enough for her to enter her sophomore year, her last year.[58]

During winter 1949 and early 1950, Lorraine Hansberry continued to escape to her old haunt—the university theater. Just as she absorbed O'Casey, she studied Strindberg and Ibsen—their defiant, oppressed women; their guarded marriages and illicit unions, their naturalistic, Scandinavian settings. Later she wrote of this time: "I was intrigued by the theatre. Mine was the same old story—sort of hanging around little acting groups, and developing the feeling that the theatre embraces everything I like all at one time.[59]

Her final year at Wisconsin was an academic disappointment. Robert Nemiroff recalls that one professor assigned Lorraine a D in a course dealing with set design. Even though the professor considered her work above average, he did not want to encourage a young black woman in a field dominated by whites, or so he said.[60] Outside the classroom, she read Jomo Kenyatta's *Facing Mount Kenya,*[61] Dr. DuBois's *Black Folk Then and Now,*[62] and many other books on African culture. Kwame Nkrumah of

Ghana, she discovered a year later, had visited Uncle Leo's home near Howard when Nkrumah was a student.[63] Poring over maps of Africa, she imagined faces, rhythms, movements of the Kikuyu, Ashanti, Yoruba, Mandingo peoples—"ancient cousins of hers."[64]

When Lorraine Hansberry told Mamie that she wanted to leave Wisconsin, the entire family was surprisingly sympathetic. Carl, Jr., Perry, and Mamie were carrying on the family business that their father had worked so hard to build. They had acquired new properties and maintained the respect of the families who rented from them. Perry was especially popular for helping renters with unreasonable creditors and merchants. Nevertheless, they had problems with the white political machine. Once Mamie went with her brother Carl to pay off a corrupt city official with "hard-earned black money"—$1,500. Much later, Hansberry Enterprises filed a million-dollar suit against Mayor Daley and the City of Chicago.[65] Although Lorraine fully understood the racial implications of these dealings, she could never share the family's enthusiasm for business matters.

As the time came for her to pack her bags and leave her room at Langdon Manor, Lorraine Hansberry knew she would miss Edythe, her other "house mates," and the young African men who had come to call. These days would serve as the basis of one section of her autobiographical novel, *All the Dark and Beautiful Warriors,* in which Lorraine becomes Candace. (Eventually, Robert Nemiroff plans to publish the total unfinished manuscript.)[66] Candace worries about her pregnant, unmarried roommate, her own African boy friend Monasse, and how to lure this "gorgeous black knight-without armor" into bed. Ostensibly, Candace brought the young man "into the twentieth century."[67]

A month or so later, Lorraine Hansberry took the train from Chicago to New York. As the familiar plains gave way to the craggy Northeastern countryside, the security of family and friends, white fur, and football fell steadily farther behind. As she emerged from the depths of Pennsylvania Station, she once again felt an outsider, now caught in this eddy of people, oblivious to their buildings stretching to the sky. New York, though, is a city of outsiders. Sometimes they form societies.

Chapter Two
Nobody Is Crying:
It's Just Quiet

The air hung heavy and warm with motes of dust suspended in the light from the stained-glass windows in the Harlem Baptist church. Nobody was crying. It was just quiet. A few friends stepped outside onto the sidewalk. They asked the minister, Why the delay? It's the middle of the week—we'll get docked. The large coffin arrived at the door of the cavernous granite church. The service was mercifully short. Nobody cried. It was quiet.[1] Lorraine Hansberry knew the cops killed the young black man, but he could have died from many dreams deferred. At twenty, she began to learn how to tell his story—in all its infinite varieties.

Many white middle-class Americans remember the years immediately after World War II as a time of peace, stability, and the protection of basic American virtues. Few people seriously questioned the Jim Crow laws—banning interracial drinking fountains, education, and marriage—still on the books since the 1880s. With the advantages of money, education, and social status, Lorraine Hansberry knew better. She had been to Wisconsin. She had heard of blacks being lynched in the South; she knew that "separate but equal schools" were a farce; she knew that many blacks in the South voted only at great risk. On a more personal level, she knew that the State Department was trying to lift Paul Robeson's passport because of his objections to American involvement in the Korean War.[2] Dr. DuBois was barred from teaching at most major universities.[3] The McCarthy Era had begun.

New York City, forever in the vanguard of political and artistic change, reflected the restlessness and creativity beneath this veneer. In 1949, Arthur Miller had challenged the American Dream in *Death of a Salesman*, just as Tennessee Williams probed beneath the charming facade of Southern families to expose a grasping, almost incestuous nature in both *A Streetcar Named Desire* (1947) and *Cat on a Hot Tin Roof* (1955). Ralph Ellison had railed against the anonymity of the black man in a white society in *Invisible Man* (1952), while Langston Hughes fused the "common man"

13

with the black experience for the New York stage. From Greenwich Village to midtown to Harlem, New York writers and artists rejected the happy vacuity of many Americans for creative vitality.

Within weeks Lorraine Hansberry began classes at the New School for Social Research and moved into an apartment on the Lower East Side with three other girls.[4] She wrote articles for the Young Progressives of America magazine. (She did *not* write for the *Daily Worker* as some sources stated.) She became fascinated by the labor struggle and the Women's Movement.[5] She remembered the man in the Harlem church.

Freedom Magazine

A block west of hustling Lenox Avenue in Harlem, the *Freedom* magazine offices on 125th Street were brimming with energy and experience. As publisher of *Freedom*, Paul Robeson attracted some of the most brilliant minds of the day. Dr. W. E. B. DuBois was a regular contributor; the noted artist Charles White wrote an occasional piece on the political mission of the artist; Alice Childress, actress and wit, frequently satirized the foibles of whites and blacks alike, through the persona of a black domestic. Above all, no one on the *Freedom* staff was oblivious to the plights of New Yorkers, Southern blacks, Kenyans, Ghanaians, and American soldiers in the Korean Conflict (1950–53). Others in the 1950s might have whiled away their Saturday afternoons watching outer-space movies, but the *Freedom* writers unmasked the political upheaval and exploitation of Africa, Senator McCarthy's intimidation of artists, writers, and actors, and the American South's faithful marriage to the Jim Crow laws.

Enthusiastic, slender, and bright, Lorraine Hansberry became the youngest member of the *Freedom* staff in 1951. Learning from editor Louis Burnham that everything is ultimately political, Hansberry brought her own fresh insights about the state of women's rights, the arts, and African history and politics to the magazine. (Her year's study in 1953 with Dr. DuBois at the Jefferson School of Social Science in New York[6] helped add a sharp, firm thrust to her African articles.) Traveling to Washington, D.C., South America, Ithaca, New York, and wherever *Freedom* bid her go, she was promoted from staff writer to associate editor within the space of a year. Most important for her intellectual growth, her assignments planted the seeds of ideas that were to ripen later in her serious drama.

From 1951 to 1955, *Freedom* served its readers as the catalyst for political growth. In June 1953, *Freedom* published a detailed, two-page map of Africa, pinpointing French, English, and American interests in the rich store of tin, cobalt, diamonds, and iron ore. This vast continent contained five hundred tribes, numerous mountains, deserts, and grassland plains, and its people spoke one thousand different languages. In its legend, the map documents that five million Kenyan natives—the Masai, the Kavirondo, and the powerful Kikuyu—were ruled by only thirty thousand Europeans. The readers learned that far to the west president-to-be Kwame Nkrumah was leading Ghana into international trade with cocoa production, while taking care to preserve the Ashanti heritage.[7] For the first time, thanks to the map in *Freedom,* many people had accurate information about African government, history, and natural resources.

Deeply concerned with events in Kenya, *Freedom* published "British Jail Kenyatta" and "Who Is Jomo Kenyatta" in the April 1953 issue. The first article revealed that seven thousand Africans were jailed in Kenya in one week.[8] The second article chronicled Jomo Kenyatta's studies at the University of London, his leadership of the Kenya Africa Union, and his hasty arrest and confinement in northern Kenya.[9]

Moving from Nkrumah, Kenyatta, and Africa, *Freedom* attacked Senator Joseph McCarthy's investigation of American artists and political activists. The magazine applauded the humor and fire of Eslanda B. Robeson (writer, anthropologist, and wife of Paul Robeson) in her confrontation with the House Un-American Activities Committee. When Mrs. Robeson invoked both the Fifth and Fifteenth Amendments, declining to discuss her private beliefs and opinions, Senator McCarthy snapped: "You have no special rights because of your race." Mrs. Robeson observed, "You're white and I'm a Negro and this is a very white committee."[10] Almost every month, *Freedom* published Paul Robeson's column, "Here's My Story," detailing his war against racism and protection of civil rights.

Despite the prestige of its staff and writers, *Freedom* was not without its critics. Harold Cruse in *The Crisis of the Negro Intellectual* lambasted the magazine as "a Negro version of the Communist *Daily Worker.*" Its failure to develop an "independent political and cultural philosophy," he felt, stemmed from the middle-class bias of Killens, Robeson, DuBois—and Hansberry. While praising Robeson for his "personal magnetism," Cruse still found him naive about American racial politics and "not an original thinker." Novelist John O. Killens was hampered by his middle-class puritanism. The magazine, Cruse felt, was interested in everything *but* the plight of the lower economic and education class of Harlem. Nevertheless, the sanction of Dr. W. E. B. DuBois, the "great intellectual scholar," lent credibility to the enterprise.[11] (Cruse is right that *Freedom* sometimes lacked the objectivity that first-class writing demands.)

During her five-year association with *Freedom*, Lorraine Hansberry contributed at least twenty-two articles, dealing with Africa, women, social issues of New York, and several reviews. Her most intriguing article is "Kenya's Kikuyus," which contains germs of folk myth and modern politics embedded in the following tale. A man had a friendship with an elephant. During a raging storm, the man let the elephant put his trunk into the man's hut to keep dry. Pushing his head and body into the hut, the elephant then forced the man out into the storm. Later the man sought justice from the lion, king of the jungle, who sided with the elephant. After all, he had saved the rather backward man's hut from being demolished in the hurricane. Undaunted, the man built hut after hut, but the greedy elephant seized each one. In desperation, the man finally built an enormous hut, where the elephants and lions gathered and began bickering about ownership. While the animals fought within, the man built a fire and burned the hut—jungle lords and all.[12] (This story evolves into the tale of the elephants and hyenas in *Les Blancs*.)

A close observer of African politics, Hansberry notes the basically peaceful Kikuyus' delegations and petitions to protest British seizure of Kikuyu land and gold deposits in Kavirondo territory and the British disregard of treaties. Never missing the opportunity for humor, she mentions the Kikuyu name for Europeans, "Muzungu"—"he who is dizzy."[13] Bright and eager to learn, Lorraine Hansberry did not squander her three active years as a *Freedom* staffer. (After her marriage in 1953, she quit full-time work but continued to contribute occasional articles.)[14]

Three years earlier as a senior at Englewood, Lorraine Hansberry had realized the stature of her Uncle Leo, whose references to Mali, Songhay, and Kenyatta came as naturally as dinnertime conversation. She was pleased, therefore, when editor Louis Burnham assigned her a feature on Ghana and its leader, Kwame Nkrumah, a student at Howard during Uncle Leo's tenure. In the article Hansberry depicted the Gold Coast casting aside its European title to reclaim its soft African name, Ghana, and legislators, exchanging business suits for native draped robes and sandals. She praised Dr. Kwame Nkrumah, who had been imprisoned for leading a general strike. He was elected prime minister, even as he sat in jail on February 10, 1951. Urging free primary education for all children, Dr. Nkrumah sought $211 million to advance Ghana's economic and social services, communications, and general administration. Hansberry's prophecy that "The promise of the future of Ghana . . . is the promise of freedom"[15] paralleled her cry for self-rule and human rights in Sierra Leone.[16]

In a factual, controlled piece about the Egyptian freedom movement, Lorraine Hansberry etched the "stark, sober quiet" of the single day when 250,000 people protested seventy years of British rule. Upper-class citizens enjoyed fine education, housing, and incomes in this "cradle of civilization," but the plight of many Egyptians was bleak. Writing the African articles increased Lorraine Hansberry's awareness of the continent's history and leaders. "Kenya's Kikuyus," particularly added a metaphorical dimension to her later work. At this point, she had not yet suffered from the polemicism Cruse found in *Freedom*.

In her articles about women, Lorraine Hansberry seemed a feminist only in the most general sense: she praised the accomplishments of women. In the fall of 1951, Lorraine Hansberry traveled to Washington, D.C., to cover a conference of 132 black women, "Sojourners for Truth," who sought an end to war and racial discrimination. From California, Virginia, and New York, these wives and mothers came to protest the death of a son in "the senseless war in Korea," the fatal shooting of a son on an operating table, the legal lynching of a husband. Having visited the home of Frederick Douglass the day before, these women were stirred by the spirit of Sojourner Truth as they said: "Dry your eyes and speak your mind."[17]

Eulogizing Florence Mills, one of New York's most beloved actresses and singers, Hansberry traced her career from child stardom to Broadway to international fame. Eleven-year-old Florence and her two sisters were so appealing as the "Mills Sisters" that two black writers booked Florence Mills for a part in *Schooldays,* a successful musical. Later she starred in the landmark Broadway musical *Shuffle Along,* written by Eubie Blake and Noble Sissle. Her talent and reputation firmly established, Florence agreed to an international tour with the Blackbirds in 1926. Returning home after a year, Florence finally found the time for an operation for appendicitis—but it was too late. Not even thirty, "Lady Florence" was driven to her funeral in Harlem as 150,000 people lined Lenox Avenue, peered through windows and packed fire escapes. *Variety* concluded: "Florence Mills—petite and pretty . . . [was] . . . the personification of refinement. . . . Her admirable work . . . [was] . . . of a quality and temperament unusual in the . . . field."[18]

Even though the Sojourner story was a journalistic limbering-up exercise, Hansberry's tribute to Florence Mills was a lucid character sketch. Carefully selecting details, Hansberry makes the reader feel Mills's nightly seventy-block trek home and the warmth of her Sunday-afternoon socials. Once again she avoided any artistic traps Cruse believed hidden in the 125th Street office.

When Editor Burnham began to assign her stories on social inequities in New York City, however, Lorraine Hansberry truly became the "intellectual revolutionary." She was outraged that Roosevelt Ward, twenty-two-year-old secretary of the New York Labor Youth League, was arrested on July 16, 1951, for draft evasion although he had never received an induction notice. Bond, she reported, was set at $5,000.[19] She interviewed George Crockett, noted attorney and defender of eleven black Communist leaders. He was cited for contempt of court and sentenced to four months of jail by Judge Medina, a man guilty of "red baiting." She agreed with Crockett that the attack on Communists could precipitate an attack on blacks.[20] Robert Nemiroff adds that at this time she also covered the Communist trials in Foley Square, including those of City Councilman Benjamin J. Davis and youth leader Claudia Jones.[21]

Shuttling about the city—from the Waldorf-Astoria to Broadway back to Harlem schools—Lorraine Hansberry did sharpen her journalistic tools. She learned to interview easily; she started to sift important figures from mazes of paper; she began to penetrate the facades of people and events. She reported on the Negro Labor Council's campaign against Jim Crow hiring practices in New York hotels. Even in November 1952, blacks were excluded from more lucrative jobs as skilled maintenance people, office workers, dining-room workers, and bartenders. By March 1953, the Waldorf-Astoria and the Sherry Netherlands had begun to upgrade employees and to consider other applications seriously.[22]

A champion of the young and gifted, black and white, Lorraine Hansberry described the sunless asphalt playground, large cheerless basement serving both as lunchroom and gymnasium, and overcrowded classrooms of Public School 157 in Harlem. The substandard physical plant was only matched by the inferior education of young blacks, who were generally forced into vocational skills rather than academic studies. As a result, 30 percent of all Harlem students were three academic years behind their age group.[23] Several years later, she would contribute an article on a related topic, juvenile crime. Many of these young blacks lacked a strong self-image, the result of ignorance of black and African heritage. Hansberry urged educators to stress the history of ancient Egypt and Ethiopia and the lives of Frederick Douglass, Toussaint L'Ouverture, and Jomo Kenyatta, rather than relying solely on European literature and history.[24] With materials she later included in The Drinking Gourd, Hansberry traced the dilemma of black and white children of the nineteenth and twentieth centuries, who labored twelve hours a day for meager wages in textile mills, glass factories, the cotton industry, and coal mines.[25]

In March 1952, Lorraine Hansberry made her most important journey for *Freedom*. She flew to Montevideo, Uruguay, to deliver a speech for the internationally famous Paul Robeson.[26] He could not attend, since the State Department had revoked his passport. In her article, she described the "illegal" conference for peace, attended by 250 delegates from eight South American countries and the United States of America. Honored at a special session for women, she was presented carnations and a doll in traditional Uruguayan dress and thrilled to the chant of 5,000 people—VIVA ROBESON. In his stead, she was awarded the honor of being seated on the presidium,[27] speaking for peace and against the Korean Conflict.

Hansberry's Uruguayan trip actually epitomizes the best and worst aspects of her *Freedom* years. Burnham and Robeson gave her responsibilities exceptional for a woman in her twenties—challenges she met as an articulate, powerful speaker and as a fervid writer. (At this time, she also coordinated several large-scale artistic programs—one on Ida B. Wells—complete with script, music, and publicity.)[28] Yet her elders at *Freedom* may not have served her growth as an artist so well. Dr. DuBois was eighty-four; Paul Robeson was chronologically fifty-four, but the peak of his popularity seemed decades rather than eight years behind. Though they meant well, Lorraine Hansberry, as the strong, young conduit through which their ideas flowed, advocated theories out of sync with the black working class and novelists Richard Wright and Ralph Ellison.

Most regrettably, the *Freedom* philosophy temporarily skewed her critical judgment. Wright and Ellison had renounced any Communist sympathies. In her review of *The Outsider*, Hansberry berates Wright for his nihilism—not a fair aesthetic criticism. Wright had chosen to create a novel of "social realism" and Hansberry should have judged it on its own merits—not by *Freedom*'s standards of an acceptable black family.

In her other notable review, Hansberry's idea of the fusion of art and propaganda does not obscure the intent of the work concerned. In a lyrical review of the Japanese movie *Hiroshima* she called the critics who isolated its propaganda from its art "insanely vulgar." As the movie opens, the Emperor's drill masters slap and abuse young girls, children stare up at the skies, hearing "the lonely hum of that single bomber," and then the bomb. In the "terrible moment" when the bomb explodes, the filmmakers do not attempt the sounds of "the million thunders." Instead, they use total silence as the "mighty mushroom rises" and then darkness fills the screen. Ending on a note of hope, *Hiroshima* still conveys a sense of the horror and futility of war, which she later achieved in *What Use Are Flowers?* Although *Flowers* is certainly a product of Hansberry's own genius, she did not forget

the silent children, the chant of "No More Hiroshimas," the flattened
landscape, and the survivors who lived to teach the young the meaning of
flowers, music, and beauty.[29]

Robert Nemiroff

During her years at *Freedom*, Lorraine Hansberry matured as a writer and
speaker. (She had even learned to write for a young audience in "Stories For
Children.") She taught classes at Frederick Douglass School on 124th
Street;[30] she traveled widely; she was recognized by New York critics and
activists. But Nannie Perry Hansberry somehow felt uneasy about her ad-
venturous "baby."

Late in 1952, Mrs. Hansberry traveled to New York to find her spirited
daughter delivering political speeches. The first time her mother and sister
heard Lorraine speak, Mamie recalled: "It really blew me away. And so
mother and I just looked at each other."[31] They had just had their first look
at Lorraine as a professional. Though her behavior was in keeping with the
activism of the Hansberry family, one problem still remained, as Mamie
explained:

Mother was bugging her about coming home after she had been in New York a
couple of years or so. She said, "Well, any middle-class lady shouldn't be in New
York so long, because you know it is time for you to think about getting married,
and you know." I think she [Lorraine] had two or three roommates, and Mother
began to say, "Well, it is time you were getting married, time you started looking
for a husband. . . ." Lorraine kept saying, "Yes, well, I am busy and I am happy."
"Yes, but you ought to think about getting married, and just girls setting in an
apartment isn't safe, and it will subject you to ridicule and all that stuff."

So pretty soon Lorraine was saying, "Well, I met a very nice person, and
we are thinking about getting married." Well, of course, that makes everything all right, get your child in . . . out . . . free.[32]

This "very nice person" was Robert Nemiroff—son of cultured Russian
Jewish parents. His mother was for many years a garment worker and later
became a dietitian. During the Depression, his father was unemployed
until the family managed to open a successive number of Russian restaurants and/or nightclubs. The last attained considerable popularity during
World War II, but "folded in the chill of the Cold War."[33] By the early
1950s, his parents had started a small international restaurant on Washington Place in Greenwich Village. A graduate student at New York Uni-

versity, half a year older than Hansberry, Nemiroff was absorbed in the
works of Theodore Dreiser, literary criticism, and various social causes.
According to Nemiroff, he and Hansberry met in 1951 at a picket line,
protesting the exclusion of blacks from the basketball team at New York
University—*not* at a family restaurant as Walter Winchell wrote.[34] Within
a year, Lorraine Hansberry and Robert Nemiroff were committed to a life
together—a life of writing, music, "changing the world," with a dash of
frivolity.
Once again with Mamie in tow, Mrs. Hansberry visited New York:

We went to New York, and we met Bob, and we went to the theater and stuff like
that. We could see he was very attentive, and in fact, he was overly attentive, for
our money, at that point because we hadn't done anything interracial really with
someone immediately in our family. Sometimes we would walk a little bit ahead.
But, you know, we could see that he was just an adorable person, and he was
completely open and free.
   Then after she said that the wedding plans were made, they came out and just
had a real great time. It was real cute at the station as they were going back
because Rick[35] had given them a television or something and it took Carl, Perry
and Bob to try to get the thing on the train. . . . And I remember when they
arrived I went to the station to pick them up. And everybody was so happy. It was
a wonderful time.[36]

   June 20, 1953, was an important day at the Hansberry home on Hyde
Park Boulevard in Chicago.[37] Fresh flowers and chairs filled the living
room, and presents were stacked on the table in the hall. The guests filtered into the large sunny room—Perry, Carl, and other Hansberry relatives, Robert's brother Leo and the other Nemiroffs, and a few close
friends—Burt D'Lugoff, Donald Jackson, Lorraine Fuchs, and Evelyn
Goldwasser. Mrs. Mae Nemiroff and Mrs. Nannie Hansberry walked
proudly into the crowded room, as Robert Nemiroff and the Reverend
Archibald M. Carey, Chicago councilman, minister, and later United
States delegate to the United Nations, stood in front of the white brick
fireplace. Elegant and subdued, Mamie as matron of honor walked down
the makeshift aisle. Wearing Mamie's lacy white dress, Lorraine Hansberry
marched toward her future husband and the Reverend Mr. Carey.[38]
   A month later, Lorraine Hansberry and Robert Nemiroff were happily
settled in their second-floor apartment above Joe's Hand Laundry on
Bleecker Street in Greenwich Village. For the next few years, Lorraine
Hansberry worked full-time at a sequence of jobs: typist at Wanamaker's,

assistant in the Fur District (stapling labels to raw fur), secretary to Rachel Productions, which produced *The World of Sholem Aleichem*, and group leader at the Federation for the Handicapped.

Foreshadowing her sympathy with the 1960s Civil Rights Movement, she also worked for the folk magazine *Sing Out*, which first published Woody Guthrie's "This Land Is Your Land" and the astonishing anthem of the striking tobacco workers, "We Shall Overcome"—later the hymn of the entire black freedom movement in the 1960s. At this time, they met Pete Seeger and other folk musicians. Before *Freedom* went bankrupt in 1955, she sent periodic articles to her old office. Meanwhile, Robert Nemiroff, having earned his MA from New York University in 1953, became a reader and copywriter for Sears Readers' Club; later, he served as promotions director of Avon Books.[39]

The next few years found Lorraine and Bob absorbing much of the creative magic of Greenwich Village. At night they would sometimes listen to the folksingers in Washington Square or drop into the Minetta Tavern or Rienzi's; on rare occasions, they visited Chumley's. More often, they invited friends in for spaghetti or went out to plays and movies. Robert Nemiroff also recalls that they spent some spare time on picket lines and at all-night vigils during the desegregation of various areas. They made friends with Gin Briggs, a photographer, who was the prototype for the principal character in the first draft of Hansberry's play *The Sign in Jenny Reed's Window*, which later, of course, became *The Sign in Sidney Brustein's Window*. Later (in 1959) Gin Briggs, an "innocent from Appalachia," happened to hang an anti-DeSapio sign in her window to help her friends. Consequently, she had her window smashed, was threatened, and was nearly evicted from her Greenwich Village apartment.[40]

After three years of marriage, Robert Nemiroff embarked on a musical venture to the amusement of the Hansberry family. As Mamie recalled,

They wrote a song together, "Cindy, Oh, Cindy," which we thought was just hilarious, because they came home Christmas or Thanksgiving . . . they brought this guitar, and they would sit around on the floor plunking at a party I had when we were sniggering and giggling. And that little song made a hundred thousand dollars. And we started hearing it on the radio. . . . So we soon stopped laughing about that.[41]

In typical sisterly fashion, Mamie exaggerated Lorraine's role in "Cindy, Oh, Cindy." Robert Nemiroff and Burt D'Lugoff had written the song; Hansberry had suggested the title. But the major point remains: the Hansberrys were beginning to take their "baby" seriously. Released in August 1956, "Cindy, Oh, Cindy" *did* earn $100,000—which freed Lorraine Hansberry to write full time.[42]

A working pattern was established: when Lorraine would complete a first draft, Robert would serve as her sounding board. In turn, she served as his sounding board for literary criticism and, years later, his drama. (His play *Postmark Zero* was produced on Broadway in 1965). In many ways, their relationship resembled the artistic symbiosis of Lillian Hellman and Dashiell Hammett.

Some amusing, though spurious, stories about the Hansberry/Nemiroff marriage have crept into print. One source reported that they honeymooned in Egypt excavating tombs, since Nemiroff (whom the reporter confused with Dr. Hansberry) was an "expert Egyptologist." Another credited him with being a descendant of "scions." In truth, she did once throw the manuscript of *Raisin* at the ceiling (not unlike Hellman's disposal of her typewriter in a snit) and, as she told a reporter, "started to sweep them all into the fireplace. Bob didn't rebuke me at all, except with a look. He just got down on the floor and picked up every sheet of it . . . put it back in order and kept it out of my sight for several days. And then one night when I was moping around, he got it out and put it in front of me. I went to work and finished it."[43]

Nemiroff's love and support of Hansberry—the artist and woman—are crystallized by an inscription he wrote in a drama anthology—a birthday present in 1956.

Honey—
From Shakespeare to Shaw—
   Because you deserve them,
   And because one day, if
   you work hard enough at
   it (and cut out the nonsense)
   You may be up there among
   them—if not Shakespeare.
   then at least Shaw
     Love,
     Bobby

The seeds of most of Hansberry's plays had been planted during her childhood on the South Side of Chicago, her years at *Freedom,* her life in Harlem, and now in the Village. For four years, she wrote tirelessly, often into the night, drinking coffee, chain smoking, letting her feet get cold when the antiquated heating system shut off. As early as 1957, Mamie was concerned about whether Lorraine was eating properly and much later reflected: "I always regret that I didn't have her physically checked then because I noted that she was really thin, and . . . I suspect maybe she was ill even then.[44] (Nemiroff dismisses this last remark as typical sisterly oversolicitude as, he reports, there was no hint of illness until six years later.)

In her more vulnerable moments, Lorraine was prey to a host of petty fears: elevators, high places, hospitals, close places.[45] With the fierce passion for privacy so vital to serious creative artists, she sometimes refused weekend visits to his relatives' homes. Mamie explained that Lorraine and Bob "loved each other dearly as two human beings, but I think Lorraine's only great love was her work." Lorraine's decision not to have children evolved from her nurturance of her art. Again Mamie explained: "Lorraine had a natural drive, and I'm aware of it, because I have it. We all [the Hansberrys] have drive in a work sense if it's creating. . . ."[46] In many small ways, Lorraine the Artist triumphed over Lorraine the Mother. But no one can dispute the joy of her near symbiosis with Robert Nemiroff. More than anyone before, he understood her mission as an artist, her commitment to her craft and art.

In the 1950s, interracial marriage was far from being acceptable in most communities and was, in fact, illegal in thirty states. But the Hansberry and Nemiroff families had few objections to the match. As Mamie explained, "Their family, in their ethnic way, was very similar to our family."[47] Both families were comfortable, articulate, and cultured. In reality, racial diversity probably strengthened the Hansberry/Nemiroff marriage. The famed actor and playwright Ossie Davis explained that *all* subcultures share the common bond of being outsiders.[48] Subcultures also tend to value a strong sense of family, of community, of nationalism, and Lorraine would probably add, a distinct sense of humor.

From the time of her marriage to Nemiroff in 1953 until her amazing success on Broadway in 1959, Lorraine Hansberry certainly received encouragement, support, and artistic advice from her husband. But the question of Nemiroff's precise influence on her work remains unresolved. Mamie believes that "he had the effect of helping her produce it. . . . In terms of the literary work itself. I don't think so. . . . But the whole text of *Raisin,* Bob Nemiroff just wouldn't have had that information because his whole life was different. And that is purely her own art."[49] A modest man, Nemiroff tends to agree with Mamie. But he was the perfect husband for a writer: supportive, brilliant, secure in his own abilities, skilled as literary critic, and no stranger to grueling work himself.

One evening in the fall of 1957, Hansberry and Nemiroff invited Philip Rose, a music publisher, and Burt D'Lugoff for dinner at their Bleecker Street apartment, decorated with prints by Picasso and drawings of Charles White and pleasantly disrupted by their "sort of collie," Spice. After dinner, Hansberry read the first draft of *A Raisin in the Sun* to the assembled company. To her surprise, they began a lively discussion and critique, which lasted until the morning hours and suddenly Lorraine realized that the play had "taken on a life of its own."[50] *A Raisin in the Sun* shoved its way to center stage of her life for the next few years.

For the next year, Philip Rose—who optioned the play for Broadway— exhausted all resources to get it into rehearsal. (Robert Nemiroff stresses that he and Lorraine Hansberry knew *nothing* about Broadway productions, especially the financing.) There would be problems with production— union laws, rehearsal restrictions, dates for the theater—but the most significant problem was money. Rose persuaded Harry Belafonte and other black cultural leaders to invest small amounts.[51] Within the next year and a half, Rose had raised the money; named the talented black Lloyd Richards the director; convinced Hansberry's long-time acquaintance Sidney Poitier to portray Walter Lee Younger. David J. Cogan, a tax consultant, became the co-producer. Finally, they arranged tryouts in New Haven and Philadelphia. Great reviews in Philadelphia prompted an offer from the Schuberts to move the play to Chicago at their own expense and then to Broadway as soon as a theater opened up.[52]

The Chicago performance was especially important for Lorraine as the city's native daughter. She had written her mother a tentative letter about her "play about Negroes." But her older sister was as concerned about her sister's appearance as with her literary merit. The Hansberrys were, after all, a prominent Chicago family.

I enjoyed shopping, and she would always love everything I'd get for her. And then when she came home for the opening of *Raisin,* it was so cute—I said, "Well, Lorraine, what are you going to wear for the opening," I said. "You know, you're really not going on the stage in blue jeans." And she said, "Oh, I don't care. Go find me something." So I went to Michigan and got a lovely black dress with floating panels.[53]

And Mamie probably sent Lorraine to the hairdresser and put on her makeup.

Variety predicted, after the New Haven tryout, that the play would "ripen into substantial Broadway tenancy"—a prophecy come true as *Raisin* endured and prevailed in Philadelphia and Chicago. Never trusting to good fortune, due to her abiding irritation that Langston Hughes had not then been recognized for his genius,[54] Lorraine was astonished that she was becoming a media name. At five feet four inches, with her size-eight black dress with floating panels, with her husband, Robert Nemiroff, at her side, Lorraine headed back to New York—to Broadway and national acclaim.

Broadway and Hollywood Success

When *A Raisin in the Sun* opened on March 11, 1959, at Broadway's Barrymore Theater, Brooks Atkinson of the *New York Times,* Walter Kerr of the *New York Herald Tribune,* and an entranced public applauded Lorraine Hansberry and her landmark play. Critics and theatergoers also heralded the superb acting of Sidney Poitier, Diana Sands, Ruby Dee, and Claudia McNeil. Tennessee Williams sent a telegram. Within hours Lorraine Hansberry was thrust into the public eye—recognition that exceeded all expectations. Less than a month later, on April 7, Lorraine Hansberry was awarded the New York Drama Critics' Circle Award. At twenty-nine, she became the youngest playwright, the fifth woman, and the first black dramatist to win the most prestigious prize at this time. *A Raisin in the Sun* had triumphed over *Sweet Bird of Youth* by Tennessee Williams and plays by Eugene O'Neill and Archibald MacLeish.[55]

As a new, exciting celebrity, Lorraine Hansberry was deluged by letters from a distinguished lady from China, a "white farm boy from Mississippi," aspiring young writers. She won plaudits from friends like James Baldwin, Ruby Dee, and Ossie Davis and later Shelley Winters and Julie Harris. In June 1959 *Variety* polled New York drama critics, who found Hansberry the "most promising playwright" of the year. *Vogue* magazine featured Lorraine Hansberry in "People Are Talking About," and the *New Yorker* highlighted Lorraine in its "Talk of the Town" section. Both Studs Terkel of Chicago and Mike Wallace in New York interviewed her at length. The Wallace/Hansberry tapes were so incisive and lively that Caedmon recorded them as "Lorraine Hansberry Speaks Out: Art and the Black Revolution" in 1972.

By 1960 Philip Rose and Lorraine Hansberry had threaded through the maze of Hollywood agents and producers to secure a lucrative contract, which more importantly, gave her some measure of artistic control. In

March 1959, she said: "Nobody's going to turn this thing into a minstrel show. . . . If this blocks a sale, then it just won't be sold."[56] They had not settled for the first option, as have many less astute writers. With sisterly pride, Mamie gave her account of the Hollywood experience.

Lorraine had a certain amount of freedom, because she was economically secure. She didn't have to kowtow to an industry. She made demands on the industry; she demanded to take her own director to Broadway, which was unheard of.

When it was time to come to Hollywood to write the screenplay, she wrote it and sent it out here. The director said, "Well, you have to come out here and do this and that, and our writers have to go over it with you." She said, "Sir, I am sending it to you. If you don't like the way it is written, you send it back, because I am not coming to California for you to do nothing." She said, "Nobody out there is qualified to rewrite one line." And that was her attitude. And, so she sent it. They used it as is.[57]

Robert Nemiroff, however, does not feel that she had any real artistic control of the screenplay. Even though she did send a list of "major serious directors" to Hollywood, the studio refused them all, including Sidney Lumet. The production also lacked a sufficient budget—even for crowd scenes and enough diverse locations — on the grounds that there was little market for movies about blacks. Furthermore, he fears that the public confuses the inferior movie with the superior play.[58] (The movie *did* win the Cannes Film Festival Award in 1961.) Such muddling may be based on published versions of *Raisin*—which feature photographs from the movie, not the Broadway play.

In some ways, though, Lorraine Hansberry placed her artistic stamp on the movie version. Despite its limitations, she was proud that the movie allowed black life to emerge at a complex and truthful level never before depicted on the American screen. Again, *A Raisin in the Sun* was blessed by outstanding performances. Sidney Poitier portrayed Walter Lee Younger, Jr., Ruby Dee as Ruth, Diana Sands as Beneatha, and the sonorous Claudia McNeil as Lena (Mama) added depth and diversity to the film. Aware of the differences between stage and movie sets, Lorraine wisely varied several scenes. In the play Lorraine Hansberry adhered strictly to the unity of place by having all action transpire in the Youngers' South Side Chicago apartment.

In the movie, Walter Lee, dressed in his chauffeur's uniform, drives his employer to his white mansion—a sharp visual contrast to the matchbox of the Younger apartment. In the movie, Mama seeks out Walter Lee in a seedy bar to give him the money from Big Walter's insurance policy (an action which signifies her recognition of her son as a man). At the end of the movie, the Youngers actually visit their home in Clybourne Park, a modest but airy tree-lined neighborhood.

The hills of Hollywood echo with sighs of writers past whose works have been slaughtered by studios—Fitzgerald, Faulkner, Hemingway. In the first draft of the screenplay, Hansberry wrote several scenes that were later cut. Travis studies, as he puts it, "poor-Negroes-in-history" (black history) at school. Lena cleans house for a white woman, Mrs. Holiday, whom Hansberry seems to view sympathetically but ambivalently. Mrs. Holiday is unaware that calling Lena "one of the family" is patronizing, though she genuinely cares for the older woman. The camera pans over the opulence and waste of Walter's employers—never focusing on their faces (a fairly didactic statement). Lena berates a white clerk who calls her "Moms" while trying to sell her "dismally scrawny" apples. A street speaker derides the White Man in the South, in Africa, in Chicago—as Walter stands watching on the edge of the crowd.[59]

The omission of these scenes is distressing to Robert Nemiroff. He feels they were deleted because of "secret memos from the studio brass to the producers." These memoranda stated that the scenes were "too controversial, 'racially' unsettling, and therefore likely to offend white audiences."[60]

While the movie did not sparkle with the wit and simplicity of the Broadway play, the studio should not be faulted for not including street speakers and scrawny apples. Hansberry did not include them in the original play, nor did Nemiroff restore them in the 1973 musical. Overall, these additions would have warped the unity of the play.

After her victory on Broadway and success in Hollywood, Lorraine Hansberry was firmly established on the national literary scene. People were indeed talking about her, but they were also listening. In May and June of 1961, a curious literary exchange took place between Lorraine Hansberry and Norman Mailer. The substance of the dispute was certainly serious: Mailer had written two *Village Voice* articles (May 11 and May 18), in which he praised Jean Genet's play *The Blacks,* calling it "the truest and most explosive play . . . ever written" about white guilt. Mailer was especially taken by one character's speech: "I order you to be Black to your very veins. . . . Let Negroes negrify themselves. Let them persist to the point of madness . . . in their odor, in their yellow eyes, in their cannibal tastes." Justifiably, Hansberry felt that Norman Mailer had a skewed notion of blacks. On June 1, she responded with her own *Village Voice* article in which she quoted passages from Mailer's essay, "The White Negro."

But the dispute had humorous overtones. The idea of the cultured, beautiful, fair-minded Lorraine Hansberry confronting the lumpy, tousled, antifeminist Norman Mailer was in itself ironic. On June 8, 1961, Mailer wrote Hansberry via the *Village Voice:* "What bugs every liberal about 'The White Negro' is that it is built upon a drear, drear word: orgasm. . . . The Negro has built his philosophy . . . on this existential moment." In "The New Paternalists," Hansberry responded: "It is, alas . . . a good idea for everyone, man or woman, liberal or otherwise, to spend at least some hours of every day *out* of bed."[61]

Having fun with Mailer's notion of himself as a "hipster," Lorraine Hansberry mentioned that black jazz musicians, with whom Mailer claimed special rapport, had told James Baldwin that Mailer was "a real sweet ofay cat, but a little frantic." All the while Lorraine considered Norman Mailer "a good man," hoping that his "arrogance not become shapeless."[62]

By the summer of 1961, reviews, letters, and interviews about *A Raisin in the Sun* had settled down to a steady, manageable pace. Still living in their Bleecker Street walk-up, Robert Nemiroff continued to handle the business details, while Lorraine Hansberry finally had ample time to work on her other writing projects. They had learned of a lovely home in Croton-on-Hudson, a sixty-minute train ride from the city. Designed with hints of Frank Lloyd Wright, whom Hansberry admired, the house featured walls of glass looking out on the quiet wooded country and dramatic, angular ceilings with exposed wooden beams. Downstairs, there was a paneled, nearly sound-proof study with room for six filing cabinets. Outside, their dog Spice ran free on the spacious lawn with the new dog, Chaka.

As successful as both their careers had been, Robert Nemiroff and Lorraine Hansberry had begun to sense a rift in their relationship. Rarely did two people work together so well or closely, but the tensions of publicity and lack of time had begun to strain their marriage. But the fissure was not complete: they would move to Croton. Not until 1964 would they finally succumb to a very private Mexican divorce.[63]

By 1961 Lorraine Hansberry was deep into completing unfinished tasks—almost as though she knew her time was slipping away. Her ideas for *The Sign in Sidney Brustein's Window* had begun germinating in 1959. Early in 1959, she had begun combing the files of the Main Branch of the New York Public Library and the Schomburg Collection and having transcripts of old *Congressional Records* sent up from Washington to do research on the history, economy, and attitudes of the antebellum South for *The*

Drinking Gourd. Later in 1960, Lorraine crystallized the basic plot and the central characters of Tshembe (initially named Shembe), his brother Abioseh, and their sister Candace (who was almost immediately deleted) of *Les Blancs.* Then, in 1961, she conceived the idea of *What Use Are Flowers?* as a fantasy for television.[64] Her speeches and essays included the rebuff of Mailer in "The New Paternalists," "The Negro Writer and His Roots: Toward a New Romanticism," and "A Challenge to Artists."

By 1960, Lorraine Hansberry had written the final script of *The Drinking Gourd* for the National Broadcasting Company. Dore Schary, former head of MGM, now an independent producer and author of *Sunrise at Campobello,* had commissioned the play, paid Lorraine a handsome fee, presented the script to NBC, and hired Henry Fonda to play the Narrator. But the network executives—after months of dickering—remained afraid to treat the Civil War and were convinced that *The Drinking Gourd* was too violent, too polemical for family viewing. So, as Lorraine Hansberry explained, they put it in a drawer. In 1962 she completed *What Use Are Flowers?* but decided to recast it for the stage. She continued to revise, polish, experiment with *Les Blancs* from time to time.

Early in 1963, Lorraine Hansberry began to feel faint when walking up stairs, to suffer unexplained attacks of nausea. She began to suspect that she was "a very sick girl." There were so many incomplete projects: her play or opera about Toussaint; the unfinished novel, *All the Dark and Beautiful Warriors;* short stories accumulated from her adolescence and early days in New York; plans for other plays—about Akhnaton (the Pharaoh), Mary Wollstonecraft, *Laughing Boy* (American Indians), and Charles Chesnutt's *The Marrow of Tradition.* And ideas seemed to keep spinning out of the air for other plays, other stories. When Dr. David Baldwin examined Lorraine, he did not immediately reveal his full diagnosis to the thirty-two-year-old playwright. But Robert Nemiroff knew the truth: Lorraine had cancer of the duodenum.[65]

The Sign in Sidney Brustein's Window was Lorraine Hansberry's farewell message to her world. Unlike Shakespeare, she could not make her peace with a hopeful, magical masterpiece, such as *The Tempest.* The 1960s were too violent, too wrenching for such a gesture. On a radio broadcast with James Baldwin and Langston Hughes in 1961, she had said: "Personally, I can't imagine a time in the world when the artist wasn't in conflict; if he was any sort of artist he *had* to be." As a dramatist, she felt she must take issue with her world, force herself to isolate its problems, and then suggest solutions. In writing the last lines of *Brustein,* Lorraine perhaps subconsciously described the last two painful years of her own life: "Tomorrow, we shall make something strong of this sorrow."

Death and Legacy

Mamie Hansberry Mitchell has observed, "The black experience creates a lot of stress, and . . . a form of cancer can evolve from the emotional stress of racism." From April 1963 until January 1965, Lorraine Hansberry endured the physical and emotional pains of her encroaching cancer. Even now, no one has discovered the exact cause of cancer, but medical researchers have not dismissed the possibility of emotional strain. While Lorraine herself was affluent, well-educated, and loved, she was too expansive a human being to ignore the very real torments of those around her. She had reported racial discrimination in the South and in New York; she felt the birth pangs of emerging African nations; she recoiled at television and best-sellers portraying women as dependent, selfless pawns, as "idiots"; she witnessed artists, actors, and writers persecuted by McCarthyism; worst of all, she saw victims of these evil institutions punishing themselves—by giving up, by doubting their own self-worth, by believing in nothing.[66] America had become an uncommitted nation. Even as she lay dying, Lorraine sought to rectify one of the most tragic ills of her time—lack of respect for the individual, lack of caring.

During her last two years, Lorraine Hansberry continued to revise *Les Blancs* and *What Use Are Flowers?*, but her main creative energies were poured into *The Sign in Sidney Brustein's Window*. The play was bound to confound critics. *Brustein* was a "play of ideas," dealing with a host of contemporary issues: politics, marriage, abstract art, prostitution, absurdist plays, black culture, loneliness, the individual versus society. But its message was vivid and clear: the individual must become committed, involved.

In March 1964, Lorraine Hansberry and Robert Nemiroff quietly obtained a Mexican divorce. According to Mamie, the main purpose of the divorce was to clarify conditions of her will,[67] a theory which Nemiroff disputes. Due to her illness, Hansberry and Nemiroff only informed close friends and family members of the divorce.

From March until October of 1963, Lorraine frequently consulted Dr. Baldwin in Manhattan and Dr. Kenneth Warren, a noted surgeon in Boston. The production plans of *Brustein* neared completion. Despite fine medical care and love and support from the Hansberry and Nemiroff families, the cancer continued to grow in her body.

On October 8, 1964, Lorraine Hansberry and a private nurse moved into the Hotel Abbey Victoria on Seventh Avenue, so that the playwright could attend rehearsals of *The Sign in Sidney Brustein's Window*. The play

had expert businessmen as co-producers—Dr. Burt D'Lugoff, Robert
Nemiroff, and J. I. Jahre. The talented cast included Gabriel Dell as Sidney Brustein, Ben Aliza as Alton Scales, Rita Moreno as Iris Parodus Brustein, and Alice Ghostley as Mavis Parodus Bryson. In the provocative
script, Lorraine Hansberry had boldly mixed styles, breathed life into abstractions, and depicted characters so realistically that Sidney even chat-
tered in the tedious manner of "intellectuals." A night with *Brustein* was
not an evening of frothy entertainment. When *Brustein* opened at the
Longacre Theatre on October 15, 1964, the play was met with mixed
reviews, which meant financial problems.

After the opening-night reviews, Robert Nemiroff knew that *Brustein*
was in trouble. But defenders appeared. One of the first champions was
Shelley Winters, who promoted the play on radio, television, and public
platforms—often on short notice—and even volunteered to play a supporting role at union minimum. In the months that followed, many artists,
patrons, and "angels" donated personal savings to keep the play on Broadway. Late in October 1964, the *New York Times* ran an advertisement, stating that "Miss Hansberry's new play is a work of distinction. . . . *The Sign
in Sidney Brustein's Window* is . . . powerful, tender, moving and hilarious. . . . We the undersigned . . . urge you to see it *now.*" The signers
included James Baldwin, Sammy Davis, Jr., Ossie Davis, Ruby Dee, Paddy Chayefsky, William Gibson, Sidney Kingsley, Lillian Hellman, Frank
and Eleanor Perry, and Shelley Winters. Similar advertisements were later
endorsed by Alan Alda, Anne Bancroft, Mel Brooks, Claudia McNeil,
Diana Sands, and Herman Shulman.[68]

During the play's short, tumultuous run, many New York artists and
connoisseurs selflessly dedicated their time and money to Lorraine Hansberry and her play. In November 1964, comedian Mel Brooks and his
wife, actress Anne Bancroft, opened their home for a mid-night strategy
meeting to keep *Brustein* alive. Sammy Davis, in the middle of his nightly
act at the Majestic, urged his audience to rush to the Longacre the next
night. The novelist John O. Killens and his wife Grace personally stuffed
thousands of envelopes. When the play was forced to vacate the Longacre,
friends of the arts redoubled their efforts and somehow raised the necessary
$7,000 for the move to Henry Miller's Theatre on December 22, 1964.[69]
Robert Nemiroff lovingly chronicled these 101 performances of *The Sign in
Sidney Brustein's Window* in a long essay.

Meanwhile Lorraine Hansberry was dying. Two days after *Brustein*
opened, Lorraine telephoned Robert Nemiroff in terror from her hotel: the
numbness had moved from her legs to her chest. He knew the cancer had

conquered her central nervous system and immediately had her transferred to University Hospital. Three days later, on October 20, she lost her sight, had convulsions, and lapsed into a coma: the disease had entered her brain. By this time, Mamie had come from California to care for her only sister.

That was the time we had together. I stayed with her from October to January, till she died. And that was a very beautiful time. It was very hard and sad, but yet it was beautiful.

She felt, you knew, secure. She wanted you to be there with her. She wanted me to comb her hair and take care of her. And when she had to go to the bathroom, well, half of the time, she couldn't get out of bed. I would wake up in the middle of the night and just know it was time. So she was very appreciative of that. She looked up one day and said, "You're good."[70]

Robert Nemiroff watched over Lorraine every minute he was not tending to complicated business of the play. Even in the times she was unconscious, he "repeated to her the words of a letter from a stranger," who praised her play, wished her well.[71]

On October 22, 1964, a miracle seemed to occur. Lorraine regained her sight and partial movement. In the last two months of her life, she never missed the opportunity to laugh, to tease, to make funny faces at Mamie and Bob. As Nemiroff explained, "It was her *funny* lines . . . of which she was proudest.[72] For Christmas 1964, Bob gave her a lovely necklace of delicate gold and amber to set off her tawny brown skin and her flashing eyes. Less than three weeks later, on the morning of January 12, 1965, Lorraine Hansberry was smiling and chatty. At 8:30 A.M. she grew faint and fell unconscious. At 8:50 Lorraine Hansberry died. That night, in deference to her memory, the lights at Henry Miller's Theatre stayed dark—never to shine on Sidney and Iris again.

On January 15, 1965, more than six hundred friends and admirers pressed into a small red brick church in Harlem to pay their final respects to Lorraine Hansberry. As the brown wooden casket, shrouded in white carnations, lay before the altar, the Reverend Eugene Callender led the congregation in singing "Abide with Me." Then he read messages from James Baldwin and the Reverend Martin Luther King, Jr., whose letter ended: "Her creative ability and her profound grasp of the deep social issues confronting the world today will remain an inspiration to generations yet unborn." After Mr. Callender delivered the eulogy, Paul Robeson rose to speak with all his power and poetry, his large hands moving ceaselessly.

After reciting several verses of a Negro folk song, he concluded: "As Lorraine says farewell, she bids us to keep our heads high and to hold onto our strength and powers, to soar like the eagle." Ruby Dee paid tribute to Lorraine Hansberry, reading passages from *Sidney Brustein.* In the warmth and still of the hour, Nina Simone sang some of Lorraine's favorite songs, as Robert Nemiroff, Shelley Winters, Sammy Davis, Jr., Ossie Davis, and Paddy Chayefsky listened quietly,[73] as did Malcom X—a few weeks from his death. Despite the blizzard lashing Manhattan, Robert Nemiroff and Burt D'Lugoff led the procession north.[74] Later that day Lorraine Hansberry was eased into her final resting place at Bethel Cemetery at her beloved Croton-on-Hudson.

Lorraine Hansberry's most valuable legacy was her literary estate—*A Raisin in the Sun, The Sign in Sidney Brustein's Window,* three unpublished plays, and a myriad of unfinished works. In choosing her literary executor, she needed a person of intelligence, dedication, and sound literary and financial judgment. She had wisely chosen Robert Nemiroff. In the years since 1965, he has kept her works alive, sharing the spirit of this sometimes timid but always profound genius of a playwright.

In 1969, he edited and produced *To Be Young, Gifted and Black*—a title now a part of our language—and then expanded the work into the full-length informal autobiography of the same title. In 1970 *Les Blancs,* with final text adapted by Nemiroff, was presented on Broadway, and in 1972 he edited *Les Blancs: The Last Collected Plays of Lorraine Hansberry.* Recasting her 1959 play as a musical, he produced *Raisin,* which won the prestigious Tony Award in 1974.

Within her literary legacy, Lorraine Hansberry willed a philosophy that defied despair, indignity, even death. Just as Martin Luther King had a dream, just as Langston Hughes yearned for "A Dream Deferred," Lorraine Hansberry nurtured a dream. Realizing that "we are such stuff as dreams are made on," she nevertheless believed that we can impose order on the universe, that we can reform evil institutions with commitment and involvement.[75] She dreamed of a world in which we become better than we are. She told us, as she told her sister, "You're good." She wrote the stories of young men who have the potential of greatness: Walter Lee Younger, Alton Scales, Hannibal. They are all variations of the young man with the handsome face and balled up fists—dead in the Harlem church. Nobody cries, but it is very quiet.

Chapter Three

The Talented Tenth and Long-headed Jazzers

During Lorraine Hansberry's childhood and adolescence, she usually felt isolated. She did not share a major part of her brothers' and sister's lives because of age differences; she was separated from her grammar school acquaintances by her relative affluence; she was one of very few blacks at the predominantly white University of Wisconsin.

Like most sensitive, intelligent, and lonely youths, she found companionship in books. Perhaps at times methodically, at other times intuitively, Hansberry absorbed from Shakespeare and her other favorite authors a sensitivity to the sounds and connotations of words. No one knows exactly why so few people are endowed with an ability to write fluently and concisely, but Hansberry was one of the lucky ones. Her plays, stories, letters, and journal are all marked by an easy, graceful, pliable style.

But the ease and gracefulness of her works do not hide any intellectual shallowness. Listening, observing, and reading in youth ideally leads to questioning, discovering, accepting, or rejecting in adulthood. So they did to Hansberry. Her favorite books in childhood introduced her to historical figures—such as Toussaint L'Ouverture—and to talented living people—like Langston Hughes. But her years at *Freedom*, where she first put her writing ability to serious use, introduced her to ideas as well as to famous people.

Understanding rejection on a personal level, Lorraine Hansberry understood even more the pain of an entire rejected race, her own race. Through her art she attempted to portray the many injustices one people had inflicted on another and the absurdity—and the danger—of ignoring a race of people that had produced so many talented leaders. In so doing, she found herself faced with a dilemma that many white writers have confronted, but that is especially acute for black writers—how to combine the necessary detachment of the artist with the commitment of the fighter against oppression. Does the work of art or the struggle come first?

Working for *Freedom* intensified this dilemma, but it was one that
Hansberry had already observed in the lives of other black artists she had
known or read about. Paul Robeson and Langston Hughes were also lifelong influences on Lorraine Hansberry, the writer and thinker, as she tried
to make her own place in the New York literary world. They are, of course,
important figures in their own right whom no young black writer in the
1950s could have ignored, but the fact that they had dealt with Hansberry's plight in opposite ways gives them a particular interest as figures in
her background. Two other men whom she had long admired—Frederick
Douglass, who had died thirty-five years before her birth, and W. E. B.
DuBois, whom we have already seen as a guest in the Hansberry household—remained important presences in her thought and writing, most
obviously in the plays she wrote near the end of her life about slavery in
the antebellum South and the struggle for freedom in Africa. Both men
spent their entire adult lives as activists for black freedom, yet out of the
intensity of the struggle itself both men paradoxically produced books that
survive as works of art.

These, then, are some figures behind Lorraine Hansberry. Without
some understanding of their lives, aspirations, and achievements, we cannot fully understand hers. Hansberry herself understood and honored the
endurance and strength of her literary heritage.

The Song of the Slave: Frederick Douglass

Negro spirituals have injected deep tones and varied rhythms into the
American musical repertoire. The lyrics suggest abiding religious faith, a
chastened but realistic acceptance of life, anticipation of the Promised Land
of milk and honey. Spirituals should be sung by solemn white-robed figures in large, hot, dim churches.

Frederick Douglass, in his 1845 *Narrative,* had no such romantic
notions.

Slaves sing most when they are most unhappy. The songs of the slave represent
the sorrows of the heart. . . . [The songs] told a tale of woe . . . they were tones
loud, long, and deep; they breathed the prayer and complaint of souls boiling over
with the bitterest anguish. Every tone was a testimony against slavery, and a prayer to God for deliverance from chains. . . . To those songs I trace my first glim-
mering conception of the dehumanizing character of slavery. [1]

"Stealing Away to Jesus" meant heading north to freedom, leaving Master
behind to chop his own cotton.

Born in 1817, Frederick Douglass recorded his first twenty-one years in a spare, yet lyrical, style in *Narrative of the Life of Frederick Douglass, An American Slave* (1845). Not only a moving autobiography, this book also describes the Slave as Everyman and is a significant contribution to American letters. Even though he personally suffered little physical abuse—besides cold and hunger—as a child, he witnessed violence that shredded his childhood innocence. He watched his master flay his aunt's back raw. He watched the master's son throw his younger brother to the ground "and with the heel of his boot stamp . . . upon his head till the blood gushed from his ears. . . ." He heard of his future wife's cousin's mistress striking her so viciously with an oak stick that her nose and breastbone shattered. The girl died within hours. Her offense: while watching the baby in her mistress's room she fell asleep in her chair and let the baby cry.[2]

Frederick Douglass learned a valuable lesson at the age of eight. He was the son of the slave Harriet Bailey and a white man (rumored to be the master). After spending his first seven years on a plantation in Talbot Country, Maryland, Douglass was sent to Baltimore to his master's relative, Hugh Auld. The country boy's excitement over moving to the city was only matched by his admiration for his kind new mistress. "Her face was made of heavenly smiles and she was not offended by a slave looking her in the face." Mrs. Auld seemed the antithesis of the jealous Captain Anthony, who had tied, stripped, and beaten the boy's beautiful Aunt Hester for seeing a young black man. A stranger to slavery before this time, Mrs. Auld soon began to teach him "the A,B,C" and then words of three or four letters.[3]

When he learned of these lessons, Hugh Auld became enraged. Teaching a slave to read was "unlawful, unsafe." If you gave a slave an inch, he would take an ell. A slave who could read became "unmanageable, discontented and unhappy." Overnight, Douglass's mistress's "cheerful eye" became cold and enraged as she snatched newspapers and books away from him. The reading lessons were over. But the real lesson he had learned was "the white man's power to enslave the black man." Later he wrote, "It was a grand achievement, and I prized it highly. From that moment, I understood that pathway from slavery to freedom."[4] The slaveholders' obsessive need to keep the slaves illiterate, and hence less than men, is one of the insights of Douglass's stark, compelling narrative of 1845.

During his next eight years with the Aulds (1825–33), Douglass enjoyed the superior clothing and food and relative freedom of movement of the city slave. He also had time to contemplate the psychology of slavery. After his "lesson," he continued to read, learned to write, befriended the

white street urchins, yearned to escape. Baltimore had become his "gateway . . . to . . . prosperity."[5]
Owing to a death in the Auld family, Douglass returned to Master Thomas in the country. After nine months of frustration over his slave's lack of submission, Auld sent Douglass to Edward Covey, a "slave breaker." In the longest and most lyrical chapter of his *Narrative*, Douglass describes his weekly beatings. But one day he determined to fight back, and "a slave was made a man." Risking his life by striking a white man, drawing strength from a magical root (possibly ginseng) and the Almighty, Douglass fought with Covey—and won. From that time on his credo was: "The white man who expected to succeed in whipping, must also succeed in killing me."[6] In 1838, at the age of twenty-one, Frederick Douglass fled to freedom in New York, married Anna Murray, and then settled in New Bedford, Massachusetts, where his *Narrative* ends.

The year 1841 marked the beginning of Frederick Douglass's public life as he nervously addressed the Anti-Slavery Society in New Bedford. By 1845, his powers as an orator were honed to such brilliance and persuasion that people began to doubt that he had ever been a slave. At that time, he wrote his *Narrative*. Fearing reprisal from Thomas Auld, he sailed for England, where he addressed the World Temperance Convention at Covent Garden in 1846. Long a foe of alcohol, he felt that drinking was especially destructive to the black man—his dignity, family, and work. Douglass's reception in England was so warm that his British friends raised over $700 to purchase his freedom and later over $2,000 to found his Abolitionist newspaper, the *North Star*.[7]

The *North Star* files (1847–60) contain Douglass's commentary on many important issues of the day. An advocate of women's suffrage, he attended the Seneca Falls Convention in 1848. He railed against the Fugitive-Slave Law, capital punishment, and African colonization; he envisioned Kansas as a free state, defended John Brown, and supported the Republican party.[8]

From 1861 until his death in 1895, Frederick Douglass was very much a public figure. His associations with President Lincoln and John Brown, his role in recruiting the 54th and 55th Massachusetts Regiments to the Union Army, his service as Minister to Haiti and as Marshall of the District of Columbia are all well known. Orator, editor, reformer, presidential advisor, writer—Frederick Douglass excelled in all of these fields. His achievements surpassed those of most educated, moneyed men of the time, let alone those born in slavery. Only recently have scholars restored Frederick Douglass to his rightful place in American history.

Of his voluminous writings, Douglass's *Narrative* of 1845 remains one of his finest. In 1855, he expanded the book, entitling it *My Bondage and My Freedom*. His final, inclusive autobiography, *Life and Times of Frederick Douglass, Written by Himself,* was published in 1881. Just as Abraham Lincoln was the Great Emancipator, Frederick Douglass was the Great Reformer, the father of the twentieth-century protest movement.[9] Even though he died an honored citizen in a twenty-room mansion, the spirit of Frederick Douglass and his message to the oppressed of America remain engraved in his 1845 *Narrative*.

A slave about to become a man in 1833, on Sundays he watched the ships on the Chesapeake Bay: "Those beautiful vessels, robed in purest white . . . were to me so many shrouded ghosts. . . . There, with no audience but the Almighty, I would pour out my soul's complaint . . . with an apostrophe to the moving multitude of ships; 'You are freedom's swift-winged angels, that fly around the world; I am confined in bands of iron.' . . . The glad ship is gone; she hides in the dim distance. I am left in the hottest hell of unending slavery."[10]

Five years later, Frederick Douglass escaped to freedom in a sailor suit. More than five decades elapsed until he died in his mansion by the river, the captain of his own soul, having steered many to freedom.

On her desk, Lorraine Hansberry kept the three-volume *Life and Writings of Frederick Douglass,* containing the essays, articles, speeches, and letters of the mature man, as well as his 1845 *Narrative*. From Douglass she learned the "wedding of intellect to action" and the importance of "internationalism"—while being inspired by the "breadth of his vision.[11]

For the literary frontispiece of *Les Blancs,* Lorraine Hansberry included a quote by Jean Genet: "But what exactly is black? / First of all, what's his color?" The other author she honored by quoting a longer passage (without citing its specific source):

If there is no struggle there is no progress. Those who profess to favor freedom and yet deprecate agitation . . . want the ocean without the roar of its many waters.

This struggle may be a moral one, or it may be a physical one, and it may be both moral and physical, but it must be a struggle. Power concedes nothing without a demand. . . . Men may not get all they pay for in this world, but they must certainly pay for all they get. If we ever get free from the oppressions and wrongs heaped upon us, we must pay for their removal. We must do that by labor, by suffering, by sacrifice, and if needs be, by our lives and the lives of others.

With the image of the sea, the fire of youth, and the wisdom of age, Frederick Douglass expressed the essence of *Les Blancs.*

The Talented Tenth: W. E. B. DuBois

A lover of music, an original thinker, and one of the great sociologists of our time, Dr. W. E. B. DuBois wrote a famous essay in 1903, "The Talented Tenth." The thrust of the essay is that one tenth of black people, the talented, should be educated to lead the masses of black people—a theory of an elite.

On February 23, 1868, William Edward Burghardt DuBois was born to Mary Burghardt and Alfred DuBois in Great Barrington, Massachusetts. Within a year, Alfred DuBois left his wife and son to support themselves in this small town notable for its absence of racism except toward the Irish Catholics. During his first seventeen years, he typified the New England schoolboy. He and his mother attended the predominantly white Congregationalist church, joined in the Town Hall meetings, and lived frugally and fairly happily except for his mother's silent depression over his father's desertion. The town took pride in his exceptional scholarship. His principal arranged for him to study Greek and other college preparatory subjects; the mother of one of his classmates bought books for him. [12]

A descendant of Frenchmen, Dutchmen, and Africans, DuBois encountered little prejudice in Great Barrington and believed that exceptional achievement would whisk away any trace of prejudice. New England thriftiness, reserve, and self-reliance had permeated his fiber. In his *Autobiography,* he explains:

I became quite thoroughly New England. It was not good form in Great Barrington to express one's thoughts volubly, or to give way to excessive emotion. We were even sparing in our daily greetings. . . . I was early thrown in upon myself. I found it difficult and even unnecessary to approach other people and by that same token my own inner life perhaps grew the richer. . . . The Negroes in the South, when I came to know them, could never understand why I did not naturally greet everyone I passed on the street or slap my friends on the back. [13]

Poverty and ignorance, DuBois thought, stemmed from a lack of opportunity, or more likely, a lack of thrift. [14]

On graduation day, W. E. B. DuBois—the only black student—spoke on the Abolitionist Wendell Phillips. With encouragement from his teachers, family, and townspeople, he began to plan for college. But that fall his plans were delayed because of the death of his mother. His reaction was curious: "I felt a certain gladness to see her at peace at last, for she had worried all her life."[15] Harvard was his first choice, but first he would go South to Fisk University.

During his three years at Fisk (he was exempted from the freshman year), W. E. B. DuBois became more aware of his blackness. He "thrilled to be . . . among so many people of . . . such various and extraordinary colors. . . ." He was impressed by the beautiful Lena Calhoun (the aunt of Lena Horne).[16] More important, he discovered the southern spiritual; he began to sense southern racism; he performed so well that he was accepted by Harvard.

Had DuBois been white, his life would have been launched into a smooth, rich course by the Harvard master's degree, his two years' study at the University of Berlin, his graduation speech on Jefferson Davis, and the Harvard Ph.D. His doctoral dissertation, *The Suppression of the African Slave Trade,* was hailed as "the first scientific historical work" written by a black man and was published as the first volume of the new Harvard Historical Studies (1896). He had the cool temperament, the mechanized discipline, and the facile mind of the northeastern scholar. He felt, however, that he must use his intellect to prove the equality of the black man. In *The Philadelphia Negro* (1899), the first sociological study of blacks ever published, he still retained his New England notion that self-reliance was the key to social mobility. This idea echoed through most of the fifteen books he edited, including *The Negro in Business, The Negro Church,* and *The College-Bred Negro,* during his tenure as a professor at Atlanta University (1897–1910).

As the years wore on, however, his identity as a black man propelled him into public life and politics. Despite opposition from Booker T. Washington, DuBois organized the Niagara Movement (1905)—the first black protest organization of the twentieth century.[17] Five years later, it evolved into the National Association for the Advancement of Colored People. His role as a founder of the NAACP led to his break with Atlanta University in 1910. He did not leave Atlanta for the New York office without regret: "My career as a scientist was to be swallowed up in my role as master of propaganda. This was not wholly to my liking. I was no natural leader of men."[18]

For the next twenty-four years he served as editor of the influential official NAACP magazine. *Crisis* became "more a reflection of DuBois' personality, thinking, and concerns than it was of the organization."[19] He forged black opinion of art, military service, lynching, Jim Crow, interracial marriage, Karl Marx, black theater, Marcus Garvey, and Booker T. Washington. Gradually he lost faith in American democracy, becoming particularly appalled by both the Democrats' and Republicans' cavalier attitude toward the black vote and black concerns. Finally, in October 1961, two years before his death, he applied for membership in the Communist party, stating, "Capitalism cannot reform itself. . . . No universal selfishness can bring social good to all."[20]

In his ninety-five years, Dr. W. E. B. DuBois wrote twenty-one books, edited fifteen more, published hundreds of essays and articles, and founded and edited four magazines, including *Crisis* and *Phylon*. (Currently, the best concise selection of Dr. DuBois's work is the two-volume *Seventh Son,* ably edited by Julius Lester.) While his fiction has its detractors, most of DuBois's works are outstanding in style and philosophy. His well-known *The Souls of Black Folk* (1903) is marked by the clarity of a man in his thirties and includes his famous essay on Booker T. Washington, a piece which indirectly contributed to his break with Atlanta University. Of his three autobiographies, the final 1968 *Autobiography* (quoted in this text) is moving and compelling, though at times vague. Who exactly, for example, are the white Burghardts? "The Talented Tenth" (1903) remains one of his most famous essays. Not the best-known of his works, *Black Folk: Then and Now* (1939) is the work of a mature scholar and political thinker.

In 1903 Booker T. Washington published a book entitled *The Negro Problem,* a collection of essays by black leaders. Washington's own essay, "Industrial Education for the Negro," was first, followed immediately by DuBois's "The Talented Tenth." For the last time, these two men were closely aligned. The points DuBois makes seem reasonable: to chronicle past leaders, or the Talented Tenth; to suggest how they be educated; and to show their relation to the Negro problem (they will solve it). His list of the Tenthers is impressive: Phillis Wheatley, Frederick Douglass, Sojourner Truth, Benjamin Bannecker, Washington himself. With overtones of a modern-day humanities director, he concludes: "Education must not simply teach work—it must teach Life."[21]

What is distressing about this essay is that DuBois avoids coping with the *other* 90 percent of the black population. Should they not learn about Life? As time passed, DuBois became increasingly derisive toward Booker T. Washington and his "Cast down your bucket where you are" philosophy—that blacks should learn trades, support themselves, acquire property, gradually earn a niche in the American economic structure. He does allude to Washington's ideas briefly. "Where ought they [Northern black leaders] to have begun to build? At the bottom . . . down in the very depths of knowledge there where the roots of justice strike into the lowest soil of Truth."[22]

DuBois never fully appreciated Washington for his pragmatism, his real accomplishments, his sensitivity to the Southern mind and way of life. Great Barrington is a long way from Franklin County, Virginia, where Washington was born into slavery. Much of DuBois's resentment stemmed from jealousy over Washington's position as the most powerful black man in America, the first black man ever invited to dine at the White House.[23] "The Talented Tenth," then, has an elitist, paternalistic overtone—ironic for a man who cherished New England individualism as a boy and then gradually evolved into a Socialist and Communist for the good of *all* people.

With the passage of thirty years, however, Dr. DuBois put aside personal dispute, devoting himself to sociology as a means of ending racism and to history for its own inherent fascination. An outgrowth of *The Negro* (1915), DuBois's *Black Folk: Then and Now* (1939) explored the richness of black African history as well as the current status of blacks in the West Indies, America, and Africa.

In addition to the accuracy of his research and the clarity of his writing, DuBois still had a clear moral purpose in writing *Black Folk: Then and Now*: to dispute the notion that the Negro has no history and to shatter the black man's image as "the clown of history" and "the slave of industry."[24] This ethical perspective, together with his intellectual edge, raises DuBois to the level of an original thinker. His belief that Negro blood was the basis of the blood of all men may have provoked some whites, but he makes a convincing argument. Stating that color prejudice is a relatively new historical concept, he theorizes that prejudice ironically evolved during the Renaissance when individual freedom included the freedom to enslave.[25]

We have already seen that Dr. DuBois was a frequent guest in the Hansberry household, but he most affected Lorraine Hansberry's work as a theorist and historian of black life. Of his numerous works, *Black Folk: Then and Now* affected her most obviously and specifically. A young woman named Candace was the heroine of her unpublished novel, *All the Dark and Beautiful Warriors,* and Candace was a main character (almost immediately deleted) in her play, *Les Blancs.* Even though Candace was a popular name for children in the 1940s, Hansberry learned from DuBois's work that Candace was the title—not the name—of an entire line of African queens.[26] From *Black Folk,* Lorraine Hansberry perhaps had her first vision of the Haitian liberator, later the subject of her unfinished play *Toussaint.*

Black Folk also teemed with details of African dance and music, British seizure of African lands, Kenya, the Kikuyu, the bronze and brass works of Benin, the Ashanti, and Bantu—integral to the backgrounds of *A Raisin in the Sun* and *Les Blancs.*

Robert Nemiroff believes that Hansberry was not influenced by this theory of the "Talented Tenth," but rather that she was affected by *The Souls of Black Folk* (1903).[27] He concurs with Saunders Redding that this book fixed "the moment in history when the American Negro began to reject the idea of the world's belonging to white people only, and to think of himself, in concert, as a potential force in the organization of society."[28]

From the time of her year's seminar on African Studies, Dr. W. E. B. DuBois played a substantial role in Hansberry's artistic life. On February 23, 1964, she paid tribute to this great thinker in a speech at Carnegie Hall:

I do not remember when I first heard the name DuBois. For some Negroes it comes into consciousness so early, so persistently that it is like the spirituals or the blues or discussions of oppression; he was a fact of our culture. People spoke of him as they did the church or the nation. He was an institution in our lives, a bulwark of our culture. I believe that his personality and thought have colored generations of Negro intellectuals, far greater, I think than some of those intellectuals know. And, without a doubt, his ideas have influenced a multitude who do not even know his name.[29]

She characterizes his legacy as one that insists that American blacks should not "follow their oppressors," should "work for a socialist organization," and should never again allow "their oppressors to say who is or is not a fit leader of our cause."[30] In all likelihood, Dr. DuBois would have numbered Lorraine Hansberry among his Talented Tenth.

The Artistic Activist: Paul Robeson

Large, and charismatic, Paul Robeson was one of the finest baritones of our time. Internationally famous by his thirtieth birthday as a singer and actor, he added arias from *Boris Godunov* to his concert program after his first trip to Russia in 1934.[31] Given the brilliant range, tone, and subtlety of Robeson's voice, a typical one-man evening program would be likely to include arias from Mozart's *The Magic Flute,* Negro spirituals, folk songs of various countries, "Ol' Man River" from *Show Boat,* and other songs from his movies and musicals. When he sang "Go Down, Moses," he introduced the spiritual by explaining its role in the slaves' escape to the

North and the parallel between Moses and the freedom fighter Harriet Tubman.[32] He admired the grandeur of "Deep River," the driving power of "Jacob's Ladder," the militancy of "Joshua Fit the Battle of Jericho."[33]

The youngest of five children, Paul Robeson was born on April 9, 1898, in Princeton, New Jersey. When his mother died six years later, young Paul became the closest companion of his fifty-nine-year-old father, the Reverend William Drew Robeson. With great love and respect for "Pop," young Paul enjoyed playing checkers with him on winter evenings. "We two would sit for hours, engrossed in our game, not speaking much but wonderfully happy together." His father was never an Uncle Tom to a white man.[34]

When Paul was nine, he and his father moved to Westfield, New Jersey, where Paul attended an integrated school; two years later, they settled in nearby Somerville. One of two black students in the high school, Robeson easily formed close friendships with his classmates. His music teacher carefully trained his voice; his English teacher introduced him to Shakespeare and directed him in the title role of *Othello;* his coach was pleased with his star fullback. His principal hated him.[35]

Spurred on by the racist hatred of Dr. Ackerman, the principal, the encouragement of his teachers and classmates, and his father's confidence, Robeson decided to enter a competitive examination, open to all seniors in the state, for a scholarship to Rutgers College. Robeson won. That spring he also entered a contest, reading Wendell Phillips's oration on Toussaint L'Ouverture. Although he placed third, he still had his Rutgers scholarship to present to the Ackermans of the world.[36]

During his Rutgers years, Paul Robeson distinguished himself as a student, athlete, and leader. He was elected to the student council, earned twelve varsity letters in sports (football, basketball, baseball, and track), delivered the commencement address, and graduated Phi Beta Kappa. In 1919 he moved to New York, rented an apartment in Harlem, and entered Columbia Law School in 1920. In 1921 he married Eslanda Goode, later an anthropologist, and earned his law degree in 1923.

While still a law student, Robeson had already begun his ascent to stardom in the Broadway lead of *Taboo* in 1922. Later that year, renamed *Voodoo,* the play ran in England—which the Robesons loved for its absence of Jim Crow laws. In 1924 the Provincetown Playhouse engaged Robeson to star in two Eugene O'Neill plays, *The Emperor Jones* and *All God's Chillun Got Wings,* a tragedy of interracial marriage. Praised by George Jean Nathan and other critics, Robeson became incapable of a mediocre performance in his remaining ten plays. His New York productions included *Black*

Boy (1926) and *Show Boat* (1930), featuring his curtain-calling rendition of "Ol' Man River." In London he starred in *The Hairy Ape* (1931), *Toussaint L'Ouverture* (1936), and with singular distinction in *Othello* (1930).

Nineteen forty-four marked the pinnacle of popularity for Robeson the artist. His New York portrayal of Othello with Jose Ferrer as Iago was so illuminating and powerful that the play made theater history as the longest-running Shakespearean play on Broadway—296 performances. Two months before *Othello* left the Schubert Theater for a national tour, the Council on African Affairs arranged a birthday party for the beloved Robeson at the 17th Regiment Armory. More than seven thousand people attended. All this time, Robeson had been performing (some would say legitimizing) the Negro spiritual. He learned more than twenty languages so that he could sing folk songs in their original form. His eleven films include *The Emperor Jones* (1933), *Show Boat* (1936), and *Song of Freedom* (1937), which features a black opera singer who discovers his royal African roots and returns to England to lead a labor strike.[37] (Paul Robeson, Jr., cites this role as the reason some people mistakenly think of his father as an opera singer).[38]

In March 1947, Paul Robeson announced, "You have heard my final concert. . . . I shall sing now for my trade union and college friends. In other words, only at gatherings where I can sing what I please."[39] Thus began a debate which continues today: Robeson the artist versus Robeson the political leader. Philip S. Foner considers him "a great political thinker with a mind both original and sound, qualities enhanced by a fine literary style."[40] Harold Cruse writes that Robeson "subordinated what should have been his specific role as a Negro artist to the role of civil rights leader in a field already overcrowded. . . ."[41]

From 1945 until 1958, Robeson the political activist overshadowed Robeson the artist. The American stage, film industry, and music world lost one of its most original talents. Robeson's role as spokesman for oppressed blacks expanded to that of advocate for the Russian people, champion of labor groups, and defender of Benjamin J. Davis, "a dear friend of mine and . . . for many years a leader of the Communist Party of this country."[42] In April 1949 Robeson addressed the World Congress of Partisans for Peace in Paris. "It is unthinkable that the American Negroes will go to war in behalf of those who have oppressed us for generations . . . against [Russia] which has . . . raised our people to full human dignity of mankind."[43]

America of the late 1940s and early 1950s did not share Robeson's love for the Soviet Union. In 1946 he told the California Un-American Activities Committee that he was not a Communist—a comment he refused to repeat to the HUAC in 1948. In 1949 he published articles in *Komsomolskaia Pravda,* and the Soviet Union named Mount Robeson in his honor. The American government did little to protect him against rioters at a concert arranged by folk singers and civil libertarians in Peekskill, New York, in 1949. The State Department revoked his passport in 1950, causing his annual income to plummet from $150,000 to $3,000. In 1952 the Soviet Union awarded him the Stalin Peace Prize. Finally, in 1958, his passport was restored.[44] Oppressed people of many races will long remember Paul Robeson's selfless, though at times naive, devotion to their cause. For Robeson the artist the price was dear.

In 1951 Robeson founded *Freedom* magazine, Hansberry's employer for nearly three years. From Robeson, she began to consider the fusion of art and politics. Just as Moses told the pharaoh to let his people go, Robeson sought to loose the chains of his people. Like Douglass and DuBois before him, his methods lacked prudence and pragmatism. He did not lack nobility and bravery. In his last years, Robeson played *Othello* at Stratford-on-Avon, toured Australia and New Zealand in his final concerts, and saw his name placed on the Rutgers University student center.[45] A more perfect world would have cherished one of its most talented artists, assuring him the peace of mind to sing his arias, spirituals, and folk songs, to create his Othellos and Toussaint L'Ouvertures. He provided to Lorraine Hansberry, however, a powerful example of "man's inhumanity to man" to inspire her writing. At a Harlem rally on May 26, 1954, Hansberry praised Robeson as a "truly great artist . . . who embodies . . . at once—not only in [his] life but in [his] art—the people from whom [he] springs: to be a voice, member and champion of the people's struggle."[46]

Long-headed Jazzers: Langston Hughes

Nineteen twenty-one was an exciting time for a young man in New York. The Jazz Age had invaded Manhattan with its flappers, blues, jazz singers, raccoon coats. Prohibition, speakeasies, bootleg gin, easy money, the Charleston. Uptown in Harlem, a significant literary revival was two years in the offing. By 1923 the population would have exploded tenfold in ten years. Many blacks came from the South, seeking better jobs and housing, but some came for an almost mystical sense of a new nation: Harlem, the Black Metropolis. While the Cotton Club and the Sugar Cane Club catered to whites, young Harlemites had heard Bessie Smith belting the blues and had seen dancers doing the Cakewalk.

In the fall of 1921, Langston Hughes arrived in New York. With tuition money from his father, he enrolled in Columbia University. Already a published poet, he would have been content to absorb the music, parades, street people of Harlem.[47] The Broadway musical *Shuffle Along* symbolized the spirit of Harlem to him with the music of Eubie Blake and Noble Sissle, songs such as "I'm Just Wild about Harry," and dancing of chorus girls Josephine Baker and Florence Mills. In "Jazzonia" (1923), Hughes captured the whirling, brassy ambience of Harlem nights:

> In a Harlem cabaret
> Six long-headed jazzers play.
> A dancing girl whose eyes are bold
> Lifts high a dress of silken gold.
> Oh, singing tree!
> Oh, shining rivers of the soul. . . .[48]

An admirer of Carl Sandburg, Paul Laurence Dunbar, and Vachel Lindsay, Hughes preferred the company of men in the street and the bar to that of intellectuals. The driving beat of the blues caught the perseverance and spunk of these unlettered men. While the blues had a despondent mood, when they were sung they made people laugh—at their troubles.[49] In 1923 Hughes wrote "The Weary Blues," faithfully copying the form of the blues, the syncopation, the steady bass, the irregular African rhythms of the treble.

> Droning a drowsy syncopated tune,
> Rocking back and forth to a mellow croon,
>   I heard a Negro play.
> Down on Lenox Avenue the other night
> By the pale dull pallor of an old gas light
>   He did a lazy sway. . . .
>   He did a lazy sway. . . .
> To the tune o' those Weary Blues.
> With his ebony hands on each ivory key
> He made that poor piano moan with melody,
>   O Blues![50]

Of all the important writers of the Harlem Renaissance (1923–33), Langston Hughes alone took jazz and the blues seriously.[51] Moreover, he was probably the single most important artistic influence on Lorraine Hansberry.

The only child of Carrie Langston Hughes and James Nathaniel Hughes, Langston Hughes was born in Joplin, Missouri, on February 1, 1902. From his mother he inherited a love of books and theater and a certain wanderlust. (Later he would tell Richard Wright, "Six months in one place is long enough to make one's life complicated.") His father bequeathed him little of value; in 1903, that embittered, pompous man made his permanent exit to Mexico, like Carl Hansberry forty years later. His mother left Hughes in the care of his grandmother from 1908 to 1914—probably the happiest years of Hughes's life. A proud and strikingly handsome woman of Indian, French, and African heritage, Mary Langston had been the first black woman to attend Oberlin College. Even though she could not always afford meals, she told him wonderful stories. Later Hughes said, "Nobody ever cried in my grandmother's stories. They worked, or schemed, or fought. But no crying."[52] These stories may well have been a source of Hughes's sense of humor and survival.

After his grandmother's death, he joined his mother in Cleveland, where his school classmates elected him class poet in 1916 because they thought blacks had rhythm. Even though his first effusive poems were terrible, these children had initiated his career. In 1919 Hughes spent the summer with his father in Mexico. Deeply upset by his father's hatred of blacks and poor people, and by his insistence that he learn bookkeeping, Langston Hughes attempted suicide. Nevertheless, he returned to Cleveland for his senior year, where he was elected yearbook editor and again class poet—an honor he now deserved.[53]

Hoping that his father would eventually pay his college tuition, Hughes spent the year after graduation in Mexico. (Resentment of patrons was a continuing motif in Hughes's life.) On the train ride down, he scribbled one of his most famous poems on an envelope, "The Negro Speaks of Rivers." With a stake from his father in 1921, he moved to New York, where he attended Columbia University for a year, wrote poetry, and worked at a series of odd jobs. In 1923, he signed up as a cabin boy on a ship to West Africa. On the day of departure, he threw all his books into the sea. This grand gesture was for naught: when he arrived, he was met by signs advising EUROPEANS ONLY and Africans' amusement at this light-skinned man's quest for his "roots."[54]

The remainder of his twenties was marked by travel, excitement, and sporadic hunger. In 1924 he worked as a cook in Paris. While working as a busboy in Washington, D.C., in 1925, he met Vachel Lindsay. That year *Opportunity* magazine awarded him first prize in a poetry contest. He went to New York to accept and met many of the Harlem Renaissance writers—

James Weldon Johnson, Zora Neale Hurston, Countee Cullen, Arna Bontemps, Jean Toomer, and Carl Van Vechten. This recognition prompted
Amy Spingarn, a patron of the arts, to award him a scholarship to Lincoln
University in Pennsylvania. While there, he published two books of poetry, wrote a sociology paper demanding integration of Lincoln's all-white
faculty, and escaped to Harlem periodically, before graduating in 1929.
   In 1928 Hughes had acquired another patron, Mrs. Rufus Osgood Ma-
son, an elderly white woman. During the two years she supported him
while he wrote his first novel, he was genuinely fond of her. When she
criticized a poem for its lack of "primitivism," however, he decided he
could accept no more money and severed all ties. The year 1931 found
Hughes traveling South with a friend, visiting Mary McLeod Bethune,
and lecturing at various colleges, including the University of North Carolina and Hampton Institute.[55]
   By his thirtieth birthday in 1932, the agenda for the rest of Hughes's
life was set. He wrote. He lectured at many universities. He traveled to
Russia in 1933, to Spain during the Civil War in 1937, and all over America. He promoted black art, establishing the Harlem Suitcase Theater in
1938 and later other black little theaters in other cities. He wrote a number of children's books, beginning with *The First Book of Negroes* (1952),
which omitted Robeson and DuBois. He celebrated life with persistence
and "no crying."
   Supporting himself with his writing after his youth, Langston Hughes
was prolific. During his sixty-five years, he published sixteen volumes of
poetry, two novels, two autobiographies, three volumes of short stories,
eight children's books, and five books about "Simple" (Jesse B. Semple)—
an untrained, honest, long-suffering factory worker whose prototype
Hughes met at a bar on the corner of 125th and Lenox. Of his many plays,
three were produced on Broadway, *Mulatto* (1934), *Simply Heavenly* (1957),
and *Tambourines to Glory* (1963). He became a Guggenheim Fellow in 1935
and was elected to the National Institute of Arts and Letters in 1946.
While his fiction was well received commercially and critically, Hughes
will probably be remembered best for his poetry. His poems "Harlem,"
"Mother to Son," and "Washerwoman" made a deep impression on Lorraine Hansberry, as will be shown in chapter 4.
   Much of Hughes's poetry is infused with jazz and the blues—indige-
nous American art forms. He captures the sensual atmosphere of the Harlem cabaret where the long-headed jazzers play. He discovers power and
pathos as the black man plays the blues "like a musical fool" and sings "I'se
gwine to quit ma frownin' / And put ma troubles on the shelf." He extols
the power of the black mother in "Washerwoman" and "Mother to Son."

In his *Dream* montage, he voices basic human needs in the poorest man's vernacular: "There's liable to be confusion / when a dream gets kicked around." He good-naturedly teases death in "Wake." Hughes's poems are shot through with brilliant colors, diverse textures, complex rhythms, nuances of black speech, the rainbow of black skin tones. There is also an archetypal quality to Hughes's poetry as he speaks of souls "grown deep like the rivers" in his early 1920 poem. Like Melville and Twain before him, Hughes uses the river to signify man's journey from childhood to adulthood, from innocence to knowledge. By juxtaposing the Euphrates, Nile, and Mississippi, he suggests the historical continuum of humanity, the mystical union of all races.

Rebelling against this reflection of pain and suffering in so much black writing, Hughes caught the humor and valor of black life in his work. He sought to refute critics who might one day say, "No wonder the Negroes never amounted to anything. There were no heroes among them. . . . Did nobody fight? Did nobody triumph?"[56] Hughes's best-known "fighter" is "Simple." His female counterpart is Madam Alberta K. Johnson, whom Hughes depicted in sixteen poems outwitting the census man, the newsboy, the rent man, the phone company, even the minister.

Grandmother Hughes would have found Madam Johnson a "schemer" par excellence. In "Madam's Past History" (1943), she gives the world a piece of her mind.

> My name is Johnson—
> Madam Alberta K.
> The Madam stands for business.
> I'm smart that way.
>
> I had a
> HAIR DRESSING PARLOR
> Before
> The depression put
> The prices lower.
>
> Then I had a
> BARBECUE STAND
> Till I got mixed up
> With a no-good man. . . .
>
> I do cooking,
> Day's Work, too!
> Alberta K. Johnson—
> *Madam* to you.[57]

She becomes the archetypal "earth mother"—strong, proud, enduring—the black heiress of Eve and Lilith.

Sometime before his death on May 22, 1967, in New York City, Langston Hughes left very specific instructions for his memorial service. His friends made sure the requests were honored, as one of them read "Wake" aloud.

> Tell all my mourners
> To mourn in red—
> Cause there ain't no sense
> In my bein' dead.

As the service ended, a jazz trio played Langston Hughes's final joke on his friends, "Do Nothing Till You Hear From Me."[58]

Lorraine Hansberry's Inheritance

Seven months before her death Lorraine Hansberry wrote in her journal, "Do I remain a revolutionary? Intellectually—without a doubt. But am I prepared to give my body to the struggle or even my *comforts?* This is what I puzzle about."[59] She had witnessed the American government's persecution of Paul Robeson; she had seen his decline from one of the highest-paid concert artists to nonentity in black studies books. Robert Nemiroff recalls: "She knew that the car purchased with funds raised at the Croton civil rights rally which she chaired had become the death vehicle that carried voter registration volunteers Chaney, Schwerner and Goodman to martyrdom in Mississippi. . . . Now, with her body wracked by . . . cancer . . . she wondered how much *she* was prepared to sacrifice—of painkillers; of so simple a thing as air-conditioning . . . [of] the time and tranquility . . . to write. . . ."[60] She did not live long enough to answer these questions.

While she lived and wrote, however, she enjoyed the life of the commercially successful playwright. *A Raisin in the Sun,* as well as Nemiroff's musical success, provided her with enough income to free her from the drab necessity of part-time jobs. She could work in peace and comfort at Croton. But like her successful black friends—Robeson, James Baldwin, Langston Hughes—she did not ignore the plight of the untalented nine tenths. All of her works reveal the depth of her concern for the black race, for all downtrodden races in America and abroad. She presented to the theatergoing public the life of the black family in *Raisin,* the life of the intellectual in *Brustein,* and the life of the slave in *The Drinking Gourd.*

Paul Robeson's influence on Lorraine Hansberry is difficult to assess. They constantly crossed paths in her lifetime. She loved his voice and the songs he sang. He was her first employer, at *Freedom*. Indirectly she learned through him and *Freedom* of the dire condition in which most blacks lived, and of the dangers of being an artist. He was an inspiration and, to some extent, a warning.

Langston Hughes's influence is much more obvious. He did not allow himself—especially in the McCarthy era—to become primarily involved in the political struggle for racial equality. His poetry reflects the lives of black people, frequently with humor, but he understates his sense of personal frustration or anger, or of impending danger to those who do not understand his poetry. Rather, he explains himself and others of his race. He did not hate those who chose to misunderstand; rather, he found them absurd. Of course, in "A Dream Deferred" Hughes does warn those who would thwart the lives of others, but it is a detached warning, an offering from a wise observer who is above all an artist.

Hansberry did not get her social consciousness primarily from Hughes. What she got from him instead was a consciousness of the poetic possibilities of her own race, an appreciation of the black American culture, and—because of Hughes himself—an awareness that, in spite of all obstacles, black people remain a dynamic, powerfully creative force in American society whose achievement must be celebrated in art.

From W. E. B. DuBois she gained an admiration for the black intellectual, socialism, and black leadership. He spent most of his long life trying, with mixed success, to get a hearing for racial equality in America. Ironically, when the black population raised its collective voice and white people began to show signs of listening at last, he moved to Ghana, where he began to edit a multivolumed *Encyclopedia Africana*.

From Frederick Douglass, Hansberry learned about slavery and its psychology. This knowledge she would put to use in *The Drinking Gourd*, a play too outspoken to be broadcast on commercial television. From Douglass, too, she learned the invaluable lesson that the sufferings of a people may be presented truthfully in ways that rise above propaganda to the level of art. This lesson, perhaps, was the key to the synthesis of action and language toward which, in her own very different kind of writing, she was working.

These four men, among many people, particularly influenced Hansberry. But they could not, finally, answer the question she asked herself. DuBois—even though he founded *Phylon* and edited *Crisis* to promote black art—and Douglass were not as deeply devoted to art for its own sake as were Robeson and Hughes. Rather, DuBois and Douglass used their considerable rhetorical skills to illuminate and investigate the black conditions. They left behind books now considered works of art, but the creation of art was not their primary intention. Robeson sacrificed his musical career to pursue justice for members of his race and to become a revolutionary. Hughes pursued his art and—when forced to choose—left the struggle to others.

One month after she questioned her commitment to revolutionary activity, Hansberry wrote in her journal: "Have the feeling I should throw myself back into the movement. . . . But that very impulse is immediately flushed with a thousand vacillations and forbidding images. . . . *Comfort* has come to be its own corruption. . . . *Comfort.* Apparently I have sold my soul for it. I think when I get my health back I shall go into the South to find out what kind of revolutionary I am. . . ."[61] Hansberry died six months after writing of her intention to go South, where militants were being murdered, and as a result never answered her question. She died with her dilemma unresolved.

That this conflict was, in principle, resolvable, Hansberry herself realized at one point. Asked during an interview what the difference was between naturalism and realism, she replied, "I think the artist who is creating the realistic work imposes on it not only what *is* but what is *possible* . . . because that is part of reality too."[62]

Both the artist and the revolutionary are devoted to the possible; both have visions of what might someday be. Hansberry's works dealt with the way life was and the way life is. Life must change if some possibilities (such as the fulfillment of individuals and races) are to be realized and others (such as nuclear self-destruction) averted. This vision of a better world is the message of the artist—and of the revolutionary.

Chapter Four

Measure Him Right:
A Raisin in the Sun

A moving testament to the strength and endurance of the human spirit, *A Raisin in the Sun* is a quiet celebration of the black family, the importance of African roots, the equality of women, the vulnerability of marriage, the true value of money, the survival of the individual, and the nature of man's dreams. A well-made play, *Raisin* at first seems a plea for racial tolerance or a fable of man's overcoming an insensitive society, but the simple eloquence of the characters elevates the play into a universal representation of all people's hopes, fears, and dreams.

On January 19, 1959, a timid Lorraine Hansberry wrote her mother about *Raisin:* "Mama, it is a play that tells the truth about people, Negroes and life and I think it will help a lot of people to understand how we are just as complicated as they are . . . people who are the very essence of human dignity. . . . I hope it will make you very proud."[1] Indeed, *A Raisin in the Sun* made not only Nannie Perry Hansberry proud but also artists—both black and white. *Raisin* was the first play by a black writer ever to win the prestigious New York Drama Critics' Circle Award. The play would become "an American classic, published and produced in some thirty languages abroad and in thousands of productions across the country. . . . James Baldwin [said]: 'Never before in the entire history of the American theatre had so much of the truth of Black people's lives been seen on the stage.'"[2] Despite the earlier contributions of Langston Hughes, David Littlejohn wrote, "It would not be unfair in dating the emergence of a serious and mature Negro theater in America from 1959, the date of Lorraine Hansberry's *A Raisin in the Sun*."[3]

The play essentially concerns the Younger family—black, poor, and hopelessly trapped in a Chicago ghetto. As the play opens, Ruth Younger, tired and thirty, is cooking breakfast in the cramped South Side Chicago apartment that she shares with her husband, Walter Lee, thirty-four; her son Travis, ten; her restive sister-in-law Beneatha, twenty; and her dominating mother-in-law, Lena, sixty, whom everyone calls Mama. (Lena's husband, Walter, Sr., is dead, but he remains an important moral force in the family.) One by one, the family tumbles sleepily into the kitchen, which also serves as the living room and Travis's bedroom, to resume a discussion that probably trailed off the night before. Today the $10,000 check from "Big Walter's" life-insurance policy arrives. Walter Lee wants the money to open a liquor store; young Beneatha vaguely hopes the money will pay her medical-school tuition; but Lena will quietly retain control of the small fortune. (The crux of their problem is money. Lena wants to buy freedom; Walter Lee wants to purchase social status.) As act 1 continues, the family's tensions quickly come to the surface. Lena dramatically slaps Beneatha's face when the young woman declares that there is no God. Then Ruth discovers that she is pregnant and consults the local abortionist. Later the young Nigerian Joseph Asagai visits Beneatha, filling her with dreams of Africa.

Act 2 explodes early into a mock African ceremonial dance with Beneatha in Nigerian robes given her by Asagai and with a drunken Walter Lee crying atop the kitchen table, "FLAMING SPEAR! HOT DAMN! . . . OCOMOGOSIAY. . . . THE LION IS WAKING. . . . OCOMOGOSIAY."[4] In the midst of this merrymaking, George Murchison, the prototype of the black bourgeoisie, arrives to take Beneatha to the theater. A smug college man, he sneers: "Let's face it, baby, your heritage is nothing but a bunch of raggedy-assed spirituals and some grass huts" (68). Undaunted, Walter strikes back at the affluent George, who considers a college degree only a work permit for his father's business. "Filling up your heads . . . with the sociology and the psychology—but they teaching you how to be a man?" (71).

In the meantime, Mama has spent $3,500 on a down payment for a house in the all-white Clybourne Park. The family is delighted that they can begin to breathe fresh air and escape the confines of the ghetto. But Walter is so bitter that he cannot buy his liquor store that he gets drunk and quits his job. (Mama's hatred of liquor is typical of many southern women—especially blacks—who have seen alcohol destroy a man and ultimately his family.) Walter then says to Mama, "*You* the head of this family. You run our lives like you want to" (80). But Mama reconsiders, turning over the remaining $6,500 to Walter Lee. "I'm telling you to be the head of this family like you supposed to be" (87).

Later while Mama is shopping, the unctuous Karl Lindner comes to persuade the Youngers *not* to move into his neighborhood. Offering the family a substantial payoff, he says, "A man, right or wrong, has the right to want to have the neighborhood he lives in a certain kind of way" (97). Finally, Walter Lee orders him out of the apartment. But tragedy falls as his friend Bobo nervously comes to tell Walter that Willy Harris, with whom Walter was to buy the liquor store, has absconded with all the money—$6,500. For the time being, the Youngers are without hope.

In desperation, Walter Lee phones Karl Lindner, intent upon accepting the Man's humiliating offer. When Lindner arrives, Mama insists that Travis remain in the room to witness his father's performance. (She intuitively knows that Walter Lee, who so loved "Big Walter," cannot debase himself before his own son.) Shifting from one foot to the other, looking down at his shoes, Walter Lee finally stands up straight to deliver one of the most moving speeches of the play, which ends: "We have decided to move into our house because my father—my father—he earned it. We don't want to make no trouble for nobody or fight no causes—but we will try to be good neighbors" (127–28). Walter Lee has delved into his soul and mined the strength of his African past, the six generations of his family in America, and his father.

With the moving men and the rest of the family outside, Mama reenters, grabs her plant (a symbol of life and survival), and leaves for the last time. Only an hour before, she had told a chastened Beneatha:

Child, when do you think is the time to love somebody the most; when they done good and made things easy for everybody? . . . When you start measuring somebody, measure him right, child, measure him right. Make sure you done taken into account what hills and valleys he come through before he got to wherever he is. (125)

Act 3 becomes a reaffirmation of the human spirit as Walter Lee regains his dignity and manhood, Ruth decides to have her child, Beneatha gains in understanding and tolerance, and Ruth and Walter restore the "sweetness" to their marriage. The ending is not blindly happy, for Clybourne Park is potentially violent, but the Youngers are once again a family—a family that symbolizes some of the aspirations of black Americans.

Today some black critics feel that *A Raisin in the Sun* is a play whose time has passed—a simplistic, halting treatment of race relations. Some are confused by Hansberry's professed nationalism, when she seems to favor integration. Harold Cruse even calls *Raisin* a "cleverly written piece of glorified soap opera."[5] Hansberry used the traditional form of the well-made play in *Raisin,* especially observing the unities of action, place, and time. The action of the play is carefully delineated: act 1 serves as the beginning, act 2 as the middle, and act 3 as the tightly knit end. Furthermore, all action is carefully and causally related. Hansberry strictly abides by the unity of place: all action transpires in one room of the Youngers' South Side Chicago apartment. Stretching the unity of time from one day to one month (not unusual for a modern dramatist), Hansberry still maintains unity of impression with the central emotional concerns of the Younger family: Walter's search for a dream, Lena's faith in God and the family, Beneatha's hope for a new world.

Hansberry needed this rather traditional form to control the innovative ideas and themes of *Raisin*. Far from being a stereotyped or romanticized treatment of black life, the play embodies ideas that have been uncommon on the Broadway stage in any period. Resurrecting the ideas of the Harlem Renaissance and anticipating the new thinking of the 1960s, Hansberry examines the importance of African roots, traditional versus innovative women, the nature of marriage, the real meaning of money, the search for human dignity. Most significantly, she addresses the sensitive question of to what extent people, in liberating themselves from the burdens of discrimination, should aspire to a white middle-class way of life.

African Heritage

During her *Freedom* years, Lorraine Hansberry continued to study African history with encouragement from Paul Robeson, W. E. B. DuBois, and Louis Burnham. "She had spent hours of her younger years poring over maps of the African continent. . . . She was at one, texture, blood . . . with the sound of a mighty Congo drum."[6] She imaginatively knew the lions, drumbeats, quiet sandy nights, respected the antiquity of Ethiopia founded in 1000 B.C. Stirred by Kenya and Ghana wresting control from Europe and England, Hansberry inevitably incorporated her knowledge of Africa in her first play. More than earlier playwrights, Hansberry made Africa a serious, yet natural, issue on Broadway.

In *Raisin* even George Murchison, Beneatha's beau, has an awareness of his African past. In the fever of Walter Lee's and Beneatha's mock African dance in act 2, George remarks sarcastically: "In one second we will hear all about the great Ashanti empires; the great Songhay civilizations; and the great sculpture of Benin—and then some poetry in the Bantu . . ." (67). George had probably learned in a college atmosphere that the Songhai empire was a powerful western African kingdom, which garnered wealth from its export of ivory and gold between 850 and 1500 A.D. (Mali and Ghana—not to be confused with the modern state of Ghana—were equally old and powerful empires.) Along the coast of Nigeria, Benin was another expansive empire, noted for its bronze and gold art objects, that came to power around 1500. Coming to power about 1700, Ashanti was still another western kingdom famous for its heroic warriors.[7]

In the stage directions, Hansberry writes that Lena has "the noble bearing of the women of the Hereros of Southwest Africa" (27), who were essentially a pastoral people. Thus Hansberry identifies Lena as an "earth mother," one who nurtures both her family and her plant as well as she can. But Lena reveals her total ignorance of African history by a parroting of Beneatha's earlier remarks in her politely naive, unwittingly humorous speech to Joseph Asagai, the young Nigerian visitor: "I think it's so sad the way our American Negroes don't know nothing about Africa 'cept Tarzan and all that. And all that money they pour into these churches when they ought to be helping you people over there drive out them French and Englishmen done taken away your Land" (51).

Most of the African material in *A Raisin in the Sun,* however, surfaces in conversations between Beneatha and Joseph Asagai. Touched by Beneatha's beauty and idealism, Asagai lovingly nicknames her Alaiyo—a Yoruban word for "One for Whom Bread Food—Is Not Enough" (52). In act 3, after Walter Lee has been duped out of his $6,500, Asagai visits an embittered, distraught Beneatha. Speaking of his beloved Nigeria, Asagai reveals his basic philosophy of life, of Africa: "A household in preparation for a journey . . . it is another feeling. Something full of the flow of life. . . Movement, progress. . . . It makes me think of Africa" (111). Perhaps he sees in Beneatha a microcosmic America—one struggling to overthrow the limitations imposed on her by an alien culture.

Asagai's village in Nigeria is one where most people cannot read, where many have not even seen a book. In the village, there are mountains and stars, cool drinks from gourds at the well, old songs, people who move slowly, anciently. But Nigeria also has guns, murder, revolution, illiteracy, disease, ignorance. Asagai understands the inevitability of change and progress in Africa; he imagines for a moment the consequences should he betray the movement. "Don't you see that . . . young men and women . . . my own black countrymen . . . [may] . . . step out of the shadows some evening and slit my then useless throat?" (115). Rebuking Beneatha for becoming discouraged over one small frustration (Walter's losing the money), Asagai views his possible death as an advance toward freedom for himself and his people. "They who might kill me even . . . . actually replenish me" (116). Asagai's beliefs certainly contribute to Beneatha's transition from brittle idealist to a more tolerant human being.

In an interview with Studs Terkel (Chicago, May 2, 1959), Lorraine Hansberry referred to Joseph Asagai as her "favorite character" in *Raisin*. He represents the "true intellectual" with no pretense, no illusions. A revolutionary and nationalist, he realizes that initially black African leaders may be as corrupt as their white predecessors (Idi Amin of Uganda bore out this theory in the 1970s). Nevertheless, he shares Hansberry's conviction that "before you can start talking about what's wrong with independence, get it." More the idealist than the practical, effective leader— compared to Kenyatta and Nkrumah—Asagai is willing to die at the hands of his countrymen for the general good and freedom. (Harold Issacs suggests that his name derives from the Zulu word *asegai,* "sawed-off spear.")[8] On a more obvious level, Asagai certainly refutes the stage stereotype of the African with "a bone through his nose, or his ears."[9]

In *A Raisin in the Sun,* then, Africa becomes a symbol of a proud heritage and a troublesome but hopeful future. To Hansberry's great credit, Africa is a natural, at times humorous, element in the Younger family—as Walter Lee shouts "HOT DAMN! FLAMING SPEAR," as Beneatha dresses in Nigerian robes, as Mama speaks of Tarzan, churches, and Englishmen.

Women—Old and New

Growing up in an affluent, urbane, but above all socially and politically active family, at an early age Lorraine Hansberry developed considerable respect for strong women. Her constant references to her mother as a "very tall woman" baffled Robert Nemiroff when he met Mrs. Hansberry, who was only five feet three inches tall.[10] But Mrs. Hansberry's commanding and dignified presence is suggested in Lorraine Hansberry's telling dedication of *A Raisin in the Sun*: "To Mama; in gratitude for the dream" (i). Seven years older than her sister, Mamie Hansberry also provided an admirable model for Lorraine Hansberry: on her first date, Mamie and her nervous escort essentially integrated an exclusive Chicago restaurant—on orders from Carl Hansberry, Sr.[11]

In *A Raisin in the Sun,* Hansberry presents us with three strong, human women—Beneatha, Ruth, and Lena. In an interview with Mike Wallace, Hansberry laughingly said that "Beneatha is *me,* eight years ago" (when she was twenty-one).[12] By logical extension, Ruth was loosely modeled on Mamie, a charming, astute businesswoman who admired the traditional, close marriage of her parents. Lena resembles the strong-willed Nannie Perry Hansberry. The primary model for Lena, however, is "the black matriarch incarnate . . . she who in the mind of the black poet [Langston Hughes] . . . scrubs the floors of a nation in order to create black diplomats and university professors." She is Rosa Parks sitting in the *front* of the bus in Montgomery.[13]

Beneatha, Ruth, and Lena reflect the different roles of women in society—the old versus the new woman. At twenty, Beneatha is very much the new woman: she is planning to become a doctor, she will delay marriage until she completes her training, she doubts God and various social institutions, and she toys with diverse forms of self-expression—playing the guitar, acting, and horseback riding. At thirty, Ruth is caught between the ideas of the new and the old. She is a full-time domestic, but she values her roles as a wife and mother. Yet she still considers having an abortion in order to prevent adding another financial burden to the family, and she understands many of Beneatha's concerns. (Ruth will be discussed later in relation to Walter Lee.) At sixty, Lena is a doting grandmother; she does not question God or marriage; she is thankful that her family need not fear lynching or beatings as they did years before; and she is troubled by the sophisticated ideas of Beneatha and Walter Lee. Even the names of the women suggest their relationship to society. Beneatha is an obvious pun, suggesting her contempt for many traditional ideas, while Ruth is clearly a biblical reference to the faithful wife.

The old world of Lena and the new world of Beneatha are separated by more than forty years of social and political change. The old world looks inward to the kitchen, the family, the home; the new world stares outward at college, medical school, Africa. Since the Younger family is searching for a center, a nucleus, the old and new world cannot orbit peacefully: like stray neutrons, the two worlds were destined to collide. In *A Raisin in the Sun,* Lena and Beneatha clash—sometimes violently.

During times of slavery and Reconstruction, the church was the center of black life. (Even in the 1960s and 1970s, the church served as the primary headquarters for the activism of Dr. Martin Luther King, Jr., and the Reverend Jesse Jackson.) Lena typifies traditional blacks who found personal fulfillment and courage for political and social action in God. Beneatha, however, does not find solace in God, believing instead that man deserves credit for his own efforts. The confrontation in act 1 begins innocently enough as Beneatha says, "How much cleaning can a house need, for Christ's sakes" (34). Lena recoils and Ruth says that Beneatha is "fresh as salt" (34). Beneatha retorts, "Well—if the salt loses its savor" (34). Mama is offended at the mild sacrilege. After some chitchat about Beneatha's hobbies, boy friends, and theory of marriage, Lena says, "You going to be a doctor, honey, God willing" (38). Beneatha replies, "God hasn't got a thing to do with it" (38). Silent and incensed, Lena and Ruth listen as Beneatha continues: "God is just one idea I don't accept. . . . I get tired of Him getting credit for all the things the human race achieves through its own stubborn effort. There simply is no God—there is only man and it is he who makes miracles" (39).

Rising slowly and powerfully, Lena crosses the room and slaps her daughter violently in the face. Shocked, Beneatha drops her eyes as silence fills the room. Then, Lena says, "Now—you say after me, in my mother's house there is still God." There is a long pause as Beneatha stares at the floor. Lena insists, "In my mother's house there is still God." Defeated, Beneatha says, "In my mother's house there is still God" (39).

Accepting traditional ideas of marriage and motherhood, Lena becomes almost a black "earth mother"—exuding fecundity and love of the land. Throughout the play, Mama is associated with her plant (a symbol of life, survival, and the human spirit). In act 1, Mama frets, "Lord, if this little old plant don't get more sun that it's been getting it ain't never going to see spring again" (28). At this point, Ruth is nauseated and pregnant, and the family is anxious about the $10,000 check. Again in act 1, after the upsetting scene with Beneatha, Mama is watering her wilting plant. "They spirited all right my children. . . . Like this little old plant that ain't never had enough sunshine or nothing—and look at it . . ." (40). Revealing her love of the land, she says, "Well, I always wanted me a garden like I used to see sometimes at the back of the houses down home. This plant is close as I ever got to having one" (41).

In act 2 when the family has decided to move to Clybourne Park, Mama is "Fixing [her] plant so it won't get hurt none on the way" (101). Her nurturance of the plant reflects the caring associated with both mothers and agrarians. When Beneatha asks why she is taking "that raggedy-looking old thing" to the new home, Mama says, "It expresses *me!*" (101). In the final scene of act 3, Mama looks at the empty living room, clutches her plant to her chest, and leaves for the last time. Even in her "measure him right" speech, Mama alludes to the land: "Make sure you done taken into account what hills and valleys he come through before he got to wherever he is" (125).

Marriage was not always easy for Lena. Early in the play she says, "God knows there was plenty wrong with Walter Younger—hardheaded, mean, kind of wild with women—plenty wrong with him" (33). (Beneatha and other new women probably would not have tolerated these qualities in a husband.) Lena values children—and grandchildren—highly, seeing in them a link with the future. Having lost a child (little Claude) through miscarriage, Lena becomes determined that Ruth will not have an abortion. She lectures Walter Lee: "When the world gets ugly enough—a woman will do anything for her family. *The part that's already living*" (62). She urges him to be "your father's son," to discourage the abortion, adding "we a people who give children life, not who destroys them" (62). Lena makes a down payment on the house because "We was going backwards 'stead of forwards—talking 'bout killing babies and wishing each other was dead. . . . When it gets like that in life—you got to do something bigger . . ." (80). When her grandson gives her a ridiculous, oversize hat, she says, "Bless your heart—this is the prettiest hat I have ever owned" (104).

Having grown up in a South that was racist, Lena is fairly content to live simply in Chicago where she and her family could survive with some dignity. She is disturbed by Walter Lee's dream of owning a liquor store, because she has seen too many Southern black men drown their troubles in bottles of beer or Bourbon. They were frustrated—by their "invisibility" in a white society, their inability to succeed because of racial prejudice, their failure to support their women financially. Deeply religious, Lena cannot shake the emotional fundamentalist conviction that alcohol—regardless of the occasion—is evil. She then avoids the deeper issue when she says, "We ain't no business people, Ruth. We just plain working folks" (30). At the same time, Lena takes pride in Beneatha's plans for medical school. Doctors, preachers, and teachers make the world a better place. Beneatha is determined to become a doctor and has little interest in marriage now. Beneatha, George Murchison, and Joseph Asagai form a romantic triangle, each side suggesting different styles of life Beneatha may eventually choose. George represents a more traditional life as he says to Beneatha: "You're a nice-looking girl. . . . That's all you need, honey, forget the atmosphere. . . . Drop the Garbo routine. . . . As for myself, I want a nice—simple—sophisticated girl . . . not a poet" (82). George might have added, not a doctor. When Beneatha tells Mama that George is a fool, she is pleasantly surprised when Mama is sympathetic: "I guess you better not waste your time with no fools" (84). Joseph Asagai is more complicated: he offers Beneatha dreams of Africa, poetry, support, sensitivity. (Murchison represents "crass materialism," while Asagai signals meaning and commitment.)[14] Still when Asagai proposes marriage, Beneatha concurs with Mama's judgment that "You ain't old enough to marry nobody" (129).

Most of the time, however, Beneatha is patient with her mother's conservative views. She is committed to blacks improving themselves and society through education, professions, social and political action, and a proud awareness of their African heritage. She ridicules her brother's business aspirations, not understanding his search for self. More sophisticated than the other Youngers, she speaks in a more cultivated manner and is the first to realize the hypocrisy of Karl Lindner. But Beneatha is not selfish, especially in her desire to become a doctor:

When I was very small . . . we used to take our sleds out in the wintertime and the only hills we had were the ice-covered stone steps of some houses down the street. And we used to fill them in with snow and make them smooth and slide down them all day . . . and it was very dangerous you know . . . and sure enough one day a kid named Rufus came down too fast and hit the sidewalk . . . and we saw his face just split open right there in front of us. . . . And I remember standing there looking at his bloody open face thinking that was the end of Rufus. But the ambulance came and they took him to the hospital and they fixed the broken bones and they sewed it all up . . . and the next time I saw Rufus he just had a little line down the middle of his face . . . I never got over that. . . .
    That was the most marvelous things in the world. . . . I wanted to do that. . . . Fix up the sick, you know—and make them whole again. (111–12)

In act 1 Beneatha is rather brittle and humorless, given to sarcasm and lack of understanding. When Walter Lee questions the cost of her medical training, she falls to her knees: "Well—I *do*—all right?—thank everybody . . . and forgive me for wanting to be anything at all . . . forgive me, forgive me" (25). In the beginning of act 2, she emerges in her African robes, fanning herself, looking "more like Madame Butterfly than any Nigerian that ever lived" (63). But by the end of act 2, Beneatha has become less egocentric: she is delighted that Ruth and Walter Lee are dancing like "old fashioned Negroes" and cheerfully accepts the criticism that she tends to "brainwash herself" (92–93). By act 3 Beneatha appears a more generous, tolerant human being as she tells Joseph Asagai about her friend Rufus's accident which inspired her to become a doctor and as she gains tolerance for Walter Lee's human frailties.

Never losing her faith in God or the family, Lena begins to understand her children's modern ideas. She gives Walter Lee control of the family money (he hungers for an identity in the society that ignores him), and she supports his decision when she says to Karl Lindner: "My son said we was going to move and there ain't nothing left for me to say. . . . You know how these young folks is nowadays, mister. Can't do a thing with 'em" (128).

The old world of Lena and the new world of Beneatha cannot remain static. As both worlds react and collide with the other, they are sure to emerge as slightly different substances. Little is lost in these transformations. Much is gained in the new structure of strength, humanity, wisdom.

The Crystal Stair

For her best-known play, Lorraine Hansberry considered only titles that alluded to the poetry of Langston Hughes. No poet has captured the spectrum, depths, and heights of the black experience as he did. Souls deep as rivers, washerwomen, madames, young men lynched, young men rejoicing, dreams deferred, America, mulattoes, Manhattan—he captured life that teemed around him. Hansberry told Studs Terkel, "The glory of Langston Hughes was that he took the quality of the blues and put it into our poetry. . . . The Negro dramatist can begin to approach a little of that quality. . . ." Hansberry finally entitled her play *A Raisin in the Sun,* the title of a Hughes poem, which reflected the more universal theme of man's search for dignity. Initially, though, she sought titles in other Hughes poems.

Lorraine Hansberry deeply admired Langston Hughes's portrait of the "black matriarch incarnate" in "Washerwoman," and she was also drawn to his understated, profound hymn to maternal love in "Mother to Son." Like the washerwoman, the mother has labored as a domestic to make a better life for her children. She typifies, Lorraine Hansberry later declared, the "epic figure who entered . . . [my] consciousness as a child."[15] Especially to black men, Hansberry explains, "The matriarchy in Negro life is . . . at once beloved and hated. . . ."[16] In an early draft of *Raisin,* she tentatively entitled the play *The Crystal Stair*[17]—a phrase from Hughes's poem.

Only the most egotistical, cold human being could fail to love and cherish a mother who scrubbed floors, ironed clothes, tended children for other people, so that he might lead a full, free life. But even a caring man might sometimes resent the power, the "bossiness" of such a strong woman. Interestingly enough, the three divisions of Hughes's "Mother to Son" parallel the three stages of the Lena/Walter Lee conflict and its resolution.

As the poem opens, the mother begins her advice to her son—in a loving, but authoritative manner.

> Well, son, I'll tell you:
> Life for me ain't been no crystal stair.

> It's had tacks in it,
> And splinters,
> And boards torn up,
> And places with no carpet on the floor—
> Bare.

Just as the mother describes the stair as hard, barren, splintered, Mama's
view of life has a wooden, unyielding quality. Her sharp comments lack a
softened edge.

At the beginning of *A Raisin in the Sun*, Lena is the unchallenged authority of the household. After she slaps Beneatha for denying the existence
of God, she forces her to say: "In my mother's house there is still God."
The emphasis on "my *mother's* house" is not incidental. In act 1, Walter
Lee screams above the hubbub of the cramped apartment: "WILL SOMEBODY
PLEASE LISTEN TO ME TODAY!" Unaware of his real frustration, Lena simply
says, "I don't 'low no yellin' in this house, Walter Lee, and you know
it—" (57). Then she meddles in Ruth and Walter Lee's marriage: "Boy,
don't make the mistake of driving that girl away from you" (59). (Even her
reference to this man and woman in their thirties as "boy" and "girl" dem-
onstrates her domineering attitude.) Her admonition to Walter Lee to "be
[his] father's son" further reinforces her treatment of him as a child.

In the middle of Hughes's poem, the mother focuses on the hardships
and triumphs of her own life. She is now too enrapt in her own world to
consider others on a conscious level.

> But all the time
> I'se been a climbin' on.
> And reachin landin's,
> And turnin' corners,
> And sometimes goin' in the dark
> Where there ain't been no light

Life, to Lena, seems dark, there is no light. Ruth is planning an abortion;
her son's marriage is fraying with frustrations; her grandson still sleeps in
the living room. Wanting to reach a landing, to turn a corner, she goes
alone to buy the house in Clybourne Park.

The culmination of Lena's authority comes in act 2 when she makes a
down payment on the house in the all-white neighborhood without con-
sulting any other members of the family. Ruth, Travis, and Beneatha are
pleased, but Walter Lee views his mother's purchase as just another dem-
onstration of her power. Bitterly he says, "So that's the peace and comfort

you went out and bought for us today" (79). Shattered that he cannot buy his liquor store, he says, "*You* the head of this family. . . . So what you need for me to say it was all right for?" (80)

As "Mother to Son" ends, the mother has returned from her private reverie to impart her strength and wisdom to her son. No longer the un-yielding authority, she calls her son "boy" and "honey"—warm terms of endearment:

> So, boy, don't you turn back.
> Don't you set down on the steps
> 'Cause you finds it's kinder hard.
> Don't you fall now—
> For I'se still goin', honey,
> I'se still climbin',
> And life for me ain't been no crystal stair.

Realizing that Walter Lee's spirit is almost broken, Lena makes a signif-icant decision: she will relinquish all power over the money to her son. She now understands that Walter Lee's life—so different from her own—is "kinder hard," that he needs the money to chisel a place for himself in the silent monolith of white society. Almost immediately, Walter Lee gives the money to the scoundrel, Willy Harris, who is never seen again. But Walter comes into his full maturity as he tells Karl Lindner finally: "We don't want your money" (128). From his now mellowed mother, he has learned not to turn back, to keep on climbing. At the end of the play, Mama says, "He finally come into his manhood today, didn't he? Kind of like a rainbow after the rain . . ." (130).

The Crystal Stair would certainly have been a magical, sparkling title for Hansberry's play. There are several obvious reasons why the change to the more earthily powerful *A Raisin in the Sun* was a sound artistic decision. While *The Crystal Stair* would have stressed the love between mother and son and her role in his coming to full maturity, this title does not indicate the deep impact of "Big Walter."

In three of Hansberry's five plays—*Raisin, Sidney Brustein,* and *Les Blancs*—deceased fathers exert such an influence over their children that we almost think they are alive. (Lorraine Hansberry's loss of her father when she was fifteen seemed to have affected her profoundly.) On the most obvious level, Big Walter bequeathed $10,000 to his family, giving Wal-ter Lee hope for a career. More significantly, Walter, Sr.—not Lena—is the source of might from which Walter Lee draws to reject Lindner's obscene offer. Always, Walter Lee will remember his father's moral and material gifts to him as he tries to give Travis education, clothing, food, and love.

As the title, *The Crystal Stair* would exude the sparkle and richness of a Tiffany jewel. But materialism for its own sake, as Hansberry stresses in numerous places,[18] was the *bête noire* of the play. *A Raisin in the Sun,* on the other hand, is about as earthy and humble as a title can be. In "Mother to Son," the narrator looks upward (which could imply social mobility, with luxuries, such as the strand of pearls Walter wants for Ruth). We normally look downward (implying "roots," solid virtues, such as the college education Walter wants for Travis) at raisins. Nevertheless, Hansberry sees Walter Lee as being duped by the American Dream as fully as Willie Loman, while Mama wants money only for necessities. Finding the lack of a central character a flaw in the play, Lorraine Hansberry wrote that "neither Walter Lee nor Mama Younger loom large enough to monumentally command the play."[19] In truth, the dual protagonists provide creative tension throughout the entire play.

Finally, *The Crystal Stair* with its spiraling, upward sense of motion might not have suggested the *real* ending of the play—an interpretation which most reviewers and theatergoers seem to miss. Superficially, Walter makes his speech and the Youngers follow the movers to their house surrounded by birds, flowers, and trees. *But* they are also encircled by white neighbors, who selected Karl Lindner as their most diplomatic spokesman. Lorraine Hansberry never forgot the brick flying through the window that almost killed her at the age of eight.

A Raisin in the Sun, indeed, was the most appropriate title for Hansberry's play. This epithet suggests the tensions and frustrations of the black man's, as well as the black woman's, existence. The central images of Hughes's poem—raisins, sores, rotten meat, crusted sugar—are images of inevitable decay if dreams are deferred. Much more than *The Crystal Stair,* the title *A Raisin in the Sun* suggests the reality and universality of man's search for dignity and self-respect.

Rebirth of a Marriage

The black family has historically been a close, fiercely loyal unit. Although denied the dignity of marriage and constantly threatened by separation, slaves often went to extraordinary extremes—risking beatings, physical degradation or deformation, or death—to protect and remain with their mates.[20] In *A Raisin in the Sun,* Big Walter was unfaithful to Mama, and he was hard-headed and "mean." But the troubled marriage of Ruth and Walter Lee has less to do with the problems of the slaves or Mama and Big Walter than with those problems haunting many contemporary marriages—the lack of personal fulfillment, unhappiness with a job or career, the scarcity of money, the fear of losing one's youth, the inability to communicate, the unthinking loss of sexual and emotional intimacy.

At the beginning of the play, the marriage is troubled. Walter Lee says, "You look young this morning, baby. . . . Just for a second—stirring them eggs. It's gone now . . ." (15). As Walter Lee ridicules Ruth's weary appearance, he may feel that *he* is growing old, that his opportunities for success are running out. They fail to communicate as Ruth is obsessed by cooking breakfast when Walter Lee tries to explain his plans. He responds: "Man say to his woman: I got me a dream. His woman say: Eat your eggs. . . . Man say: I got to change my life, I'm choking to death, baby! And his woman say—Your eggs is getting cold" (21–22).

Not only does Walter Lee feel powerless in his own family before Mama gives him control of the legacy, but he feels impotent within the black community. His admiration for the "upwardly mobile" black, in fact, leads to a serious flaw in his judgment: he considers Willy Harris a successful businessman when he is really an untrustworthy hustler. Walter Lee also admires another man of whom Ruth is suspicious—Charlie Atkins who grosses $100,000 a year in a dry-cleaning business. Some critics have mistakenly considered all blacks part of one homogeneous group, but this community has many factions. When Walter Lee starts an argument with George Murchison, we see the lower-income black in bitter confrontation with the black bourgeoisie. Walter Lee reveals his frustration and venom toward George, who has the advantages of money and education, when he says: "I know [there] ain't nothing in this world as busy as you coloured college boys with your fraternity pins and white shoes . . ." (71).

Much of Walter Lee's desire for money and position revolves around wanting to give Travis a strong image of his father:

One day when you 'bout seventeen years old I'll come home and I'll be pretty tired, you know that I mean, after a day of conferences and secretaries getting things wrong the way they do . . . 'cause an executive's life is hell, man—And I'll go inside and Ruth will come downstairs and meet me at the door and we'll kiss each other and she'll take my arm and we'll go up to your room to see you sitting on the floor with the catalogues of all the great schools in America around you. . . . Just tell me where you want to go to school and you'll *go*. . . . (89)

Walter Lee does not always want money just for its own sake, but as a means of acquiring education, decent housing, human dignity—positive goals to Lorraine Hansberry. He also wants money and social position so that he can give Ruth the leisure time, peace, clothes and jewelry that she has never had:

I want to hang some real pearls 'round my wife's neck. Ain't she supposed to wear no pearls? Somebody tell me—tell me, who decides which women is supposed to wear pearls in this world. I tell you I am a *man*—and I think my wife should wear some pearls in this world! (123)

Hansberry would consider these aspirations negative, "materialistic."

As exhausted as Ruth is from domestic work for whites, her pregnancy, and her tension with Walter Lee, she does not share Walter Lee's mono-mania about money, business, and social position. She would be satisfied with a peaceful home life and an adequate income. But as she begins to understand the compulsion of Walter Lee's dream, their relationship be-comes closer. Even Ruth's unselfish willingness to have an abortion shows her understanding of Walter Lee's plight: she does not want to add to the financial burden or to crowd the apartment with one more person.

But Ruth and Walter Lee restore the sweetness to their marriage when they begin to talk, to go to the movies, to dance in the living room, to realize that they have a problem. Walter Lee has said that a man needs a woman to back him up (20), to build him up (22), and Ruth is in equally desperate need of support. Ruth tells Mama, "Something is happening between Walter and me. I don't know what it is—but he needs some-thing—something I can't give him any more" (30). Later Walter Lee says, "It's been rough, ain't it, baby? How we gets to the place where we scared to talk softness to each other" (74).

When Walter Lee and Ruth begin to "talk softness" again, we witness the rebirth of a marriage. They have not solved their financial problems, but they are beginning to fulfill their dreams. And with this rebirth of self comes the rebirth of marriage. A marriage in which two people laugh, love, listen, touch, and celebrate themselves and each other.

Far from being a measured plea for racial tolerance or a mere fable of man's overcoming a callous society, *A Raisin in the Sun* goes out of its way to universalize a family and its hopes. As a child, Lorraine Hansberry sat quietly when the noted poet Langston Hughes came to visit her father. Even then the seeds for this quiet celebration of life—*A Raisin in the Sun*—may well have been germinating. Surely she was moved by Hughes's poem, from which the final title of the play derives:

What happens to a dream deferred?
Does it dry up
Like a raisin in the sun?
Or fester like a sore—
And then run?
Does it stink like rotten meat?
Or crust and sugar over—
Like a syrupy sweet?

Maybe it just sags
Like a heavy load.

Or does it explode?

The Youngers' dream neither dries up nor explodes; instead, it takes forms that were widely accepted by American society in 1959. The tangible achievement is a part of the American dream, a house in the suburbs. But the more important part of the dream is freedom for the individual, for the family. The Youngers are indeed a "young" family, for they are beginning to grow spiritually and socially. To varying extents, each of the Youngers changes during the course of the play, thus beginning the painful, yet creative act of examination—of heritage, of values, of self. One day someone may hurl a brick through their window, but the Youngers will withstand the attack together. As they begin to take pride in being young, gifted and black, their neighbors may relent and accord them the respect due all men and women.

Chapter Five
Trying Not to Care: *The Sign in Sidney Brustein's Window*

The Sign in Sidney Brustein's Window is a still-life study of modern man and woman caught up in the conflict between not caring and caring too much. As critics have noted repeatedly, it is a play of ideas in which Lorraine Hansberry scrutinizes many contemporary issues: family relationships, prostitution, marriage, psychoanalysis, homosexuality, politics, absurdist plays, abstract art, anti-Semitism, racism. At the center of the play is Sidney Brustein—a man torn between the torture of not caring and the weight of commitment. The play is more than a philosophical treatise, however; Brustein approaches the form of a dialectic as each character confronts another with alien ideas, in the attempt to make himself and his desires understood. Conflict arises, of course—that is, intellectual conflict—but a synthesis occurs by the time the curtain falls.

Opening on Broadway on October 15, 1964, *The Sign in Sidney Brustein's Window* was roundly criticized by the reviewers. Some felt that the play was too philosophical; some were distressed that Hansberry had mixed comic and tragic styles, as well as realism and fantasy. One thought the playwright harbored a hostility toward "homosexuals, liberals, abstract artists, nonrealistic playwrights, white people unwilling to commit suicide. . . ."[1] The last phrase is telling—"white people unwilling to commit suicide." Underlying many of the negative comments was a feeling that the darling of black playwrights—who had only five years earlier won Broadway with *A Raisin in the Sun*—had had the audacity to switch subjects, to waste her time bemoaning the plight of *white* Greenwich Villagers. The critics did not understand Hansberry's perception of all people—black and white, male and female, Christian, Jewish, and agnostic. Because of their perplexity over the complicated context of the play, many missed its point entirely, a point that Hansberry made repeatedly in her other works: that people must commit themselves to a goal. He who is committed, whether to art, social causes, another person, is truly a valuable member of society, a person whose deed will help to bring about a more humane society in which all may prosper. Yet, in defense of these critics, the play may indeed be too complicated in terms of the sheer number of issues the characters discuss and represent.

The Action

As the play opens, Sidney Brustein and Alton Scales are lugging metal racks of restaurant glasses into the Brusteins' Village brownstone. Sidney, thirty-seven and bedraggled, wears a white dress shirt open at the sleeves and mismatched jacket and trousers. In comparison, Alton, a handsome black man of twenty-seven, seems casual and stylish in his mustard sweater and corduroy slacks. In the background looms Greenwich Village with its narrow, twisted streets, panes of glass with frosted corners, a refuge for "many who fancy revolt, or at least, detachment. . . ."[2] More an intellectual than a businessman, Sidney has just closed the Silver Dagger, his failed night club, and has purchased a newspaper. As Sidney tells Alton to avoid causes and commitments, Sidney's wife, Iris, enters with a bagful of groceries. Iris immediately starts an argument with Sidney which prompts Alton to leave. As usual, they quarrel about Sidney's failure to manage money, Iris's psychoanalysis, and an undefined sexual problem.

After some time, Alton returns with Wally O'Hara, an earnest political candidate in his early forties. Carrying a VOTE O'HARA FOR REFORM poster, they want Sidney's newspaper to endorse Wally. But the uncommitted, uninvolved Sidney refuses, saying, "I no longer even believe that spring must necessarily come at all" (207). Sidney's fantasy-laden perception of Iris begins to emerge as he urges her to "do her dance"—an exotic combination of a Greek Miserlou with Indian and Appalachian movements. Iris's two sisters, Gloria and Mavis, are introduced when Alton passes around a photograph of Gloria, the "high fashion model," and when Mavis, the irritatingly conventional uptown sister, telephones. Sidney has been goaded and challenged by Wally's and Alton's arguments that the individual must commit himself to his community, perhaps to his world, despite the limitations of politics. He silently wrestles with Wally's poster and finally decides to endorse him. The scene closes as Alton and Wally leave.

A week has passed when scene 2 opens. Max, an abstract artist who wears "sandals, stained jeans, a black turtleneck and a pained expression" (217), is helping Sidney with the artwork for the newspaper. Max frivolously suggests that they place the masthead at the bottom of the front page and change the type weekly. A startling change has transpired: Sidney has thrown himself into Wally's campaign. He then hangs the sign in his window "CLEAN UP COMMUNITY POLITICS Wipe Out Bossism VOTE REFORM" (218). Meanwhile, Iris learns in a letter from Gloria that Alton has asked her to marry him. Again Sidney asks the Iris of his fantasy to do her mountain dance.

When Mavis Parodus Bryson, Iris's oldest sister, enters, a war erupts between bohemian and uptown values. The meddlesome Mavis is a fashionable, heavier, red-headed version of Iris, for whom she has brought a dress—at odds with Iris's usual blue-jean couture. Unaware of her prejudices, Mavis is given to such statements as "I thought . . . Jews didn't drink" (231). A comically cruel scene unfolds as Iris tells Mavis that Gloria (who we finally learn is a high-priced call girl) is planning to marry Alton, who is black. Mavis reveals herself when she says, "What do you think Gloria is?" (236). Meanwhile, David Ragin drops in from his upstairs apartment to borrow typing paper. He is a young homosexual absurdist playwright, whose most recent work deals with two men married to each other who live in a refrigerator (240). Here, obviously, Hansberry indulges in rather broad satire.

As Alton enters, Mavis is frozen in conformist helplessness. Iris is preparing dinner for the Villagers, who make sport of Mavis. As she leaves, Mavis delivers a moving plea for tolerance: "I am standing here and I am thinking: how smug it is in bohemia. I was taught to believe that—creativity and great intelligence ought to make one expansive and understanding" (245). Shaken by the speech, Alton attacks David on his way out the door: "After a while, hanging out with queers gets on my nerves!" (246). The dinner party is totally disrupted as Sidney shouts "I care! I care about it all. . . . Yesterday I counted twenty-six gray hairs . . . all from trying *not* to care" (247). Hurt and disgusted, David leaves Sidney and Iris alone with their problems. As Sidney goes out to a political rally, Iris cries that they must fight for their marriage. "Let's fight like hell for it" (250).

Act 2 opens with the most lyrical scene of the play (possibly inspired by *Dark of the Moon,* which Hansberry had seen many years earlier). In the quiet before the dawn, Sidney is transported by reverie to his imaginary world of the mountains where he plucks his banjo and the Iris-of-his-mind, barefoot, with flowing hair and mountain dress, embraces him, does an Appalachian dance, kisses him, and flees. Then the real Iris awakes and offers to make coffee. Throughout the rest of this scene, Sidney remains dreamily in the mountains, while Iris is always aware of the city. As Sidney becomes one with the clear brooks, pines, and mist, Iris quietly tells him that she hates her long hair and that her father was "crude and stupid." But the moment is tender. We begin to understand why they are bound together, as Sidney says: "There is no pollution, no hurt; just me and this ball of minerals and gasses suddenly shot together out of the cosmos . . . I love you very much" (256).

In sharp contrast to the mountain illusion, scene 2 opens to the raucous strains of "The Wally O'Hara Campaign Song." To everyone's amazement, Wally is winning the election, and David's play is a hit. Sidney is elated. But his high spirits are quickly grounded when Iris tells him that she is going to a party. He forces her to tell him that theater acquaintance Ben Asche (who Sidney suspects is her lover) will also be a guest. Iris concedes that she is "the world's *lousiest* actress," but says, "I just want something to happen in my life" (268). When Iris leaves, Sidney is depressed and calls upstairs for David to come down. For once in his life, David is personable, almost boyish. He "feels pretty good," he is "famous," he is going outside to "wear it in the streets" (269). But Sidney ends David's happiness by asking him to write Iris a part in his next play. Sidney, in effect, is offering to write David a good review—whether he deserves it or not—in "payment" for creating a part for Iris. David is justifiably appalled; "Prostitutes interest me clinically; I've not the least intention of ever becoming one" (271). Wally enters jubilantly, and Sidney recites a monologue about his ulcer and Modern Man, ending with "One does not *smite* evil any more: one holds one's guts, thus—and takes a pill" (275).

By election night Sidney is ecstatic: "Little old ladies and big tough truck drivers and little skinny Madison Avenue ad men" (227) have kicked out the bosses and elected Wally. In the midst of this merriment, Alton enters, his eyes trained on Sidney. "Is it true? Is it true she's a hooker? And you were going to let me marry her?" (278) The scene becomes emotional as Alton describes his father, a railroad porter, wiping up spit and semen of white men, and his mother, a maid, always bringing home white people's leftovers—some jelly, a piece of ham, a broken lamp, a sweater. He almost screams: "I ain't going to have the white man's leavings in my house, no mo'! I ain't going to have his *throw-away* . . . no mo!" (280). Alton leaves a note for Gloria and exits.

Mavis enters the Brustein apartment. While she is there she reveals emotional depths rarely expected of an uptown matron, shattering yet another stereotype in this play. After giving Sidney a sizable check for Wally's campaign, she tells him: "I've enjoyed conversations I've heard down here. And, Sidney, I've understood some of them" (283). Unlike Iris, Mavis idolized her father, who she says read Greek classics aloud and was a "backwoods poet." Her most touching revelation is that her husband, Fred—whom she lovingly quotes as an authority on all topics—has a girl friend who bore his son. With bitter restraint and no hostility toward the girl,

Mavis explains: "I just wanted to meet her. So I got in a cab, got out, rang a bell and there she was. . . . There's this sandy-haired kid standing in pedal pushers and an apron, pregnant as all get-out. So I said I rang the wrong bell" (287). But Mavis has accepted her lot: "A divorce? For what? . . . There was no rush years ago at home to marry Mavis Parodus; there was *just* Fred *then*. . . . And, let's face it, *I* cannot type" (287). As she leaves, Sidney says, "You're tough, Mavis Parodus" (289).

Act 2 draws to a close as Iris enters with her hair cut, teased, sprayed stiff, and tinted a metallic yellow for the Golden Girl television ads she will be doing. She does not want to play Appalachian anymore. Iris is leaving Sidney for some time and delivers the *coup de grace* as she leaves: Wally is *owned* by the political bosses. In disgust, Sidney removes the sign from his window.

The first scene of act 3 finally introduces us to Gloria, Iris's younger sister and erstwhile prostitute. She sits with Sidney and David, and all three question the meaning of their lives. Sidney is drunk and describes himself as: "Modern Man: flat on my back with an oozing intestine, a bit of a tear frozen in the corner of my eye, a glass of booze which will saturate without alleviating . . ." (298). Gloria dislikes David immediately when he says, "Isn't it the greatest tradition for writers and whores to share the world's truths?" (300). After learning from the note that Alton will not marry her, Gloria begins drinking and taking pills. She, too, has her own vivid memory of her father: he called her a tramp on his death bed. After much drinking and singing, Gloria plants a long, wet kiss on David's mouth, at which point he asks her to come upstairs and watch him have sex with a beautiful golden boy. As Sidney lies drunk and self-absorbed on the couch, she goes into the bathroom and kills herself. Sidney has failed Gloria; he has let her die.

As the play ends, a detective has come to investigate Gloria's death. Mavis and Fred have left when Wally arrives. Sidney tells Wally he will fight him and the machine, because he believes that "death is waste and love is sweet and . . . people wanna be better than they are . . ." (317). Iris has returned, and Sidney declares: "Tomorrow, we shall make something strong of this sorrow" (318).

Three Sisters

Just as Lorraine Hansberry believed *Raisin* lacked a "central character," *Sidney Brustein* is as much the Parodus sisters' play as Sidney's. The Parodus sisters enjoy a close relationship. They are also close to each other in age: Gloria is twenty-six; Iris is twenty-nine; Mavis is in her early thirties. Yet Hansberry carefully delineates each character in terms of names and physical appearance. Iris's name suggests a flower of delicacy, beauty, femininity. Mavis's name lacks imagination. Mavis was the name of a popular, very sweet chocolate soft drink of the time as well as the brand name of a cheap, scented talcum powder—both emblems of depressing conventionality. Gloria's name has vague religious overtones which may suggest her essential innocence. At the same time, she may have been named for the ever-glamorous Gloria Swanson. Since hair is an ageless symbol of fertility, Iris with her long flowing dark hair may be considered the most sexual; Gloria with medium-length blonde hair *appears* sexual, but hers is a cold, often twisted sexuality; and Mavis's short, sculptured red hair denies sexuality, although she is the only sister with children. Iris's blue-jeaned style suggests a free spirit, Mavis's simple, elegant clothes reflect the control she imposes on her life; and Gloria's girl-next-door clothes reflect the person she would like to be.

Although their mother is never mentioned, all three sisters have strikingly different, sometimes frightening views of their late father. Iris considers "Papa . . . so crude and stupid. . . . You know, I never heard my father make an abstract thought in his life. . . . Didn't work that steady" (255). Mavis sees Papa Parodus as a "dreamer," a "sort of backwoods poet, kind of a cross between Willy Loman and Daniel Boone. He just loved sitting and thinking" (284). Mavis recalls his reading Greek classics to them, directing little productions in the living room, letting Mavis play Medea (285). Gloria sees her father only in terms of his relationship to her: he played "creepy music" and called her a tramp on his deathbed (308).

Such vivid, contradictory views are bound to have a profound effect on one's life. Each of these women seems to feel that her life was predestined by her father. Considering her papa crude and stupid, Iris thinks that she is not very bright, which leads to a feeling of real insecurity. She tells Sidney: "When I met you I thought Kant was a stilted way of saying cannot; I thought Puccini was a kind of spaghetti; I thought the louder an actor yelled . . . the greater he was" (267). The only sister who admired her father was Mavis who has created a respectable, painted veneer for herself, seeing the spontaneity of a "backwoods poet" as an impossible goal. Gloria is perhaps affected most deeply: her father called her a tramp; she became a prostitute. Even though she has recently quit prostitution, she feels branded for life. David tells her, "Trying to live with your father's values can kill you . . ." (308). Gloria replies, "No, Sweetie, living *without* your father's values can kill you" (308). Shortly thereafter, Gloria commits suicide.

Not only does Mr. Parodus (we often forget he is dead) affect his daughters' views of themselves, but he also influences their choice of the men they love and marry. Iris tells Sidney: "And each of us; I think we've sort of grown up wanting some part of Papa that we thought was the thing missing in him. I wanted somebody who could, well, think; Mavis wanted somebody steady and ordinary. And Gloria, well you know—rich men" (255). But since each woman's vision of herself is skewed, her vision of her husband or lover is also warped. In Sidney, Iris indeed found a thinker, but one who lacks the empathy and compassion to understand her desire to become an actress, to escape her rural background, "to know that when I die more than ten or a hundred people will know the difference. I want to *make it,* Sid" (256). Until the end of the play, Sidney sees Iris as an unspoiled mountain girl, an adolescent beauty.

At first seeing Fred as having a touch of the poet, Mavis was happy. Before they were married, Fred drove forty miles to see her and then drove forty miles back home in a decrepit car. But after their marriage, Fred became "steady and ordinary"; their sexual appeal for each other faded, and Fred took a mistress. Despite this lapse, Mavis is still *grateful* that he married her: "There was no rush at home to marry Mavis Parodus" (287). So Mavis is trapped. "I take care of my boys. I shop and I worry about my sisters. It's a life" (289). Beneath her polished exterior, she lacks a sense of self-worth. She also suspects that Fred has become dull.

Thinking that she wants "rich men," Gloria takes the short cut to success by becoming a prostitute. Her guilt causes her to try suicide four times, her last attempt succeeding. She has accepted her father's deathbed proclamation as fact: she *is* a tramp. But she chooses Alton Scales as a fiancé: he is attractive, intelligent, and compassionate. Perhaps she could have averted Alton's rejection of her had she told him the truth before he learned it from someone else. She *had* given up her business; she planned to lead a new life. But she felt she could not escape her past; she was doomed by her father. Gloria's suicide is as much a form of noncommitment to herself as is Sidney's initial refusal to become involved in his community, in politics.

Not surprisingly, all three sisters are in psychoanalysis. Like many playwrights and novelists of the 1960s, Hansberry did not see psychiatry as a real solution. For example, Gloria continues to accept clients who are sometimes cruel and violent. When she arrives at the Brustein apartment, she is badly bruised. Perhaps the analyst helps her make the break from prostitution, but he does not steel her against the world.[3] Mavis began analysis five years before, when Iris married Sidney and, more important, when Fred began his affair. The analyst no doubt helped her cope, but her life is depressingly asexual, segmented, and hollow. Iris talks more about her doctor than do her sisters, but comments about his treatment become a satire on psychiatrists. For twenty dollars an hour (in the economy of 1965), she has learned to "swear *out loud*!" quips Sidney (198). Iris bandies about terms such as love-hate obsession, mother complex, unconscious versus subconscious motivation, but Sidney never exposes the fact that the terms have no real meaning to her—they are only jargon, a substitute for facing her real problems.

What partially rescues these three women from a spiritual wasteland is that they all care deeply about each other. Iris resents the dresses Mavis buys her, but she wears one to a party where she hopes to make contacts for an acting job. Iris pretends a tolerant attitude about Gloria's misadventures, but she begs Sidney not to tell Alton the truth so that Gloria may start a new life. As annoying as Mavis is, she genuinely tries to understand the ideas of Iris and her Village friends. Perhaps if Gloria had lived to marry Alton, Mavis could have accepted his blackness just as she attempts—often humorously—to cope with Sidney's Jewish background. Gloria says little about her sisters, but significantly she comes home—to the Brustein brownstone—to die. Their caring extends beyond the family—to Sidney, Fred, and Alton, however flawed these unions may be—and, in Mavis's case, to Fred's young "sandy-haired kid," and her son, whom Mavis goes to the park to see.

In one of her more vulnerable moments, Mavis Parodus Bryson tells Sidney that her father changed their surname from "plain old everyday Parodopoulos" to Parodus—a Greek chorus. "No matter what is happening in the main action of the play—the chorus is always there, commenting, watching. . . . We were like that, the family, at the edge of life—not changing anything. Just watching and being" (285). Indeed, the three Parodus sisters—Iris, Mavis, and Gloria—function as a modern-day Greek chorus in *Sidney Brustein,* commenting upon and watching life around them. As the modern Furies of ambivalence, nihilism, retreat, and denial descend upon Sidney, the Parodus women serve individually and collectively to remind him that fate offers him a choice. The proper choice, of course, is for Sidney to abandon his retreat and to become once again a leader in the cause of justice. But the Parodus sisters also change and influence events, and they have small victories, unlike the Greek chorus. Iris

secures a job as a Golden Girl permanent model,[4] even if that falls short of
starring in a Broadway play. To save him further embarrassment, Iris tells
Sidney that Wally is "owned." Gloria has the fortitude to quit being a
hooker, even if she cannot cope with the outside world. More than anyone
else, she understands David's homosexuality. Mavis questions Sidney's
business deals and Gloria's way of life, but she tries to understand ideas
different from her own. She buys Iris clothes, she gives Sidney money, she
forgives Fred, she cares. The three sisters have an impact on people around
them. Near the end of the play, Sidney says: "*This world*—this swirling,
seething madness . . . has done this . . . now it has taken my *sister*" (317).

Homosexuals and Artists

In *The Sign in Sidney Brustein's Window,* sexuality and creativity seem to
be closely linked. On the simplest level, the physical sexual act can lead to
the birth of a child, just as the mental act of creation can lead to the birth
of a painting, a play, or a jazz piece. Of course, sexuality is mental and
emotional as well as physical, and creativity is physical and emotional as
well as mental. Given this equation, the homosexual David Ragin would
seem to be the least creative character in the play: he will not produce
children. In reality, he is the most productive, having written fourteen
plays. Significantly, he is also the character whose sexuality is the most
meaningful and integrated, though lacking in maturity.

David Ragin is perhaps the most complex character in the play. At first
he seems little more than a vehicle for satirizing absurdist plays. But David
is an attractive, soft-spoken homosexual, genuinely devoted to his art and
to selected friends, among whom are Sidney and Iris.

Absurdist plays, of course, are based on the premise that life is absurd,
that life has no innate meaning. Popularized by Sartre, Beckett, Ionesco,
and Albee, the absurdist play deems that we must *impose* meaning on life,
but frequently these impositions are trivial. Ionesco's characters find meaning by repeating monosyllables to each other; Albee's women derive value
by shopping and bringing home brightly wrapped packages that have
nothing inside. Many absurdist plays take place in one room, reinforcing
the concept of modern man's entrapment in a ridiculous life. Thus David's
setting his play in a refrigerator carries absurdist tendencies (perhaps cli-
chés) to a ridiculous extreme. Intolerant of marriage, religion, government, and other institutions, absurdist plays stress the difficulty of human
communications. David's play, therefore, may also be an unintentional
stab at homosexual marriage. The most noble action of an absurdist char-

acter is suicide—the ultimate imposition—which is an act of sterility, of noncommitment. David's characters are not necessarily suicidal, but their marriage is sterile and exhibits hostility to usual social commitments. While the content and format of absurdist plays is frequently baffling to the uninitiated, they do adhere to their own dramatic unities. The action—if it may be called that—is limited to twenty-four hours, frequently less, and consists of involving only the minimum number of characters in minimal activity—to the point where the beginning and end of the play are sacrificed entirely for the middle. In short, an absurdist play begins with and ends *in media res.*

Absurdism was in its heyday in the 1960s, and a young avant-garde playwright would naturally have been attracted to the form. More important, David Ragin takes his work seriously: he has written fourteen plays; he is astounded when his own drama is a hit; and he even considers writing the night after the rave reviews—a night for celebration. A careful observer of human behavior, David is a sensitive recorder of human experience and a disciplined craftsman who strives for integrity in his work.

David's personal life, however, is not so well ordered as his writing career. Modern psychologists do not agree on the origins of homosexuality, but late in *Sidney Brustein,* David describes his first love to Gloria:

I was seven. So was Nelson. We were both exactly seven. We used to make a great deal out of that. We used to play all day in my yard. He had fine golden hair and a thin delicate profile—and Mother always said: "Nelson is a real aristocrat." Then, just like that, one summer his family moved to Florence, Italy. Because that is the sort of thing that aristocrats do when they feel like it. And I never saw him again. (309)

Apparently, David has been searching for Nelson ever since. David's loves are important to him: he describes Nelson with an artist's eye—golden hair and a delicate profile; he views Nelson with dignity and respect—he was an aristocrat. Unlike Max, David is not looking for an easy mark in a bar. At the same time, David's sexuality is rooted in the myths of childhood.[5] By freezing Nelson in time as a seven-year-old, David does not confront mature homosexuality.

In a less than admirable moment, David whines about his sexuality. Alton has stomped out, after telling David he is tired of "hanging out with queers" (246). With seeming innocence, David begins to set a trap for Iris. "*You* accept queers, don't you, Iris?" (246). Iris answers, "Sure," and David continues, "Yes, because you accept *anything.* But—I am not *anything.* I hope he never has to explore the *why* of his discomfort" (246–47). But

Sidney is on to David's game. "You have written fourteen plays about . . . the isolation of the soul of man . . . the desolation of all love, all possible communications. When what you really want to say is that you are ravaged by a society that will not sanctify your particular sexuality!" (247). A bit boorishly and simplistically, he tells David to sock his detractors in the jaw, to start a petition, to love little fishes if he likes. He can do anything but think his "thing" is "something that only the deepest, saddest, the most nobly tortured can know about. . . . It's just one kind of sex—that's all" (247–48). David goes out, pouting.

David comes into his finest moment, however, when he refuses to compromise his integrity. Iris has left Sidney because she wants "something to happen" in her life. Still in a state of euphoria over his success, David is even considering having his phone unlisted and misses the import of what Sidney is asking him to do—at first. Unable to look David in the eye, Sidney says: "Write her into your play, David. Something for her. Something simple that she can do. With dancing" (270). Compounding his error, Sidney even offers to review the play. David becomes increasingly outraged:

Such a tiny little corruption. Not three people in the whole world would ever really care whether or not my little insignificant play did or did not have its unities stretched to just happen to include a part for your wife in trade for a patch of glowing praise in your paper. Not three people in the whole world. That's the magic of the tiny corruptions, isn't it, Sidney? Their insignificance makes them so appealing. (272)

David may whine over Alton's insults, but he is an artist's artist. He is shocked that Sidney would ask him to violate the unities of absurdist drama, but he is appalled at the thought of compromising his personal integrity—and Sidney's and Iris's, too—in order to accommodate an actress of little promise. David is honest with himself and with others, at least when his art is involved.

Near the end of the play, David makes Gloria a proposition that many people would consider perverted: he wants her to watch while he and another man make love (310). His partner is a "beautiful burnished golden boy" from a distinguished New England family who wants a young woman of his own class present. David's manner in asking Gloria is respectful, quiet, and strained; he would find his lover the "snows of Himalayas" if he desired them. As awkward as his situation is, David has rediscovered the Nelson of his childhood in another man. David the artist and David the lover merge into one of the few characters in *Sidney Brustein* who are committed, involved, and caring.

None of the other major characters in *Sidney Brustein* is homosexual. The quality of their heterosexual love is, however, linked inextricably with the state of their emotional stability and creative potential. In sharp contrast to David is the painter Max, a minor character whose presence on stage, though short, tells us all we need to know. Max, whose last name is not given, has no sense of history; he hates Michelangelo; his free-form paintings lack a real sense of color or design. Hansberry is not condemning all abstract art: she is merely using Max as another example of the uncommitted. He is casual about his work. As the art consultant for Sidney's newspaper, he is useless; he wants to use three-point type at the bottom of the page for the masthead so readers will *look* for it (219). An aging macho type, he is torn between eating dinner with Iris, Sidney, and Alton and meeting a "chick" at the Black Knight Tavern. Sex—and we gather casual sex—is victorious. Alton says, "The *loins* triumph! See, Max, you're *not* a true primitive or you would have put *food* first! You only *paint* like a savage" (221). Max leaves for the Black Knight Tavern and does not return.

For Iris Parodus, creativity and sexuality mingle in a state of arrested development. Her acting is obviously in an embryonic form: she is attractive, she dances gracefully, but she has not studied her craft seriously. David describes one of her performances as horrible (270). At the same time, Iris and Sidney share an unspecified sexual problem. Hansberry seems to be saying that not until one's sexual behavior is mature, devoid of fantasy and therefore honest, will growth or personal satisfaction be possible. The play implies that Iris will pass through the stages of Golden Girl and mountain lass and mature as both an actress and woman.

Although Gloria Parodus could only metaphorically be considered an artist, she has a sensitivity and compassion normally associated with the artist. She understands David; she loves and is loved by Alton; she appreciates the surrealistic horror of a Goya print. But Gloria's sexuality is distorted, almost schizophrenic: she endures sex, sometimes sadistic sex, for money, while she longs for the warmth of Alton's love. She can break into the Stravinskyesque frenzy of a death dance with David and Sidney, yet she has made her fortune as the model of the bright American girl. Unable to reconcile all these forces, she kills herself. Her death is the antithesis of creativity, of life.

In *The Sign in Sidney Brustein's Window,* then, Lorraine Hansberry pleads for maturity and commitment in sexuality and creativity—whatever form each may take. Despite his sporadic emotional torture, David is a commit-

ted and therefore fulfilled being who gives more than he takes. Iris and
Sidney are searching for fulfillment, sometimes at cross purposes, and
sometimes meeting with failure. Yet the search for commitment continues
because they care. Gloria could not recognize her own power. And Max—
shallow as he is—does not deserve a last name.

From Politics to Commitment

Caught in the maze of modern society, Sidney Brustein is a Broadway
version of the modern Everyman, financially comfortable, idle, and intellectual, sometimes quietly hovering in corners, painfully strutting into
false passages, and finally finding his way to the lighted exit. He seeks
defensively the false security of drinking, glib philosophizing, and ill-ad-
vised business deals. He stumbles into the treacherous world of politics,
religion, and racial issues. By the end of the play, he and the others begin
to understand the puzzle, where there is meaning—both in the outside
world and in themselves.

In act 3, Gloria, Sidney, and David deliver a profane litany on contemporary life. They rationalize themselves into an absurdist philosophy. In
their musical, subconscious trance, they celebrate the terrible forces bom-
barding modern man and woman—nihilism, absurdity, primal fears and
urges, commercialism, selfishness, basic guilt and innocence. Intoxicated
by liquor, they reveal their own vulnerability. Gloria begins the rites with
a masterpiece of circular logic: "Things as they are are as they are and have
been and will be that way because they got that way because things were
as they were in the first place" (306). Life, she is saying, defies change, and
free will is but an illusion. Defeatism, of course, is at the base of Hansberry's fears for modern man: he is in a state of ennui because he believes he
has no options; he must conform to the corrupt institutions of his uncaring
society.

Sidney flirts with the Judeo-Christian notion of original sin and deprav-
ity: "Society is based on complicity in the common crime . . ." (306). He
then regresses to man's primal urges and fears: "We all suffer from the
murder of the primal father who kept all the females for himself . . ."
(306). For a moment, the three speakers seem to find some hope in the
following syllogism: "We are all guilty. Therefore all guilt is equal. Therefore none are innocent. Therefore—None are guilty" (306). But the minute of optimism is shattered when Sidney declares: "Any two of anything
is totalitarian" (307). They espouse the most negative aspect of Ayn Rand's
theory of selfishness, "He must be dedicated to his own interests" (307).

They stress the obscenity of using sex as a commodity: in his newspaper, Sidney will feature Lucy Jones upside down and women doing the splits juxtaposed with a treatise on Etruscan excavation. All will be justified by unprincipled commercialism, as Sidney says, "I'll prove I'm right—by growing rich!" (307). Intermingled with all these drunken ravings are references to *Hamlet,* situation ethics, and Zen Buddhism—all values and morals that are irrelevant to their situation.

As the lighting shifts from deathly blue to hot pink, Gloria, David, and Sidney dance to the frenzy of the frug, the Watusi, and twist—popular dances of the 1960s. Beautiful modern jazz weaves in the background, but the music disintegrates into nonmeaning as they debase two children's songs: "Here we go round the mulberry bush" becomes "This is the way the cheese will rot," and "Who's afraid of the big bad wolf?" becomes "Who's afraid of absurdity?!"

What is so frightening about this scene is that it mirrors what is wrong with Sidney the modern man and his society. There are no priorities, no meanings, no exits. Intense and surrealistic, this scene reveals the depths of modern man's and woman's frustrations. With tongues and hearts loosened by alcohol and the moment, Gloria, Sidney, and David expose private tortures that usually do not surface. But most of their problems exist on a more conscious, mundane level: voting for the right candidate, if voting at all; coping with racism, filling the void left by a forgotten God; finding inner peace despite a turbulent world.

The political subplot of *The Sign in Sidney Brustein's Window* borders on the simplistic: Man decides to run for office. Man plans to undercut the corrupt political machine, to stand up for the little man. Man gains "grass roots" support of old ladies, truck drivers, businessmen, intellectuals. Man wins. Man is discovered to be a part of the political machine, but he still believes that he can "do good." The man is Wally O'Hara, candidate for an unspecified office—an ambiguity which renders the campaign both universal and commonplace.

What gives this political cliché freshness and vitality is the involvement of Sidney Brustein, the floundering intellectual. After proclaiming his apolitical stand, Sidney makes a rather rapid conversion to Wally's cause—the main reason being his concern for Sal Peretti. Although Sal is mentioned only twice, we learn that he is a seventeen-year-old boy who swept floors for Sidney at the Silver Dagger and whose involvement with narcotics has left him near death. Understandably, Sidney is taken by Wally's argument that he wants to rid the community of crime, narcotics, and the "machine." As Wally explains: "We're not talking about the world, we're

talking about this community . . . your own little ailing neighborhood
. . ." (207). Wally himself is an attractive candidate. He is a successful
lawyer with a sense of humor who is attuned to current issues. Furthermore, he can quote Thoreau as well as Sidney. Aware of the women's movement, he engages in a little coterie wit: "Woman's place is in the oven"
(209). Sidney mistakes his glibness for sincerity and devotes himself without reservation to the campaign.

Exhilarated when his dark-horse candidate wins, Sidney feels a sense of
renewal in himself, his neighborhood, in the world:

Alton, old baby, do you know the main trouble with us believers in this world?
We don't believe. . . . Do you know what we proved today, Alton? . . . We proved
that what the people need, what they want, is alternatives. Give them alternatives
and all the dull stupid negative old shiboleths go up in smoke *Poof!* (276–77)

Sidney digresses to point out that the planetary system is 5 billion years
old, that primitive apes evolved 25 million years ago, that human beings
were preceded by the "sub boys"—Java, Peking, Neanderthal and Cro-
Magnon Man, that man is just an *infant*. And this infant made the right
choice—in electing Wally O'Hara.

But Sidney's euphoria evaporates quickly. No political novice, Sidney
has belonged to committees "To Save, To Abolish, Prohibit, Preserve, Reserve and Conserve" since he was eighteen. But he made the mistake of
letting his defenses down, of trusting Wally completely. With no pleasure,
Iris finally has the grim duty of telling Sidney that Wally is "owned" by
the political bosses he is ostensibly fighting. "Don't you hear me? ... They
own Wally. . . . The people you've been fighting. . . . Own him completely; the house he lives in, the clothes on his back, the toothpaste he
uses" (294).

One reason Sidney may have been vulnerable to this masquerade is that
he has a few moral lapses himself. He cannot help or understand Iris. He
refuses to recognize Mavis's tough inner fiber. He and Alton cart baskets
of glasses from the bankrupt restaurant to the Brustein apartment. Strictly
speaking, this action is illegal: all equipment should be intact for the even-
tual audit. Sidney also asks David to write Iris into his next play—obviously a matter of artistic and professional compromise for the younger man.
Granted, Sidney is desperate about his troubled marriage, but his request
is still morally suspect.

After learning of Wally's deception, Sidney could easily revert to his
apathetic, cynical state. Wally enters making direct threats, telling Sidney

that he plans to erect stop signs but to ignore the narcotics traffic, warning him that his newspaper will be destroyed. But Sidney can no longer accept corruption or the cruelties of man against man. Near the end of the play, Sidney tells Wally:

Every time we say "live and let live"—death triumphs. . . . I am going to fight you, Wally. . . . You have forced me to take a position . . . the one thing I never wanted to do. . . . And what you have to worry about is the fact that some of us will be back out in those streets today. Only this time—thanks to you—we shall be more seasoned, more cynical, tougher, harder to fool. . . . (316)

Like Lorraine Hansberry, Sidney Brustein has learned that everything is political, that to remain aloof and uninvolved is to die. So Sidney will fight for the death of the old order,the political machine, so that the new order, the living individual, may be reborn.

Sidney's best friend, Alton Scales epitomizes black identity and pride. When Iris playfully accuses him of being a "white boy playing black boy," he replies, "I *am* a black boy. I didn't make up the game, and as long as a lot of people think there is something wrong with the fact that I *am* a Negro—I am going to make a point of being one" (224). For this reason, he has no choice but to reject Gloria after he learns of her tawdry past. Lorraine Hansberry explains, "Alton . . . could not consciously have known the day before that he would have made such an assessment of the woman he loved." The hour for the unequivocal dignity of the black man had arrived and prevented his taking white man's leftovers. "He could not, if his life depended on it, transplant his decision."[6] Alton himself is guilty of racism when he admits that he could accept and forgive a past of prostitution if the woman he loved were black (281). Likewise, Gloria bitterly condemns Alton when she declares that other prostitutes deliberately sleep with black men because these men cannot look down on them (304). She is, however, speaking of the man she loves, who rejected her only minutes before. Their love was a casualty of the white man's oppression of the black—a history which Alton could not forgive.

The racial issue, however, is a minor theme of *Sidney Brustein*. Set in 1964, certainly a time of racial turmoil, the play basically reflects harmony and acceptance between blacks and whites, Jews and Christians, and peoples of varied backgrounds. Representative of the middle class, Mavis is not a hopeless racist. Iris and Sidney tell her of Gloria's engagement to Alton in a taunting, insensitive manner, but just as she has become more accepting of Sidney's Jewish heritage, she will eventually understand Al-

ton's blackness and David's sexuality. Set in Greenwich Village, the vanguard of social and artistic growth, the play beckons a society aware of rich
ethnic backgrounds but free of racial strife.

For Sidney Brustein, organized religion satisfies no thirst in his spiritual
and moral wasteland. His Jewish background mainly serves as a source of
humor: he makes stock references to his Jewish mother, and Wally teases
him about being a "nice middle-class Jewish boy." In a more serious moment, Sidney hums an old Yiddish melody, "Rozhankis Mit Mandlen"
(296). More often, he considers the despair and imposed meanings of
"Father Camus." Only Mavis seems to need organized religion, as she bitterly says to Sidney and his guests: "Where indeed might we look for understanding . . . in this quite dreadful world. Since you have all so busily
got rid of God for us" (245).

Sidney has come full circle in his search for meaning. He finds no solace
in drinking, superficial philosophizing, making poor business deals. Politics provides an outward sign of inner commitment, but he cannot control
the evils of Wally and his machine. Drawing strength from his friendship
with Alton, Sidney knows that Mavis's racism typifies middle-class insu-
larity, which intensifies man's isolation from his fellow man. Organized
religion, as comfortable as it can be, offers Sidney no real solution. The
answer then lies within man himself—who must explore the depths and
heights of his own soul and mind to find meaning.

Sidney the modern Everyman becomes Sidney the contemporary Henry
David Thoreau as he searches for self-reliance and inner strength so that he
may use this power to improve society. A lover of mountains and streams,
Sidney identifies with the introspective side of Thoreau. In *Walden* (1850),
Thoreau writes that he went to the woods and solitary pond because he
"wished to live deliberately, to front only the essential facts of life." He
prided himself on his self-reliance, closeness to nature, and time for contemplation. In the lyrical mountain scene of act 2, Sidney revels in banjo
music, Iris's natural beauty, the solitude of pines and the "thin line of
dawn" (252)—reminiscent of Thoreau's reverence of nature. Like his friend
Emerson, Thoreau believed in the innate goodness of man and in the Over-
soul—that Man, God, and Nature are equal and interdependent. In the
mountains, Sidney echoes Thoreau's belief: "Coming here makes me believe that the planet is mine again. In the primeval sense. Man and earth
and earth and man . . ." (256).

A foe of commercialism, Thoreau rejected the society that forced men
to think that "a stitch in time saves nine, and so they take a thousand
stitches to-day to save nine to-morrow." After closing the Silver Dagger,

Sidney rejoices that Manny, his materialistic brother and former business partner, is "free" of him—no longer will Manny feel obliged to finance Sidney's business ventures. And Sidney is free of Manny, the prince of Philistines: "I do not, for any reason, want to become part of Emmanuel Brustein, Inc." (239). Free of daily concerns at Walden, Thoreau could "live deep and suck out all the marrow of life," just as Sidney Brustein's conversations and introspection in the Village have led to a sense of self.

But a sense of self is not enough for Sidney Brustein or Henry David Thoreau. Leaving Walden after two years, Thoreau had "more lives to live and could not spare any more time for that one." One of his "other lives" became his prophetic *Civil Disobedience* (1849), in which Thoreau deplores the Mexican War and southern slavery and insists on passive resistance to unjust laws to the point that "the true place for a just man is . . . a prison." After Alton Scales tells Sidney that he admires "the wrong parts of Thoreau" (213), Wally O'Hara ironically recounts the tale of Thoreau's famous day in jail:

How about . . . the Thoreau who was standing in jail one day when that holy of holies, Mr. Ralph Waldo Emerson, comes strolling by and asks, "Well, Henry, What are you doing in there?" And Thoreau, who was in there for protesting the evils of his day, looked out at him and said—"The question is, Ralph, what are you doing out *thay-ah?*" (214)

Like Sidney Brustein, Henry David Thoreau is trying not to care: "I came into this world, not chiefly to make this a good place to live in, but to live in it. . . ." But such detachment is not possible for either man. Sidney Brustein has always been a thinker, even though he is sometimes pretentious and self-pitying. But the moment when he chooses to become involved in Wally O'Hara's campaign is the turning point in his becoming a reformer. Just as Thoreau grieved for the southern slave and men leading lives of "quiet desperation," Brustein mourned for Sal Peretti and other Greenwich Villagers entrapped by narcotics and crime. That Wally's cause was unjust and corrupt does not alter Sidney's commitment; he was naive but sincere. Suffering major setbacks when he learns that Wally is "owned," that his marriage is troubled, that Gloria is dead, Sidney is briefly plunged back into the role of the thinker—troubled and shattered. This short stage parallels Thoreau's realization that all laws are not just and that his "only obligation . . . is to do at any time what I think is right." Just as Thoreau found that he had other lives to lead in *Civil Disobedience,* Sidney Brustein discovers that his disappointment and hurt will only make him a stronger husband, brother, and reformer. As the play ends, Sidney is prepared to suffer the consequences of losing his newspaper, perhaps going to jail, or being ridiculed so that he can help create a better world: "Then, tomorrow, we shall make something strong of this sorrow . . ." (318).

In her final speech, Iris Parodus speaks of Gloria Parodus but alludes to the ancient myth of the Fisher King:

When she was little . . . she had fat, pudgy hands . . . and I used to have to scrub them . . . because she couldn't get them clean. And so I would pretend that they were fish and I was the Fish Lady cleaning these little fish to sell them. . . . That always tickled her, and she would laugh and laugh. . . . (318)

In *From Ritual to Romance*, Jessie Weston explains that the Fisher King was an old man who ruled a country where crops and animals were dying, streams were dry, people were starving. Not only was the land physically blighted, but it was a moral and spiritual wasteland. Sometimes the old king attempted to fish in muddy, shallow streams. But his efforts were feeble and futile. After a period of time, a young man came to the kingdom, having endured many hardships and passed through many trials. Then the young man either seized control of the kingdom or restored youth to the reigning monarch. The land and its people were then reborn.

The Fisher King is impotent and worn out like the land he rules. His attempt to catch fish symbolizes his desire to rejuvenate himself and his land. Fish have always been a symbol of life, predating the Christian age. He fishes in lifeless water, however, which symbolizes his spiritual corruption. He cannot accomplish what he set out to do because he is physically and spiritually decayed. Only virtuous youth can restore the ravaged land to its previously fruitful state.

Hansberry had a knowledge of mythology and perhaps saw her *Sidney Brustein* as a modern-day version of the Fisher King myth.[7] In essence, the Fisher King society of Wally and his ilk, sterile and corrupt, will prevail only as long as its members are spiritually dead. To Hansberry, spiritual decay was tantamount to a lack of commitment, yet both can be reversed. With commitment comes renewal of both self and society. Hansberry thought it possible to make the water pure again.

A Limbo Play

After 101 performances, *Sidney Brustein* closed on January 12, 1965—just hours after Lorraine Hansberry died. It survived on stage as long as it did partly through the devotion of numerous actors and actresses, such as Shelley Winters and Ruby Dee, who considered the play a brilliant assessment of society's ills. Though the audiences could not as easily understand or as spontaneously respond to the play as to *Raisin,* they received *Brustein* on balance with respect and even warmth. In addition to buying tickets, they donated $40,000 in small amounts to *Brustein*[8]—too much in 1965 for a sentimental gesture to a dying woman. The critics, however, were divided. Max Lerner dubbed *Brustein* a "limbo play," one that is "full of insights, striking characters, fine writing, even theatrical brilliance . . . in [which] the playwright . . . has not *broken through* with that touch of finality. . . ."[9]

Rex Reed praised the play unequivocally. In the *New York Express,* he wrote, "She knows more about the bloody world we live in than any living playwright working in the theatre today (with the possible exception of Tennessee Williams). . . . I shall never, as long as I live, hope to see such perfection in the theatre again. . . . It is a mirror to the life of the human race."[10] Martin Gottfried did not like the play. In *Women's Wear Daily,* he blasted "the stinking triviality of it all" and condemned Hansberry's "extremely poor writing, almost ridiculous plotting and a set of characters that, for sheer implausibility, should win some sort of award."[11] Howard Taubman of the *New York Times* seemed to share Lerner's "limbo" theory. He praised many scenes "that shine with humor, tremble with feeling and summon up a vision of wisdom and integrity." At the same time, "the truth must be faced that Miss Hansberry's play lacks concision and cohesion. . . ."[12]

Production problems arose over which Hansberry had little control. Mort Sahl, who would have been the perfect Sidney, was the original star. He had probably inspired the line: "Woman's place is in the oven." Unfortunately, he and director Carmen Capalbo were replaced a week and a half before opening night.[13] At this time, Gabriel Dell had not even learned all his lines. Even Harold Taubman noticed that "Mr. Dell . . . struggles in others [scenes] for a line and seems to lose his concentration."[14] Furthermore, Lorraine Hansberry was too ill to "fix" the play with important rewrites by October 15, 1964—the night reviewers Reed, Gottfried, and Taubman came.[15]

Since 1965, critics have continued to probe the artistic merit of *Sidney Brustein.* Emory Lewis, a prominent member of the New York Drama Critics' Circle for twenty years, included the play in his 1969 anthology, *Stages: The Fifty-year Childhood of the American Theatre.* He noted that "No contemporary playwright . . . has captured so vividly the fervor and *Angst* of certain big-city intellectuals. . . ."[16] John Gassner and Clive Barnes incorporated *Brustein* into their 1971 anthology, *Best American Plays*. Many critics agreed that the play was "flawed" and in need of revising and cutting. Still, Lewis thought it deserved a "key place in the history of modern American drama."[17] In the prestigious black newspaper, the *New York Amsterdam News*, Lionel Mitchell wrote in 1980: "In many ways, *Brustein* is her greatest triumph."[18]

Apart from production problems, the script of *The Sign in Sidney Brustein's Window* still keeps it in "limbo." First of all, it *is* a "play of ideas." Hansberry's merger of homosexuality and absurdist drama in the character of David Ragin at times seems a petty attack; the fusion of Gloria Parodus the prostitute and Gloria Parodus the family member almost descends into "soap opera."[19] To her credit, Hansberry skillfully and naturally embeds the other six main "ideas": marriage, psychoanalysis, politics, abstract art, anti-Semitism, racism. This inclusion of so many ideas creates the impression that the play is simply too long.

By mixing styles of genres, Hansberry defied commercial and total artistic success. *Brustein* fails to provide the catharsis of tragedy. As a comedy, the play would have profited by a few lessons from George Bernard Shaw, one of Hansberry's mentors. *Major Barbara* (1905) works as a drama of ideas because Shaw presents two memorable characters, the idealistic Barbara and her bombastic, realistic father, Sir Andrew Undershaft, who are so compelling and lively we do not mind hearing their sermons about poverty, capitalism, women's rights, and war. Shaw does not include homosexuality or the 1905 equivalent of absurdist drama. His minor characters remain minor and do not push toward center stage as do Alton Scales, David Ragin, or Max.

Probably the most subtle, but significant reason for *Brustein's* lack of total success, however, was the time in which it appeared on Broadway—1964–65. The play was in direct competition with Arthur Miller's *After the Fall*. In 1949 Miller had alerted the public that he was no defender of the American Dream with *Death of a Salesman*; ten years later, Hansberry had seemed to suggest just the opposite in *Raisin*. Perhaps critics could not tolerate another play about self-tortured Manhattan intellectuals—particularly from someone capable of writing a paean to the family, to hope in *A Raisin in the Sun*.

The Sign in Sidney Brustein's Window was also ahead of its time. A few astute critics hinted at this dilemma. Julius Lester wrote: "The play was produced a year and a half before white liberal intellectuals were to be confronted by the spectre of black power. 'Sign' was a conscious warn-

ing."[20] Lionel Mitchell believed "her view of the course of village liberalism
. . . proved prophetic."[21] In 1976 the talented playwright Ntozake
Shange included a brief tribute to one of *her* mentors—Lorraine Hansberry—in *For Colored Girls who have Considered Suicide when the Rainbow is Enuf.*
Hence, little more than a decade after Hansberry's "failure," Broadway
raved over an infinitely more "talky" play of social ideas.

As early as 1966, Brooks Atkinson assessed the critical reputation of the
play: "[*Brustein*] is overcrowded with miseries and neuroses and . . . some
of the transitions are awkward. . . . But Miss Hansberry was a genuine
dramatist. . . . Although *The Sign in Sidney Brustein's Window* failed at the
box office, it lives in Miss Hansberry's vigorous prose. Even in print it is
theater."[22] In the 1980s or 1990s, perhaps a writer will emerge who can
"put in the commas and the periods," who will tighten up the slightly
paunchy *Sidney Brustein*. Perhaps a director and producer can hone a fine
performance. Perhaps then, the play will more fully and clearly fulfill the
promise of *A Raisin in the Sun.*

Chapter Six

Some Cold Wind Blew:
Collected Last Plays

A powerful triumvirate of plays, *Les Blancs: The Collected Last Plays of Lorraine Hansberry* at first seem to be linked by nothing but Lorraine Hansberry's signature, humor, and artistry. Set in Kenya around 1952, *Les Blancs* painfully investigates the bloody Mau Mau Revolution against the British and European rulers. Set in the American South before the Civil War, *The Drinking Gourd* is a balanced treatment of both slaves and their owners. A futuristic fable, *What Use Are Flowers?* sketches the savagery of a group of children, who are redeemed by an elderly professor after an atomic holocaust. Spanning continents and centuries, these plays portray hermits, missionaries, mothers, fathers, revolutionaries, doctors, slaves, slaveowners, surly children, confused young men, brave people, fearful people, and those who know what they must do.

Although *Les Blancs* and *The Drinking Gourd* have obvious parallels—tensions between blacks and whites, urgency for action, tendency toward violence, necessity for freedom—all three plays are connected by one central idea: the cold wind of deliberate action. This cold wind is especially startling in warm climates—the farmlands of the American South, the Kenyan deserts, the tropical islands of the Caribbean, lands parched by atomic fallout—mañanalands where people have long suffered passively under tyranny. As the cold wind blows, people must fasten their coats tightly around themselves—chilling their smiles, straightening their backs, becoming silent. Often they must forego summer pleasantries and friendships and cast aside Thoreauvian nonviolence—if passive resistance has not worked. Propelled by the cold wind, they must gamble for total freedom or anihilation. *What Use Are Flowers?* is Hansberry's horrific vision of what lies in store if freedom and tolerance are finally denied. Moving away from the personal point of view of *Raisin* and *Sidney Brustein,* these posthumous plays are Hansberry's warning to despots—benevolent and otherwise.

94

In 1972, Robert Nemiroff edited and published *Les Blancs: The Collected Last Plays of Lorraine Hansberry.* Hansberry had died in 1965, leaving Nemiroff, Ossie Davis, Charlotte Zaltzberg, and others to "put in the commas and periods." Hansberry had begun *Les Blancs* in 1960 but discovered that the play needed more revision when act 1, scene 3, was staged for the Actors Studio Writers' Workshop in 1963.[1] She worked on the script until her death, but *Les Blancs* did not open on Broadway until 1970—to mixed reviews. The last two plays were never produced. After solidly researching and writing *The Drinking Gourd,* Hansberry sent the play to the National Broadcasting Company, but the network was squeamish about the script and did not produce the show. Hansberry originally wrote *What Use Are Flowers?* for television but planned to recast the play for the stage—a plan foiled by her death. Robert Nemiroff deserves credit and appreciation for editing these plays for the Random House edition—and for keeping alive the works of this remarkable playwright.

Les Blancs

Nineteen fifty-one was a landmark year for Lorraine Hansberry. In New York, she completed a year's seminar on African history under Dr. W. E. B. DuBois, for whom she wrote a research paper on the Belgian Congo. She had read key African studies, including Jomo Kenyatta's *Facing Mt. Kenya,* Basil Davidson's *Lost Cities of Africa,* and DuBois's own *Black Folk: Then and Now.* She published articles on Kwame Nkrumah of Ghana and the struggle of other African countries for self-rule. Clive Barnes, in his negative *New York Times* review of *Les Blancs,* must not have been aware of Lorraine Hansberry's background when he wrote: "I wonder how much Miss Hansberry knew or Mr. Nemiroff really knows about Africa?"[2]

Nineteen fifty-one also marked a time of drastic change in Kenya with the eruption of the Mau Mau Revolt. From 1902 to 1907, the British had moved into Kenya, primarily attracted by the fertile land, ideal for cultivating coffee, cocoa, cotton, and peanuts. Other Europeans moved into nearby countries to mine diamonds, silver, and other precious metals. Such industry could well have brought twentieth-century wealth, education, and health care to the black Africans, but many Britons sought to keep the Africans at the bottom of the economic ladder. In 1912 Lord Delamare introduced legislation—which passed—to limit the crops an African might cultivate on his own land (thereby making it impossible for him to support himself) and to impose a heavy Hut and Poll Tax.[3]

From 1920 to 1951, the Kikuyu people—who comprised one third of the Kenyan population—tried to bring about reform through nonviolent means. A peaceful, religious people, the Kikuyus valued democratic, non-centralized government and leadership based on wisdom and ability, rather than on inherited power. In 1920 they formed the Kikuyu Association, which tried to end the African loss of land to whites and to alter difficult labor policies through mass meetings and petitions. Then in 1922 the Kikuyus formed the East African Association, led by Harry Thuku. When Thuku made a public speech, denouncing the white government theft of land, the missionary imposition of "the word of the devil," and the very fact of British occupation, he was arrested. When other EEA members gathered outside the jail in peaceful protest, the frightened police opened fire, killing twenty-one people and injuring many more.[4] This incident typified British reaction to Kikuyu protest.

Still the Kikuyus attempted peaceful negotiations. In 1924 the remnants of the East African Association formed the Kikuyu Central Association, which continued to press for reform with meetings and petitions. Most important, a powerful leader emerged: Jomo Kenyatta, a large man dedicated to peace and conciliation. During the 1930s he was living in England, where he and his delegates demanded: return or payment for their lost land, freedom in planting on private property, relief from the ever-increasing Hut and Poll Tax, more educational opportunities, and— the most radical request—representation on the Legislative Council.[5] In 1940 the KCA was declared illegal, and its leaders were imprisoned for four years.[6]

In the late 1940s, a strong underground movement was forming. Resuming their African names, the members took the secret Oath (Muma), vowing allegiance to the movement for freedom (Muingi), placing their loyalty to Muingi above self, friends, and family, and declaring death to whites. (The term Mau Mau was an English invention. The closest East African equivalent was "greedy eating"—a term used by mothers scolding their children for overeating.) Opposed to violence, Kenyatta did not approve of the movement. When Kenyatta was arrested on the charge of plotting insurrection, Kenya exploded.[8]

Much of the popular literature about the Mau Maus portrays blacks mercilessly slaughtering their white masters in the quiet African nights. While these were violent times throughout colonial Africa, Hansberry seeks to explain the reasons and explore the plight of men forced to let blood for freedom. Typically, Hansberry does not preach. Nor does she fail to show us that all people—black and white—are a fusion of good and evil, fear and courage, confusion and conviction. But the Kikuyus were forced to act. In *Les Blancs,* Madame Neilsen, an aged white woman who is blind but sees, explains the situation eloquently: "Some cold wind blew in over our people here and chilled their hearts to us. It is the times, you know. I'm afraid he'll never understand it—the Reverend" (51). The Reverend Neilsen should have understood: he had been spoken to for more than thirty years.

The Action. Act 1 opens in the gray-green glow of African twilight with the sound of crickets, frogs, and bush babies. Black-skinned and imposing, The Woman freezes in a dance pose, her cheeks painted for war, a spear planted in the earth beside her. A hyena laughs.

Twilight yields to mid-afternoon in an African mission as Dr. Marta Gotterling, a handsome, blonde woman in her mid-thirties, examines a small black boy. Peter, a middle-aged porter with graying hair, leads Charlie Morris into the hospital, distressing the liberal journalist by repeatedly calling him "Bwana." Armed with typewriter and brief case, Morris is an American in his late forties, who has come to write the story of Reverend Neilsen, who founded the Mission forty years earlier to provide the Africans with spiritual and medical aid. The reverend has been missing for some days. As Marta jokes with Charlie about the lack of sanitation, Dr. Willy DeKoven enters—a slight, deeply browned man, who later emerges as one of the two white sympathizers with the revolution in the play. A colonial officer in his fifties, Major Rice blusters in and rails against the "terrorists" and whites who are "being butchered in their beds." Rifle shots are heard in the jungle, as Charlie speaks reverently of Kumalo (Hansberry's name for Kenyatta).

Leaning on a cane, Madame Neilsen enters—a genteel European with flinty inner strength: she too becomes a white revolutionary, or sympathizer. After chiding Willy for giving the confused adolescent Eric whiskey, she speaks of the drums and their messages, the Kwi (Hansberry's name for the Kikuyu), her departed friend Aquah, and the "cold wind" that blew in. Fairskinned and drunken, Eric enters, wearing filthy clothes but a clean pith helmet. Madame Neilsen says to Charlie Morris, "I shall think you an exceedingly poor journalist . . . if you . . . are in the least confounded by either the name or the complexion of our Eric" (32).

As dusk falls on the Matoseh hut, Eric and Tshembe embrace, exchange the Kwi sign of greeting, and mourn the death of their father—old Abioseh. Wearing rumpled city clothes, Tshembe is a handsome, pensive young African with a European wife and son. When he shows his brother a photograph of his wife, Eric teases him, saying that she looks old and

wrinkled with veins peering through her skin—like a chicken. Abruptly
serious, Tshembe says, "Kumalo is coming home," adding derisively,
"What has he done in Europe? *Talk!* Talk, talk, talk" (56). As Eric tells
Tshembe that their father went to his death rubbing lizard powder on his
breast and chanting his kula, the third brother arrives. Taller, older, and
wrapped in a great African blanket, Abioseh smiles at Eric and "Tshembe,
who is Ishmael," and is alarmed when he suspects that his brothers may be
involved in the "terror." Calmly Tshembe replies: "All Africa is involved
in this trouble, brother" (58–59). After reminiscing about pigeons in
Hyde Park, Tshembe tells Abioseh they must dress for the funeral. Abioseh reveals that he will take his final vows for the Catholic priesthood in
the spring, and a religious argument ensues.

Tshembe has adopted existentialist views in Europe, dismisses the Kwi
religion as so much harmless "lizard powder," and finds Catholicism—
indeed, Christianity—merely "another cult." Perhaps his childhood memories of the Reverend Neilsen—his condescension, his urging of Christian
"humility," his racism—resurface as he suddenly flings his brother's crucifix across the room. This desecration sends the novice Abioseh to his knees,
to supplication. As the scene ends, Tshembe wears African ceremonial
robes as a tribute to his father; Abioseh kneels in his mystical priestly
robes, and Eric is terrified.

As evening descends on the Mission, Madame Neilsen sits on the porch.
Charlie asks Marta to take a walk with him, but she tells him that a white
family has just been murdered in this "very same incredibly beautiful
moonlight" (65). Marta again asks when Reverend Neilsen will return.
Major Rice comes to announce that another family has been killed and
implies that Kumalo is a savage. Still dressed in his ceremonial robes,
Tshembe visits Madame Neilsen, who is ecstatic to see her former student.
Major Rice's demand that all whites must be armed is met with amused
scorn by Dr. DeKoven and Madame Neilsen. When Charlie enters, all but
Tshembe retire to bed in exhaustion.

Charlie and Tshembe began an argument that lasts throughout their
uneasy association. They become black versus white, Africa versus Europe,
tired cynic versus eager neophyte. Constantly placing barriers between
himself and the journalist, Tshembe insists that they address each other
formally—Mr. Matoseh and Mr. Morris. Trying to shatter Charlie's idealism, Tshembe calls Kumalo "a scholar, a patriot, a dreamer and a crazy old
man" (75). Tshembe does not hate all white men, but desperately wished
he did. Like the uncommitted Sidney Brustein, Tshembe insists that this
revolution is not his war. As the act draws to a close, The Woman again

appears—dancing, beckoning, insisting urgently. She becomes the "sleeping lioness," the life force, sweeps up a spear, as Tshembe screams: "I HAVE RENOUNCED ALL SPEARS" (81).

As Act II opens two days later, Charlie is helping Marta pack medicine in banana leaves, the Kenyan mode of refrigeration. When he asks her about the men in her life and poses the question of Eric's real father, she brushes him off gently: "You're working too hard" (85). Unlike DeKoven and Madame Neilsen, Marta lacks total sympathy for the revolution.

When Eric wanders in drunk again Tshembe grabs his brother's bag and discovers women's cosmetics. As Charlie walks in, he and Tshembe resume their bitter harangue. This time Tshembe erects a physical barrier, laying swatches of fabric about him in a circle. Amused by Charlie's pleas for nonviolence, Tshembe explains that race is a *device*—"An invention to justify the rule of some men over others" (92). After Charlie leaves, Peter brings Tshembe a strip of bark (a Mau Mau symbol) and reveals his African name—Ntali. The subservient Peter has taken the sacred Oath. Uttering one of the most poetic speeches of the play, Peter recounts a folk tale about the land of the elephants and the hyenas, concluding: "Tshembe Matoseh, we have waited a thousand seasons for these 'guests' to leave us. Your people need you" (95). Praising Kumalo (in Charlie's absence), Tshembe again resists personal involvement.

Late that afternoon, Major Rice continues as the ugly Briton declares that the life of the native child whom Willy has brought in from the jungle cannot endanger the European community (99–100). Those at the Mission are astounded to learn from a telegram that Dr. Amos Kumalo has been arrested for plotting insurrection. Rice points to Peter as an example of a faithful servant, and Peter complies by saying. "Without de white man— de jungle close on Africa again" (103–4). Once again The Woman appears, eyes fixed on Tshembe, who stiffens and slowly turns to face her.

The next day at noon, Tshembe and Abioseh argue about religion and discuss Eric's future as though the boy were not even there. Eric reveals that Peter has given him the name Ngedi and has asked him to take the Oath. Horrified, Abioseh says that Peter must be stopped. Tshembe urges Abioseh not to betray Peter: "You believe in nothing! You act on nothing!" (110).

An hour later on the veranda, Charlie is typing and DeKoven is nursing a drink. For "whatever little" it is worth, DeKoven's twelve years in Africa have "saved his life" (113). But DeKoven is one of those rare individuals who value country—even if adopted—above self, freedom more than life itself. Unlike Charlie, DeKoven understands the paternalism that has sti-

fled—almost smothered—Africa. The Mission could have a modern hospital: electric lines could be laid in weeks, a road built in three months;
the money has been given by people all over the world (113). But there is
no modern hospital. The British have struggled to keep the African away
from the twentieth century (113–14). Even the saintly Reverend Torvald
Neilsen has been paternalistic: when old Abioseh brought Neilsen a petition asking that Africans be allowed to govern themselves, Neilsen said:
"Children, children . . . my dear children . . . go home to your huts!"
(115). DeKoven's most amazing revelation is that Eric's natural father is
the racist George Rice. Then Major Rice stomps in to announce another
raid in which Reverend Neilsen has been killed. He asks Peter to get him
a drink. Rice says, "Thank you—*Ntali*"—and shoots the porter dead
(117). Tshembe sinks to his knees beside Peter.

In the most vibrant and electric scene of the play (2.6), the Freedom of
the Land Army (Muingi) has gathered for a ritual in the darkness, as the
Old Man presides and Ngago, a graceful, robust warrior, delivers a cascade
of beautiful, destructive nature imagery: "They drop lakes of fire from the
skies on our village, drive our women and children fleeing before them,
herd our men into the great camps they have built for this hour . . . KILL
THE INVADER!" (119–20).

Late the next afternoon, Madame Neilsen sits by the coffin, depressed
in mourning black, as Charlie comes to pay homage to the reverend. Crossing the compound, he meets Tshembe for their last harangue. Tshembe
continues to plague Charlie, saying: "The whole world is waiting to hear
about the martyred Reverend and this temple in the wasteland . . ."
(122). Charlie finally erupts: "Stop writing my book. Stop telling me
which side to come out on . . . I'm Charlie Morris—not 'the White man'"
(122–23).

In a touching scene, Madame Neilsen and Tshembe talk for the final
time. She speaks of Reverend Neilsen ("a good man . . . in many ways"),
of Aquah (Tshembe's mother and her friend), whom Neilsen allowed to die
in childbirth because "the child was the product of . . . the races." She
asks Tshembe, "Do you—hate us terribly?" (125). To the older lady and
her culture, Tshembe is all-forgiving, all-loving, the heavens can afford a
galaxy, Madame's mountains have become his mountains. But he breaks
off: "I *know* what I must do. . . ." Prepared to face death, the wise old
woman replies: "Then do it, Tshembe" (126).

Several hours later in the darkness, the Mission is washed with moonlight as a hyena laughs and the sounds of night surround Madame Neilsen
at the coffin. Coming to pay his respects, Abioseh tells Madame: "Your

husband was an extraordinary human being, above race, above all sense of
self. . . . Today it looked as if the edge of earth was melting. God was
raining down glory" (127). Warriors glide in quietly; Eric is among them.
As Abioseh sees Tshembe, he moves backward, knowing intuitively what
his brother must do. Abioseh and Tshembe stand facing each other.
Tshembe shoots his brother dead. As the warriors open fire, Madame
stands erect, fatally wounded. Eric throws a grenade .into the Mission,
which explodes into flames. Holding Madame in his arms, Tshembe
stands alone. Gently setting her down, Tshembe throws back his head and
an animal-like cry of grief rises from his very being.

   Of Lizards and Lions.   Certainly a political play, *Les Blancs* urges
action and commitment, insists on freedom at almost any cost, and pleads
for the creation of a New Africa. Kenyans hoped to forge a new land with
thriving industry, modern health care, just labor policies, and fair taxa-
tion. But Lorraine Hansberry and her characters reveal that a sense of history is vital for an understanding of the present and future. Until forced
into the violence of the Mau Mau Revolt, the Kwi (Kikuyu) peoples were
basically peaceful and democratic. Aware of the rich and varied Old African myths, folk tales, and religious ceremonies, even the sophisticated
Tshembe Matoseh dons traditional robes for his father's funeral. Kenya,
like two-headed Janus, looks both forward and backward searching for the
freedom of New Africa but peering backward at Old Africa—a land of
lizards and lions, of hyenas and elephants.

   In *Le Blancs,* Old African myths add depth and meaning to at least two
rites of passage—death and initiation. (Rites of passage are mystical ceremonies which serve to redefine the individual's relationship to his society.)
When Tshembe asks Eric to tell him of their father in his last hours, Eric
says, "He was just an old savage who went to his death rubbing lizard
powder on his breast . . ." (57). In African religions, the lizard symbolizes
the messenger who brings the news from God that men should die. Fast as
summer lightning, the overconfident lizard, like the hare of the western
story, often dallied along the way, thus postponing his decree of everlasting
death. Generally the lizard was overtaken by another messenger—usually
the slow chameleon—who brought news of resurrection and immortality.[9]
After the Matoseh brothers paint their cheeks with yellow ochre and pre-
pare to dance and shake bone rattles (60), they can go to the funeral ceremony, not only recognizing their father's death but celebrating his
immortality.

   Tshembe has come home to his village uncommitted and uninitiated.
He dreams of feeding the pigeons in Hyde Park, of watching the "telly"

with his auburn-haired wife, of playing with his infant son. Having traveled more than a thousand miles to see his dying father, he has no desire to become involved in Africa's problems. The Woman appears, reminding Tshembe of his heritage and wordlessly urging him to fight for his people. A hyena laughs three times (41). In African myth, the hyena evolved from dogs and represents God's means of showing his intentions.[10] In *Les Blancs,* the hyena urges Tshembe to forego his own desires, to dedicate himself to the African cause. When the Woman appears the second time, Tshembe is stricken by her power, beauty, and sensuality.

I have known her to gaze up at me from puddles in the streets of London; from vending machines in the New York subway. Everywhere. And whenever I cursed her or sought to throw her off . . . I ended up that same night in her arms! Even when I held my bride, she lay beside me, her arms on my thighs caressing, insisting that I belonged to her! (80)

She circles in movements, symbolic of life, the slaughter and enslavement. She becomes the "sleeping lioness" (81).

In African myth, the lion symbolizes the punishment and protection of God in his most terrifying form. As the woman joins the lion, they become archetypes of the initiation rite, of man's coming into maturity. The sensuous woman signifies sexual initiation; the lion represents either the blessing or condemnation of God. When the man ventures into the jungle to catch the dangerous lion, he becomes a full member of the tribe.[11] For Tshembe, initiation and capture of God (the lion) are modernized: he must commit himself to the Kwis, to Africa, to freedom. But Tshembe recoils, screaming, "I HAVE RENOUNCED ALL SPEARS!" (81). When the Woman appears for the third time, there are no lions or hyenas—only drumbeats rising to a fevered pitch—then silence. Tshembe stiffens and turns slowly to meet her eyes (106). The next day Tshembe makes a full commitment to Africa. When Abioseh betrays Peter (Ntali), Tshembe finally allows Muingi to triumph over self and family: he knows that he must kill his own brother.

Not only does Lorraine Hansberry use African myths to enhance rites of passage, but she employs old folk tales to heighten the drama of the revolution. In a moving speech, Peter urges Tshembe to dedicate himself to his country:

Men have forgotten the tale of Modingo, the wise hyena who lived between the lands of the elephants and the hyenas. . . . A friend to both, Modingo understood each side of their quarrel. The elephants said they needed more space because of their size, and the hyenas because they had been *first* in that part of the jungle and were accustomed to running free.

When the hyenas called on Modingo, he thought and thought, seeing justice on each side. The hyenas sat and waited while Modingo continued to think. Knowing of the hyenas' stillness, the elephants gathered their herds, moved at once—and drove the hyenas from the jungle. Now the hyena laughs his terrible laugh at this bitter joke—the product of reason and caution. (95).

In his folk tale, Peter obviously equates the elephant with the white man occupying the land. Basically a symbol of goodness, the elephant is also associated with men and murder. According to one myth, the elephant originated from the transformation of wicked people whom God destroyed. [12] The elephant therefore is both the victim and the embodiment of evil men, and in Peter's tale white people in Africa are victimized by their own narrow prejudice and personify huge, selfish beasts crashing through the jungle. Hyenas, on the other hand, are sacred and holy, having evolved from dogs, which were used as sacrifices to God. [13] The hyena, which is associated with the noble black man, represents God's means of showing his intentions, but he also signifies God's gift to men. Of course, Tshembe becomes Modingo, the wise hyena.

Robert Nemiroff reports: "It is unclear whether Hansberry knew the mythic origins and significance in African folklore of the elephant and hyena. . . . But whether she did or not, her use of these animals to create, as a metaphor for the conflicts in *Les Blancs,* a myth of her own about a Hamlet-like hyena and how the species got its 'laugh,' is an interesting example of how intimately and imaginatively the playwright entered into the culture and psychology of her tribal characters."[14]

Just as Modingo wishes to settle the dispute by reason, Tshembe like Jomo Kenyatta desperately hopes to solve the problems of his people with petitions, delegations, and discussion. But that time has passed. Like the hyena, the black man was there first and was used to running free. When the white man, like the elephant, gathers his herds or armies, the hyenas must revolt or be destroyed.

Using gossamer, destructive nature imagery, Ngago, the poet warrior, exhorts his people to kill the invaders. He describes the British dropping "lakes of fire" on the people, as the English "hummingbirds of death" whir soundlessly over the fields. While referring to bombs and planes, Ngago still implies that British power will destroy the very union of man and nature. There are no definite African allusions, but we may borrow slightly from Western mythologies. The hummingbird may be one of the birds who formed a bridge between heaven and earth,[15] which is destroyed by death. As the source of life itself, the lake becomes contaminated by fire—which drives God from men.[16] Although the Kwi are basically peaceful, they must defend themselves and their sacred land against fires and invaders.

Throughout *Les Blancs*, Lorraine Hansberry suggests the strong bond between the Kwi and nature—the basis of African religions. Tshembe is a well-educated man; old Abioseh was courageous in presenting the petition to Reverend Neilsen; Peter plays the role of obsequious servant but he is truly Ntali; Ngago wears modern khaki dress. But none of these men have forgotten African myth and religion, the source from which they wrest their strength to fight for their lives and their country. Even young Abioseh, who believed that he must rid himself of his past to embrace Christianity, says to Madame Neilsen just before his death: "What a marvelous light. How beautiful this day has been. How I wish you could have seen the sunset. . . . Do you remember the stories you used to tell us to explain the sunset? . . . that the sun was eaten by a giant who rose out of the ocean" (127–28).

Knowing What Must Be Done.   Jomo Kenyatta moved to London in 1929, where he would live for the next seventeen years. During these years, he studied English, addressed specialists of phonetics at London University on the Kikuyu language, and began his study of anthropology with the world-famous Professor Bronislaw Kasper Malinowski of the London School of Economics. Inspired by Malinowski's lectures and methodology, Kenyatta made voluminous notes, wrote several key papers, and published his controversial *Facing Mt. Kenya* in 1936—with an introduction by Malinowski. Stressing the order, self-reliance, and virtue of the Kikuyu people, *Facing Mt. Kenya* challenged the white man's view of history, asserting that African history was different from but equal to the British and Western past.[17] Flamboyant, seemingly devious, and something of a ladies' man, Kenyatta astonished some of his British friends by shedding "crocodile tears" when his humble landlady begged him to pay his overdue rent of £200 (at least $1,000 by 1980s standards), by marrying a British woman who bore him a son (despite his vague marital status), and by signing on as an extra in a somewhat racist movie, *Sanders of the River*, starring Paul Robeson.[18] A lover of children, the underdog, and the outsider, Kenyatta kept the idea of Kenyan independence before him all these years. By the mid 1930s, he was even more assertive in his efforts to win African self-rule by petitions, discussions, and leading delegations. Returning to Kenya in 1946 with a patina of British education and rhetoric, Kenyatta retained the loyalty of his Kikuyu countrymen, whom he urged on to nonviolent protest. On July 26, 1952, he delivered a typical speech, making the usual pleas for better education and wages and for elimination of land control and the color-bar. But he spoke of freedom in a different cadence, as he pointed to the KAU flag. The flag had a background of black and green with a red circle in the center inscribed with a shield with the letter *U,* a spear, and an arrow. Kenyatta explained that the red signified the identical nature of African and European blood; the green, the fertile land; the shield, spear, and arrow signified the forefathers who protected the land; the *U* meant the protection of the Union from all evils.[19] Kenyatta was imprisoned three months later. His fellow Kikuyus were no longer satisfied that red meant equality of African and British blood; red meant death to the white man.

In *Les Blancs,* Dr. Amos Kumalo (who resembles Jomo Kenyatta) is as crucial a touchstone to black and white Africans as Charles Parnell is a test of conscience for Stephen Dedalus in *A Portrait of the Artist as a Young Man.* Kumalo is mentioned at eight critical stages in the play, and he has a different meaning for each character. Charlie Morris worships him as the nonviolent "leader of the independence movement" (90), while Major George Rice dismisses him as a savage (66) and a "half-demented darkie prophet" (101). To Peter (Ntali), Kumalo is a British puppet, who will merely "trade white overseers for black" (97). Madame Neilsen deplores his arrest (106), but Dr. Willy DeKoven implies that Kumalo is no longer the Great White Hope (112).

For Tshembe Matoseh, coming to terms with Amos Kumalo is no easy matter. In many ways, Tshembe is a younger version of Kumalo/Kenyatta. While enjoying the good life, Tshembe was educated in England, where he charmed many young women with his classic good looks and repartee and married a white British girl who bore him a son. Accepted as an equal by most Britons, as was Kenyatta, Tshembe could have passed the rest of his days in relative peace and affluence. Like Kenyatta, Tshembe basically believed in the power of discussion and delegations—until the urgency of action was almost forced upon him. Tshembe Matoseh alternately sees Kumalo as a "scholar, a patriot, a dreamer and a crazy old man" (75), someone who should be given a chance (97), and a man who "wanders around in the cold in his thin suits and . . . *talks*" (56). In short, there are two Kenyattas in *Les Blancs:* Kumalo, the returned expatriate, and Tshembe Matoseh, who wishes for a peaceful resolution of the conflict, but who finally recognizes and then welcomes revolution as Africa's only hope. He becomes one of Hansberry's celebrated revolutionaries.

In *Les Blancs,* the revolutionaries are those who know what must be done. Charlie Morris, who tries to understand, is the essence of the earnest white liberal. He sympathizes with the black African, but he feels no personal responsibility. He tells Tshembe as the African smiles ironically at the British helicopters overhead: "I didn't put those things up there! I'm me—Charlie Morris—not 'the White Man'" (123). But Charlie *is* the White Man, for he shares in the collective white guilt of oppressing the black peoples. Furthermore, he naively hopes that change can occur without bloodshed. For all his good intentions, Charlie remains merely a liberal, not a revolutionary.

For Hansberry, a revolutionary is someone willing to die for a cause—in *Les Blancs,* that of total African self-rule and freedom. Yet she was a perceptive judge of human behavior and did not limit greatness to blacks. Dr. Willy DeKoven is a striking example of the white sympathizer. He told Charlie that Africa "saved his life," but he became an alcoholic—largely because of the injustice he has seen the white man mete out to the black man. He told Charlie of Reverend Neilsen's patronizing his black African "children," of the European's passive refusal to bring modern health-care and education to the African Mission. When Dr. DeKoven says, "They will murder us here one day—isn't that so, Tshembe?" (116), he is not accusing. He is calmly accepting his lot: he is prepared to die so that others will live in freedom.

Even more complex than Willy DeKoven, Madame Neilsen is a white sympathizer who loves her husband but sees the destruction he has wreaked on the black African. As she sits beside the coffin of her husband, she tells Tshembe of their arrival in Kenya forty years earlier: Torvald was resplendent in his helmet and new pair of boots; she was assured in her linen culottes, with her malaria shots and helmet; and together they bought a cello and forty crates of hymnals. But she is honest about his inner feelings: he believed the white races superior to the black; he allowed Tshembe's mother, Aquah, to die; he called the black Africans his "children." To atone for her husband's harmful ignorance, Madame Neilsen consciously risks her life. She urges Tshembe to become committed, to fight for freedom in the land she has come to love: "Our country needs warriors, Tshembe Matoseh. Africa needs warriors" (126).

As tragedies usually require, heroes die that we may feel a sense of catharsis, or cleansing. Young Abioseh does not die the death of a hero: he is perhaps less aware of the real price of freedom than is Charlie Morris. The tragedy of Abioseh's death lies in fratricide: nation has triumphed over family. Having taken the Oath early, Peter dies the death of a martyr to a dream. Tshembe becomes a black Hamlet, torn between thought and action: had he remained a man of thought, he would eventually have inherited his earth. But he chooses painful action and freedom.

Les Blancs closed after forty-seven performances in December 1970. James Earl Jones's powerful performance as Tshembe Matoseh seemed the only point upon which critics—and probably the audience—had agreed since its opening at the Longacre Theater on November 15, 1970. Rex Reed in the *Sunday News* found the play racially divisive, "too black and white." Clayton Riley of the *New York Times* considered it a tribute to the "brilliant, anguished consciousness of Lorraine Hansberry." *New York*'s John Simon dubbed it an "unmitigated disaster," while Walter Kerr in the *New York Times* praised the play as "vivid, stinging, intellectually alive."[20]

Underlying these criticisms was the issue of whether whites should be offended, or somehow feel personally threatened by the suggestion that whites (albeit in Africa) should be murdered so that black Africans could rule their own countries. One might argue likewise that Robert Ruark's novel, *Something of Value,* should be judged solely on its potential for embarrassing black readers as he depicts Mau Maus wildly and mindlessly butchering whites in Africa—an impression still more embedded in the American consciousness than Hansberry's more judicious, better-researched depiction of Kenya. The black/white confrontation, then, is simply not an appropriate artistic concern here.

Les Blancs failed to achieve the consensus of critical acclaim that Hansberry and Nemiroff (who adapted the final text) might have wished for other reasons. At times the play is "talky." Tshembe anguishes over his identity and commitment; he debates religion with Abioseh; Charlie presents his ineffectual white liberal views—both with the kind of dialogue that distressed many viewers of *Sidney Brustein.* Nevertheless, such scenes are often punctuated by nice theatrical touches—Tshembe throws the crucifix at his brother; the Woman periodically beckons and dances; the Muingi ritual; Tshembe's final cry of grief as he holds Madame Neilsen. Some critics found fault with the violence of the play, but most of it is offstage. Too, the 1950s and 1960s in Africa were violent times, and Hansberry takes care to delineate the psychological violence that both blacks and whites visit upon themselves and others.

Reviewers failed to note one reason that the play lacked the popular appeal of *A Raisin in the Sun. Les Blancs* does not cater to one of America's most cherished and sentimentalized ideals—the family. Rarely does an American send his or her child to a private boarding school, whereas the upper-class British parent does so almost routinely. Marriage in America becomes a legal, moral, religious, social commitment; children are nurtured, educated, often at great sacrifice; siblings ideally love one another despite actions they would never tolerate in friends. Nineteen seventy—the year of *Les Blancs'* run—may have marked the end of the turbulent, socially conscious 1960s, but the white American 1950s—with the focus on family, the subservience of women, the American dream—lay only ten years behind. Thus, when Tshembe kills his brother, when Madame Neilsen understands why her husband must die, when Eric participates in the shooting of his surrogate mother, Madame Neilsen—freedom, an abstraction, triumphs over family. The American theatergoer recoiled. He reveled in *Raisin,* in which freedom and family are neatly fused.

Les Blancs remains, however, a vitally important play for what Lorraine Hansberry taught Americans about Africa. She taught them that many Africans were peaceful, religious people, that they respected the Old Africa with its lizard and lion, the elephant and hyena, the lake and the hummingbird. She illustrated the power of such diverse leaders as Kenyatta, Nkrumah, and Lumumba; she reinforced Kenyatta's idea that African history was different from but equal to the British and Western past. Had she included some particular American touchstone—such as the sentimentalized family—perhaps the audience could have realized that freedom from British rule was as important to Kenyans in 1955 as it was to Americans in 1776. But *Les Blancs* is more than a political treatise: it is a drama of human courage and cowardice, of ignorance and awareness, of ennui and involvement. American audiences are rarely entertained by abstractions—even when they are embodied by the talented—James Earl Jones—or inscribed by the gifted—Lorraine Hansberry. Had she created one more character as memorable as Tshembe Matoseh in *Les Blancs,* perhaps Hansberry would have engaged the emotion—as well as the intellect—of Americans as she did in *A Raisin in the Sun.*

The Drinking Gourd

In the 1850s, the Right Reverend Stephen Elliott of Georgia, the Reverend James A. Lyon of Mississippi, and Edward A. Pollard of Virginia risked public censure by leading a movement for slavery reform. Their demands included the sanctioning of slave marriages, the prevention of the separation of families, the education of slaves, the sheltering of slaves from cruelty and inhumanity, and the admission of black testimony against whites in courts of law. Courageous as these men were, they believed that such rights would not alter the essential slave/master relation.[21] But granting slaves basic human rights would probably have destroyed the very foundation of the institution (a theory certainly proposed by Hansberry in *The Drinking Gourd*). Much of our modern-day abhorrence of slavery focuses on the physical brutality—whippings, physical mutilation, strapping a man's legs and arms to two saplings until the trees bent down in opposite directions, placing a surly slave in a stuffy, cramped "sweat-box."[22] (Not always a physical or sexual crime, rape was often motivated by the white man's need to intimidate and overpower the black woman.) But the psychological damage wreaked by slavery proved as devastating as physical abuse. Even Elliott, Lyon, and Pollard subconsciously recognized this factor: four of their five demands related to emotional and intellectual needs—marriage, family stability, education, and legal credibility. The very fact that one man could *own* another was bound to create aberrations in the minds of men—both black and white.

Slavery and the Civil War have intrigued popular writers from the 1850s to the present day. In 1852, Harriet Beecher Stowe published *Uncle Tom's Cabin,* a bitter indictment of slavery. The cruel overseer, Simon Legree, the deferential Uncle Tom, the syrupy Little Eva—all have become American folk figures, unfortunately oversimplified in some stage and movie versions. Published only nine years before the beginning of the Civil War, this novel was important in dramatizing the abuses of slavery to the American people. Subconsciously, though, Stowe may have presented "plantation portraits" of blacks. Uncle Tom is the "fawning slave who puts his master's interest above his own." Sam "capers, rolls his eyeballs, and acts foolish." Eliza flees to save her son from being sold; she has little concept of the "idea of freedom."[23]

In 1936, Margaret Mitchell published the runaway best-seller *Gone With the Wind,* at times a melodramatic novel. American readers were fascinated by Mitchell's historically accurate battle scenes, intricate plot, detailed accounts of white economic ruin during Reconstruction, and vivid portrayals of Scarlett O'Hara and Rhett Butler. Nevertheless, *Gone With the Wind* is clearly a white interpretation of slavery and the Civil War. The black characters are filtered through a white lens: Mammy is the black Earth Mother, nurturing yet having no illusions about the sometimes unprincipled Scarlet; Prissy provides humor as she declares that she "don't know nothin'" about birthing and babies; and Big Sam rescues Scarlett from a group of marauding Yankees. Although Mitchell portrays blacks with kindness, she never sees them as equals or penetrates their deeper emotions. Twelve years after Hansberry's death in 1965, Alex Haley published *Roots,* a powerful study of African heritage, spanning seven generations and stressing the physical and mental anguish of slaves. Assuming the role of *griot* (storyteller), Haley created memorable portraits of Kunta Kinte, a warrior in Gambia, West Africa; the strong-willed Kizzy; and her son, Chicken George. But Haley's white slaveowners are not far removed from Stowe's Simon Legree.

The Action.   Set in the 1850s, *The Drinking Gourd* transcends such popular literature as a fair, balanced treatment of slavery. Skillfully plotted with subtle foreshadowing and a chilling climax, the play still derives much of its power from realistic characters—all a mixture of good and evil, perception and ignorance, strength and weakness. Lorraine Hansberry is acutely sensitive to the psychology of both slaves and their masters: her Hannibal bears little resemblance to the long-suffering Uncle Tom, while the southern slaveowner Hiram Sweet has little of the ignorant cruelty of the northern overseer, Simon Legree. Superficially, Rissa parallels Margaret Mitchell's Mammy, but when Rissa is forced to choose between her own son and her white master, she can no longer remain the black Earth Mother. As Maria Sweet tries to "keep peace in the family" and to protect her husband's expansive ego, she is reminiscent of Ellen O'Hara and a host of Faulknerian white southern women. But when Hannibal's disaster strikes and the Civil War is declared, Maria's strength and intelligence belie our image of a genteel southern lady.

Throughout the play, Hansberry displays considerable knowledge of cotton and tobacco cultivation, specific hours that slaves spent in the fields, erosion of the lush southern land, and nuances of southern dialects. But she is not confused about the real issues. At a symposium with James Baldwin and Langston Hughes, she said: "People spend volumes discussing the battles of the Civil War, and which army was crossing which river at five minutes to two . . . but the slavery issue we have tried to get rid of."[24] Hansberry never forgets that slavery was the deepest cause of the Civil War.

At the heart of *The Drinking Gourd* lies Hansberry's premise that institutions—unlike the individuals within them—are evil and all-consuming. Seemingly, Hansberry never resolved the internal conflict about the contradictory demands of individuals and institutions. Basically, she saw most *white* institutions as malevolent, while viewing *black* institutions—such as black rule in Africa and Haiti—with more charity. Robert Nemiroff writes: "*The Drinking Gourd* depicted . . . the crimes of American slavery. . . . The purpose . . . was to focus on the system that *required* the crimes, the culture that shaped the Southern white personality in its countless variations, maimed it, turned ego into a monstrous and all-devouring thing" (*Les Blancs*, 153). Assuming its own separate identity, slavery had attained a malignity beyond the imagination of its creators. At the end of *The Drinking Gourd*, the narrator says: "Slavery is beginning to cost this nation a lot. . . . It is possible that slavery might destroy itself—but it is more possible that it would destroy these United States first . . . . It has already cost us, as a nation, too much of our soul" (217).

Act 1 opens in a small wooded enclosure with Hannibal picking a lively tune on his banjo and young Tommy clapping to the driving beat. Hannibal is a nineteen-year old slave; Tommy is the ten-year-old son of Hiram Sweet, Hannibal's master. This idyllic scene serves as a cruel foreshadowing to the climax of the play.

The camera pans down a long coastline to the stark figure of a man, who walks with a troubled gait. Tall and narrow-hipped, the man wears side whiskers, longish hair and a military uniform of no particular army. Symbolizing the thoughtful American, the narrator explains that the cotton seed and earth only have power with the force of labor—slaves. In the background, slaves plaintively sing "Steal Away to Jesus." Labor is so inexpensive, he explains, an owner could work a man to death and buy another more cheaply than treat the first one humanely. As the driver calls out "Quittin' time," silent, drooping field hands file into their quarters— a sharp contrast to the mythical carefree slaves. Since slaves earn no wages and are forbidden education, they are easily maintained for $7.50 a year. But in the nineteenth century, he explains, the white children often work twelve hours a day in factories and women are denied many legal rights, including the vote—for they, too, are considered property.

As the narrator turns away, the camera focuses on a large iron skillet, crackling with bacon and corn pone, hanging over a roaring fire. Indifferent past resignation, Rissa the cook spoons small portions of food onto the plates of waiting slaves. Sarah, a girl of nineteen, holds out her plate while she stoops to play with Joshua, a small boy of seven or eight. He has been clutching at his grandmother Rissa's skirts and is bored by Sarah's romantic interest in his Uncle Hannibal. Teasing Sarah about "that wild boy of mine," Rissa recoils when Sarah tells her that Hannibal slipped away from the fields that afternoon. Rissa quietly asks if the driver Coffin knows. Sarah replies: "Coffin knows everything" (172).

Later in the moonlit woods, Sarah meets Hannibal on a small grassy hill. When Hannibal speaks romantically of moonlight and falling stars,

Sarah responds urgently: "Coffin noticed you was gone first thing" (173). Still the lover, he says: "Me and you was *born* in trouble with Marster" (173). As Hannibal looks up at the Drinking Gourd (the Big Dipper), which points up to the North Star, he talks of escaping and softly sings: "Follow—follow—follow . . . the Drinking Gourd" (174). Becoming even more distressed, Sarah says he is just like his brother Isaiah, who ran away to the North when Master Sweet sold little Joshua's mother. Hannibal's dreams are limited—he hopes Isaiah is working in a lumberyard—but his thirst for freedom is boundless. Embittered over his plight, he tells Sarah, "There ain't nothin' hurt slave marster so much as when his property walk away from him" (176).

Back at the "Big House," the Sweet family is entertaining Dr. Macon Bullett at dinner—a meal lavish in comparison to the slaves' bacon and corn pone—attended by two male servants. Kindly and obese, Hiram Sweet is in his mid-sixties and retains much of the frontier spirit of many masters. His patient wife, Maria, is trying to maintain peace in the spirited discussion. More polished and less humane than his father, Everett Sweet is nearing thirty but still clearly resents being dominated by the master. A frequent household guest, Dr. Macon Bullett wears the mantle of "old money" and education easily and quietly. The two black servants are merely servants.

Voices and tempers rise as each of the three men argue distinct positions about the impending Civil War. Everett Sweet, romantic and indignant, knows that the superior Southern generals can lick the Yankees in six months. Always the aristocrat, Dr. Bullett suspects the "blubber-fronted Yankee industrialist" really wants control of Congress. But Hiram Sweet is skeptical: the South cannot win; no one will be left to mind the slaves.

Igniting the fires of father/son rivalry, Hiram calls Everett a "polished little pepper" who learned how to run a plantation in Paris cafés. Trading mightily on his age and stature as a self-made man, Hiram boasts that he came to this country thirty-five years ago with $50 and four slaves, decreeing that there will be no overseer on his once-fertile land. Dr. Bullett waits until Maria leaves the dining room before he tells Hiram, "It's all over": he must spend the rest of his life reading, due to his heart condition. After a brief explosion, Hiram meditates about the "gray hours," when every man "wonders why the stars hang out there . . . and what he's here for" (184–85).

Coming out of the shadows, Rissa is alone with Hiram—for a time, her master's equal, friend, cut of the same cloth of individualism. Hiram at times is more comfortable with Rissa than with Macon or Everett. One of

his four original slaves, she came with him years ago to wrest the plantation out of the wilderness. The most stubborn man she knows, Hiram will
have no more salt in his greens: "If you aimin' on killin' yourself, Marster
Hiram, don't be askin' Riss' to hep you none . . ." (186)—a statement
which later proves ironical. They laugh over the day Ezekial fell into the
molasses vat and then had his head shaved like an egg. They remember
when Hiram frightened Farmer Burns, who thought Hiram was shooting
at him instead of the wild hogs eating his corn. But they had pork for
months. Fetching her master's old, well-oiled gun which his father gave
him at fourteen, Rissa reminds him that he promised Hannibal would be
a house servant.

Act 2 opens the next afternoon as Everett steeps himself in melancholy
and alcohol until he is called to his father's bedroom. Hiram Sweet has had
a heart attack. The old man raves quietly about the "old horseman" (death)
and "fifty dollars and four slaves." Minutes later, Maria Sweet casts aside
southern softness for adamantine resolve: Everett will be the new master.
"Every night if necessary, you must sit with pencil and pad and let him tell
you everything he wishes. And then—well, do as you please" (190).

Zed Dudley is the prototype of the "poor white"—hated by whites and
blacks alike. He stands momentarily regarding his worn-out cornfield then
storms toward his cabin. His wife is inside tending their sick baby. In
frustration over his hopeless poverty, he smashes an empty whiskey jug.
Preacher comes to call. He praises Zeb's father, who owned no slaves. Zeb
calls his father a fool, who died "eatin' dirt" (193–94). Soon Everett Sweet
rides up on his horse. "I'm looking for a good overseer, Zeb Dudley." They
settle on a salary of $2,000—a fortune in the 1850s. As Everett rides off,
Preacher says, "Cotton and slavery has almost ruined our land," but Zeb
declares in his newfound pride: "*I'm a white man, Preacher*" (194–96).

Late that night in Rissa's cabin, a circle of slaves is singing a forbidden
round, "Raise a Ruckus," when Coffin enters. He objects to the song and
warns Hannibal about leaving the field. Hannibal calls the driver "'bout
the lowest form of life known" (199). Rissa sends the evil Coffin back to
his cabin. Hannibal is furious at the thought of being a house slave, a
position Rissa wants for him, but he calms down and confesses—"Mama,
I kin read" (202). At first, Rissa is thrilled that her son can read, but then
she drops to her knees in fear, telling him he must stop. Hannibal is hurt:
"You ain't fit for nothin' but slavery thinkin' no more" (203).

Next morning in the fields, Zeb glories in his new power. He has the
accoutrements of power as well—a horse and a gun. He tells the drivers
that hands will now work thirteen hours in the fields, and he relishes Cof-

fin's news that Hannibal is "a bad one, suh" (204). He calls Hannibal aside, verbally harasses him, and strikes his whip across his face. Doubled up with pain, Hannibal hears Zeb say, "There ain't goin' to be no more foolin', no more sassin', and no more tool breakin'" (205). Lounging on the veranda, Everett tells Zeb he should have punished another slave. As they eye each other with contempt, Everett says: "This is my plantation . . . I alone am master" (206). Coffin appears to tell them that Hannibal has run away, that he is with "young marster."

Back at the small wooded clearing of act 1, Hannibal is teaching Tommy Sweet to play the banjo. They are surrounded, however, by books and papers. They have made a deal: Hannibal will teach Tommy to play the banjo and Tommy will teach Hannibal to read and write. As Hannibal concludes the lesson, the sighing young boy begins to read his story, "The Drinking Gourd." "'I do not know why, but when a man lie on his back and see the stars, there is something that can happen to a man inside that be'—*Is,* Hannibal—'bigger than whatever a man is'" (208). Everett, Coffin, and Zeb appear suddenly. Everett orders Tommy back to the house and shouts at Hannibal in a dazzling rage: "You have used your master's own son to commit a crime . . ." (209). Inspecting Hannibal's face, Everett says, "When a part is corrupted by disease—one cuts out the disease" (210). Hannibal understands his master's meaning and attempts to escape but he is caught by Coffin and Zeb. Coldly, Everett says to Zeb: "Do it now." The woods reverberate with the tortured screams of an agonized man. Like Gloucester before him, Hannibal's eyes are put out.

Late that night on the plantation grounds, a man is strung by all four limbs to two saplings, which have been bent to the ground in opposite directions. Two other men cut him down because gangrene has set in.

Meanwhile Hiram Sweet is throwing a violent fit in his bedroom, smashing his medicine bottle against the fireplace, denouncing Everett, and threatening to shoot Zeb, who speedily leaves. Hiram is horrified by Everett's cruelty toward Hannibal. But Everett is occupied with another matter. He and Dr. Bullett are joyous that the South has fired on Fort Sumter. Saying that the South is lost, Hiram prophesies that "They will pour out of the South by the thousands—dirty, ignorant and uncertain what the whole matter is about. But they will be against us" (213). Then Hiram announces that he is going to Rissa's cabin.

As Hiram stands outside Rissa's cabin, he hears a soulful slave song, perhaps "Sometimes I Feel Like a Motherless Child." Entering the cabin, he sees Rissa boiling quinine in a pot and placing clean cloths on Hannibal's eyes as the young man cries out softly. Rissa looks at Hiram with unforgiving wrath; she is unmoved when he says he had nothing to do with this atrocity. Rissa says, "Why? Ain't you *Marster?* How can a man be marster of some men and not at all of others—" (215). Hiram, defeated, leaves the cabin and collapses on the ground outside. He cries for help. Rissa sits in her caneback chair, and listens until Hiram's cries finally cease.

Sitting on the veranda some weeks later, Maria is dressed in black. Everett comes up wearing a Confederate officer's uniform. Shocked and embittered by recent events, she refuses to visit the Robleys, whom Hiram disliked, and accusingly asks: "Peaceful? Do you really find it peaceful here?" (216). In the background, a hymn rises from the quarters—"Steal Away to Jesus."

Meanwhile, in the darkened dining room, Rissa quietly removes Hiram's cherished gun from the cabinet and goes out through the kitchen. Outside she takes Joshua by the hand and together they hurry to Hannibal's clearing where Sarah and the blind Hannibal wait, ready for travel. Wordlessly, Rissa gives Sarah the gun, embraces her, and watches the three young people disappear into the woods to the strains of "The Drinking Gourd." As the "Battle Cry of Freedom" rings in the distance, the narrator reappears, buttons his coat, puts on his cap, and picks up his rifle—ready to join the Grand Army of the Republic.

Master of Every Soul—The Psychology of Slavery. At the end of their cozy chat, the culmination of a thirty-five-year friendship, Rissa asks Hiram Sweet to elevate her son Hannibal to the prestigious position of house servant. He agrees that he will when cotton picking is over, but he turns to see the smoldering anger of his wife. He answers her unspoken question by bellowing: "Because I am master of this plantation and every soul on it" (188). Many writers have chronicled the physical suffering of slaves, but Lorraine Hansberry had the rare insight that the institution of slavery maimed the psyche and soul of whites and blacks alike.

Hiram Sweet is certainly not an evil man, but the system of slavery has given him the delusion, at times the reality, of grandeur. The Sweet plantation is a tiny kingdom, complete with serfs (slaves), an heir apparent (Everett), a lovely, but overtly powerless queen (Maria), an absolute, unquestioned monarch (Hiram), and, interestingly enough, no princesses at all. Even the local peasant (Zeb Dudley) and the poor clergyman (Preacher) acknowledge the monarch's power. His question tinged with resentment, Preacher asks Zeb: "You figger you kin get to be somebody, eh. Like the Sweets, mebbe?" (193). Zeb responds seriously, "If I ever got my chance, I make that Sweet plantation look like a shanty" (193). To his neighbors, to his slaves, and most dangerously, to himself, Hiram Sweet is master; Hiram Sweet is a god.

One of the problems with a mortal becoming a god is that he begins to think himself infallible—a blindness which ultimately leads to destruction. He admits no error, which allows no self-examination, and thus stymies any growth. Intolerant of other opinions, he becomes stagnant. A god, furthermore, has absolute responsibility as well as total power, which would prove taxing to most mortals. Unlike many masters, Hiram does have moments of self-doubt: he questions the institution of slavery, but he does not dispute his role in this flawed system. Hiram's failing heart is a fitting outward and visible symbol of his inward rejection of the crushing weight of the crown.

While the progeny of monarchs must show respect to the king in public, they may at times resent merely being another's property. Yet they wish to appear every bit the monarch themselves. When Dr. Bullett chastises Hiram Sweet for his lack of manners, Everett dutifully says: "Sir, I must remind you that this is my father's house" (184). But privately Everett deplores his lack of free will: he becomes a spoiled child, carousing with the wild Robley boys, drinking by himself, brooding. When Everett challenges his father, Hiram tells him: "I'll be what I please in this house and you'll mind your manners to me in the face of it" (179). Reaching a full awareness of his father's role, Everett says, "I have asked no man's permission for the life I have lived—and I will not start now" (188).

When the monarch arrests the emotional maturity of the heir apparent well past physical maturity (Everett is almost thirty), the young prince may react with serious errors in judgment. Shortly after Everett has covertly wrested control of the kingdom, he tells the peasant Zeb: "This is my plantation. I alone am responsible, for I alone am master" (206), echoing his father's assertion that he is "master of this plantation and every soul on it" (188). But Everett lacks his father's experience and makes the tragic mistake of mutilating Hannibal. Ironically, one of Hiram's few vulnerabilities—his friendship with Rissa—leads to his own death. Inheriting the sins of their parents—the system of slavery—both sons carry the system to its awful, but logical extreme. When the black son gains a measure of freedom by learning to read, the white son reacts violently to the direct challenge, thus seeling his own inward vision as surely as he does Hannibal's eyes.

Existing on the periphery of the kingdom, the peasant is a pitiful figure, reveling in his supposed superiority to serfs. Free to cultivate his own almost barren land, he is despised by royalty and serfdom alike: he is considered lazy, dirty, and ignorant. His very freedom from the monarch's rule, ironically, denies him any real identity in the kingdom. In the American South, "poor whites" (peasants) outnumbered slaves (serfs), thus subtly but surely reinforcing the necessity of the institution of slavery. In the absence of his social inferior, the poor white would be forced to confront his own uneducated, virtually powerless self.[25]

Proclaiming "I'm a white man, Preacher," Zeb Dudley knows that the caste system and the color barrier place him above the slave, however slightly. Many overseers were members of the poor-white class and used their power to persecute slaves. Zeb is horrified at being ordered to put out Hannibal's eyes, but the system will not allow him to refuse. The poor white never engages our total sympathy; he is not a tragic figure. He is merely a pathetic footnote in an evil history.

Only imprudent serfs question the absolute power of the monarch. The king, after all, provides the essentials of life—food, clothing, and shelter. After a twelve- to fifteen-hour workday in the fields, the serf is often too exhausted to ponder more cerebral issues: the king's failure to provide education or to grant outright wages. There is always hope that he might ascend to manservant, or she to lady-in-waiting, in the castle, where one might be given cast-off finery or bask in the reflection of elegant manners and guests.

In *The Drinking Gourd,* Coffin typifies the slave who has capitalized on a corrupt situation. Believing that master "treats him good," Coffin is too unconsciously paralyzed to consider the ethics of one man owning another. So he adapts and survives, a study in situation ethics. Popular literature aside, most slaves nurtured deep resentments, which they only allowed to surface in the relative safety of their own quarters. As her friends sing "Raise a Ruckus" in Rissa's cabin, Sarah pantomimes a verse about the mistress:

> My old mistress promise me
> "Say-rah! When I die I'm going to set you free!"
> But a dose of poison kinda helped her along
> And may the devil sing her funeral song! (197)

The price was too dear for open hostility or escape. Hostility met with brutality. Runaways who were caught and returned likewise felt their owner's wrath. If the master did not capture the runaway slave, he or she still had to overcome illiteracy, poverty, and, most binding of all, the slave mentality, in the New World of the North. But these obstacles did not prevent thousands of slaves from trying to escape.

Hannibal has gone beyond anger to iron determination. With passive aggression, he annoys the slavedriver, breaks tools on the sly, dawdles in the fields. Talking with Rissa late into the night, Hannibal asks who gave master the power to be master, questions Sweet's right to beat him at all, and concludes that "all marsters come from hell" (201). In a dramatic moment, Hannibal says:

I am the only kind of slave I could stand to be—a *bad* one. Every day that come and hour that pass that I got sense to make a half step do for a whole—every day that I can pretend sickness 'stead of health, to be stupid 'stead of smart, lazy 'stead of quick—I aims to do it. And the more pain it gives *your* marster and the more it cost him—the more Hannibal be a man. (201)

Thus, we come to the crux of the psychology of the male slave—he has been castrated—sometimes literally—and he despises himself for allowing himself to be owned.

Many writers have dealt with the external black-white conflict, but Lorraine Hansberry probes deeply and painfully into inner conflicts of slaves. Much like childhood, slavery can be comfortable: the parent or master provides food, clothing, and shelter. No reasonable child expects outright wages but enjoys periodic gifts of clothing or special privileges. Only in the twentieth century does a child reasonably hope for a strong education. Parents will shower love and praise on an obedient child, but the nonconformist can anticipate punishment. As long as a child lives in the family home, he or she must conform to the parents' values or wishes.

Wanting to "be a man," Hannibal hates himself for having to accept the "marster's" food, clothing, and housing. Feeling his own sexuality threatened and sharing the male need to protect his women, he longs to come back and buy his sweetheart and mother. An unreasonable child, hence verging on adulthood, he craves outright wages or a share in the fields he tills, the cotton he picks, the tools he uses. He says to Coffin: "None of it *mine*" (199). Hannibal knows that education is one path to independence to adulthood, even if he must defy state law by learning from "young marster." To become an adult, he must physically escape the suffocation of his paternalistic master. He has already broken the spiritual bond by reading—an emblem of self-knowledge—and becomes childlike as only an adult can when he says quietly: "Mama, I kin read" (202).

For many years, Rissa has seemed an obedient child, praising her master for his kindness, seemingly sharing his friendship and garnering privileges as houseservant and cook. She has made peace with her lot; she yearns for no wages or education. But even model children have limits of tolerance. When her own child is wounded, she refuses Hiram Sweet's offer to send for Dr. Bullett: "He put his eyes back?" (211). Dismissing her master's ethics, she too becomes a revolutionary—an adult.

The tiny kingdom prospers, then, as long as the young prince, the serfs, the peasants, and even the poor clergyman remain dutiful children to the absolute monarch. A treasured possession, the queen must also defer to her king: she does not intrude on matters of state; she must fend off any stabs at the king's ego; she may not own property; and, above all, she will not inherit the kingdom. The king provides well for each property and bauble. But all does not end happily ever after. The king lies outside the cabin of a humble serf, his heart no longer beating, his crown toppled in the burnt-out dirt.

Molasses, Greens, and Wild Hogs. *The Drinking Gourd* is a remarkably balanced study of slavery, but the play also captures southern life in the 1850s with careful, often humorous details. Always the artist, Lorraine Hansberry says: "What I think a dramatist has to do is to thoroughly innundate himself or herself in an awareness of the historical period and then dismiss it" (147). Still, she creates an antebellum South that can be heard, seen, felt, and tasted. Aware of southern thought, including the sometimes curious reasons with which white southerners defended slavery, Hansberry is equally skilled at catching the squeak of the caneback chair, the squeal of wild hogs, the tang of turnip greens, and the ooze of molasses.

Even the names of *The Drinking Gourd*'s characters ring true to Southern heritage. Black characters' names reflect the only literature available to them, the Bible, and recall vague memories of ancient African royalty, while the less evocative names of white characters refer to specific character traits or to European background. Hannibal's name especially recalls the royal history of slaves; even the Roman satirist Juvenal unwittingly praised his military genius: "This is the man for whom Africa / Was too small a continent." At the precocious age of nine, Hannibal joined his father Hamilcar Barca in a religious ceremony, a sacrifice to Zeus, vowing destruction to Rome. Brave, brilliant, and rebellious, Hannibal in his mid-twenties provoked the second Punic War in 203 B.C., leading his soldiers and elephants across the Alps, to Italy, staving off Roman destruction of

Carthage for nearly sixty years. As he declares war on the system of slavery, Hannibal's namesake becomes a bold leader of his people.

Most of the other black characters have biblical names. As the wife of Abraham, the first patriarch of the Hebrews, the biblical Sarah was as loyal to her husband as Hansberry's Sarah is devoted to Hannibal. Young Joshua escapes to the North with Sarah and the blinded Hannibal; his name recalls the biblical hero who led the Israelites to the Promised Land. Three off-stage characters are named for Hebrew prophets: Isaiah, Hannibal's run-away brother; Ezra, one of Hiram's four original slaves; and Ezekiel, whose name signifies "God strengthens"—fitting for an original slave who finally escaped. Betrayer of his race, Coffin, the driver, has a name of no depth of allusion: he is merely the receptacle of death.

The names of the white characters include the obviously ironical name of the Sweet family: masters gave little sweetness or joy to their slaves, Hiram simply means "Hire 'Em"; Maria's name alludes to the Virgin Mary, in keeping with the southern white man's propensity to place white woman on a pedestal; and Everett may allude to the town in Massachusetts (wealthy southern fathers often sent their sons to Harvard for education and polish, just as Hiram sent Everett to Paris). Dr. Bullett's name suggests violence and death, even though physicians are supposedly restorers of life and health; his first name, Macon, refers to the Georgia city. (Unlike Hiram Sweet, Macon Bullett never perceives the moral compromise of owning slaves.) Hansberry clearly gives Zeb (Zebediah) Dudley a biblical name, thus subtly linking him with the slaves, whom he hates.

After two years of intensive research for the play, Lorraine Hansberry was able to portray southern thought and life in scrupulous detail. Slavery was essential to the agrarian economy of the South: that fact is indisputable. But the southern aristocratic planter, generally well educated and prominent in his Protestant church, still had to wrestle with the morality of the system: therefore, he invented some interesting vindications. Dancing about the real issues in the lively Sweet dinner, Dr. Bullett says that the North wants to free the slaves solely to gain control of Congress and that only lazy slaves try to escape. Lorraine Hansberry could have been even more brutal in introducing banal rationalizations. As late as the 1920s, some of the Nashville Agrarians tried to defend the southern point of view in *I'll Take My Stand:* slavery was defensible since the system was mentioned in the Bible; black southern slaves were treated more humanely than white European servants; working close to the land enhanced a person's humanism (twelve to fifteen hours a day surely provided a cornucopia of humanism); and, after all, blacks lacked the intelligence of whites. Through the narrator and Everett Sweet, Hansberry also conveys accurate information about crop cultivation, hours worked in the fields, erosion of land, and the hierarchy of slaves.[26]

Mark Twain, who boasted seven distinct dialects in *Huckleberry Finn,* would have been pleased with Hansberry's ear for southern idioms and speech patterns. Of all the characters, the narrator has most nearly the accent, syntax, and inflection of "standard English"—the speech used today by television broadcasters. But the rich poetry of southern dialects resounds through the speech of all other characters.

Five distinct dialects reflect the character and vision of each group. Hiram Sweet's speech reflects the rough, yet colorful planter (similar to Gerald O'Hara in *Gone With the Wind)* who sees the South as a new frontier. Confusing subjects and objects, he says: "you and me and every other planter . . . tried . . . to get the fugitive slaves laws passed." (Standard English would dictate "you and I.") Yet his imagery is bombastic and vital: his son is "a polished little pepper"; the Civil War is a "river of stupidity" which will drown the South; his friend Macon descended from a "long line of lace-hankied Bordeaux wine-sniffers." Coldly aristocratic, Dr. Macon Bullett speaks with precision to the point of prissiness; he flavors his otherwise bland speech with "malcontent" and other French derivatives. With a veneer of Dr. Bullett's European thought and customs (and his obliviousness to the plight of slaves), Everett Sweet retains some of his father's vibrance as he speaks of southern land as once "pure and fertile as a dream." Still, he represents the "new master," the scientific planter, the repository of facts and figures.

One mark of deep southern black speech in *The Drinking Gourd* is the embedded tenses of verbs. Rissa tells Hiram, "don't *be askin'* Riss' to hep you none"; Sarah says, "Coffin *know* everything"; Hannibal says, "the more pain it give . . . the more Hannibal *be* a man!" Unlike Standard English, "be askin'," "know," and "be" as spoken here suggest a complexity of thought and action. Hannibal is really saying, I am a man, I will be a man, I will continue being a man. One might argue that such complexities are simply the product of Hansberry's intellect and imagination. On the other hand, linguistic studies reveal that black English possesses a richness and variety not fully appreciated by some Americans. Regardless, Hansberry accurately records southern speech. Rissa uses a series of negatives for emphasis, when she says Hiram promised Hannibal "was*n't never* gona have to be *no* field hand. . . ." (Standard English forbids double or triple negatives.) Dropping the final *g* in "ing" constructions and using "y'all" as a plural for "you" are other marks of a softer southern speech—shared by blacks and whites alike.

Only Hiram Sweet rivals the nature imagery embedded in the speech of Rissa and her family. Thinking Hiram looks "white as cotton," Rissa suspects that Hiram sees "the horseman" (death) on his way. Hannibal cautions young Tommy against placing the "fat of his finger" on the banjo string, and Hansberry has him echo a Jamesean abstraction—"a man is bigger than whatever a man is"—in conveying his reference for the Drinking Gourd. Rissa and her family display a depth of character and experience in their speech—as complex as the caste system of the South.

The nadir of the southern social system, the poor white Zeb Dudley shares some speech traits with blacks—"ain't," double negatives and embedded tenses of verbs. But several verbal mannerisms reveal his "cracker" status: he says "mebbe" instead of "maybe"; he says "I reckon" instead of "I suppose"; he adds pronouns for emphasis, "I heard *me* some good things." Lacking the poetry of slaves and masters alike, Zeb Dudley's speech is as barren and wasted as the soil he tills.

For a writer who has "dismissed" Southern history and lore, Hansberry certainly understands southern love of land and the deep faith of slaves. Hiram and Rissa argue about the amount of salt in turnip greens; they laugh about the riot of wild hogs; they chuckle over Ezekiel's spill into a vat of molasses. At his most introspective, Hiram alludes to his beloved land during "The gray hours when every man . . . wonders why the stars hang out there and this planet turns and rivers run—and what he's here for" (184–85). Even Zeb Dudley, in his rough way, is aware of nature when he says that his father, the fool, had died "eatin' dirt." When Coffin berates Rissa about her "wild boys," she hints at her deep religion: "What was I supposed to do—send 'em back to the Lord?" (199). Popular slave songs, such as "Steal Away," "The Drinking Gourd," and "Rocka My Soul in the Bosom of Abraham," held hidden messages of freedom but also merged the love of God and nature: "My Lord he calls me / He calls me by the thunder." Shortly before Hannibal is blinded, Tommy reads his friend's essay aloud—an eloquent blend of southern reverence for land and God:

When I was a boy I first come to notice . . . the Drinking Gourd. I thought . . . it was the most beautiful thing in the heavens. I do not know why, but when a man lie on his back and see the stars, there is something that can happen to a man inside that be . . . bigger than whatever a man is. . . . Something that makes every man feel like King Jesus on his milk-white horse racing through the world telling me to stand up in the glory which is called—freedom. (208).

A fine moment in American drama, *The Drinking Gourd* is an objective study of southern slavery in the 1850s. Lorraine Hansberry illustrates that evil institutions or systems may try to consume the individual, but he or she can triumph through personal strength and courage. Hiram Sweet must die. He cannot abandon the rule of his tiny kingdom; he cannot fully see the evil inherent in the system of slavery. Hannibal sees only too clearly—as did Frederick Douglass—that the white man's power to enslave the black man lay in the denial of literacy. Hannibal "saw" that education equaled freedom. His horrendous penalty for learning to read, his blinding, becomes both a literal and symbolic punishment. He will still prevail, for young Joshua, biblical namesake of the leader of the Promised Land, guides Hannibal and Sarah to freedom.

Military historians will continue to study the battles and generals of the Civil War. Hansberry is slightly myopic in demeaning historians who "spend volumes discussing the *battles* of the Civil War, and which army was crossing which river at five minutes to two, and how their swords were hanging. . . ."[27] Nations need their heroes. The South (a nation for four years) needs Robert E. Lee and Stonewall Jackson and America needs Nathan Hale and "Mad" Anthony Wayne as surely as Haitians need Toussaint L'Ouverture and Carthaginians need Hannibal. War is, indeed, one of Hansberry's evil institutions, but one she can tolerate in Africa and the Carribbean—for there war is a black institution. Despite this logical inconsistency, she nevertheless acknowledges in *The Drinking Gourd* that the South believed its cause somehow divorced from the issue of slavery. She reminds us—eloquently—that the South ignored a fundamental ethical premise—that men and women cannot, must not own one another. But no knowledge, no freedom, no act of personal courage is without cost.

What Use Are Flowers?

In 1939 Bertolt Brecht created a stark tableau of war, *Mother Courage and Her Children,* a drama spanning twelve years of the Thirty Years' War. Traveling through Germany, Poland, and Sweden in her cart, Mother Courage is blindly and stupidly dependent on war. She ekes out a survival by selling goods to war victims. Nevertheless, she is witty, spirited, and dedicated to her two sons, Eilif and Swiss Cheese, and her mute daughter, Catherine. Despite a brief insight, she remains ignorant of the fundamental truth that one rarely profits from war. At the end of Brecht's epic drama, Mother Courage believes that her dead daughter is only sleeping, harnesses herself to her rickety wagon, and leaves for another country as the soldiers sing: "Dangers, surprises, and devastations—'the war takes hold and will not quit.' " Although a Marxist and at times a nihilist, Brecht still places his art above politics: he refuses to render Mother Courage a political activist at the end of the play, forcing his viewers to discover their own perceptions of the horrors and dehumanization of war splashed on his fragmentary and episodic canvas.

In 1952 Samuel Beckett espoused his personal view of the human condition in his brilliant play, *Waiting for Godot*. True to the absurdist tradition, there is little action, little change of scene, scant character development, much contemplation, and vacillation between hope and despair. Throughout the entire play, two middle-aged tramps wait in a quiet country setting, barren except for one tree. They wait for Godot. Several times they quarrel but always reconcile. Vladimir (the Intellect or Mind) and Estragon (the Emotion or Body) may be two halves of the same universal Man or the tramps' dependency on each other may represent the secure but often suffocating symbiosis of all men. Godot, who never appears, may be Christ for Christians, God for believers, meaning for existentialists, freedom for the two vagabonds. A materialist and his servant arrive, plagued by the same dilemmas as the tramps, searching for belief, wavering between the sublime and the ridiculous. Near the middle of the play, Vladimir and Estragon engage in a wild exchange of three hats: this seemingly trivial game signifies the futility of all action and the absence of personal identity. As the play ends, a boy comes to announce that Godot will come tomorrow. The two tramps agree to hang themselves on the tree (reminiscent of Christ's crucifixion) if Godot does not come. While some critics view the play as a testament to man's persistence and endurance, many viewers find *Waiting for Godot* a tedious, excruciating denial of meaning in life and action—a waiting for a Godot who has not come, will not come, and does not exist.

In response to Beckett's depressing yet compelling questions about life, Lorraine Hansberry conceived *What Use Are Flowers?* in late 1961. Just as she cried out against trying not to care in *The Sign in Sidney Brustein's Window*, she replaced despair with hope, death with life, destruction with rejuvenation in this fable for television (Even though *What Use Are Flowers?* and *Lord of the Flies* share a common setting, Lorraine Hansberry was not influenced by the William Golding novel, which she read a year after completing her play.) Moved by the artistry and pacifist fervor of Bertolt Brecht, she first chose as the working title of the play, "Who Knows Where?"—a line from Mother Courage's dirge to her daughter—which serves as the prelude to *What Use Are Flowers?*

> Lullaby baby
> What's rustling there?
> Neighbor's child's in Poland
> Mine's who knows where?[28]

By the spring of 1962, Lorraine Hansberry considered recasting the play for the stage but set the script aside temporarily—a delay made permanent by her death three years later. In its current form, the play has some artistic shortcomings. Yet Hansberry's basic intentions in *What Use Are Flowers?* remain clear: the play is an illustration of her romantic realism, her conviction that the human race will survive and prevail, as well as her vision that, if man abandons hope, he will surely destroy himself and his world.

   The Action.   Scene One opens on a vast rocky plain on the edge of a great forest. The Hermit, an old bearded man dressed in tattered clothes and animal skins, walks with a stick and carries his possessions in a hobo's bundle. After surveying the area, he crawls onto an outcropping of rocks and goes to sleep. The light rises on a group of children, no more than ten years old, all naked with long hair, totally silent as they stalk a small animal. When their rock fells the animal, they rush shrieking to tear into the raw flesh. The Hermit awakes to this melee and is confused, especially by the savage young girl. He screams that they are animals. Astonished at his voice and sudden appearance, one boy stoops for a rock while the other children grow taut for fight. Chiding them for their lack of manners, which merely "hide . . . greater crimes" (231), he then asks for directions to the city—unaware of the atomic holocaust. Always the disciplinarian, he thinks these "little uglies" would benefit from a "repetitive touch of the cane" (232).

   Sounding like a futuristic Henry David Thoreau, the Hermit tells the baffled children that "one of the reasons I left is because I could no longer stand the dominion of time in the lives of men. . ." (232). When he left society twenty years earlier, he had thrown away his watch but soon "*longed* to know the hour of the day"; he made rock calendars, but animals knocked them down. To the Hermit, time has an intrinsic value, but "Men invent time*pieces,* they do not invent time" (232–33). His time has come to die, so he has returned to bid society a final farewell.

   The Hermit concludes his monologue. He, the former English professor, Charles Lewis Lawson, settles himself and a small cloth on the ground and prepares for breakfast. Suddenly throwing themselves on the Hermit, the children consume the scraps of food like hungry dogs. Horrified, the old man screams: "Animals! . . . animals! . . . I'm an old man! Don't you know anything!" (234). Stalking off, he returns after some time to the sleeping children, who awake when he again begs for directions to the city. As he strikes a flint to a pile of dry twigs and dead leaves, the children are first fascinated and then frightened by the fire. He places a skewer of wild birds above the fire and sits back placidly to wait. The antithesis of Rousseau's "noble savages," the children again affirm their primitivism: perplexed by the smell of food cooking, they attack and devour the birds raw. Finally, the Hermit has a flash of recognition: the children are prelingual. "Why . . . you're not playing . . . you are wild!" He screams in fury to the quiet world: "WHAT HAVE YOU DONE!" (237).

Many weeks later, scene 2 opens on some lean-tos and a tiny garden, crudely fenced off. The children are now somewhat cleaner and their hair is combed. They gather for their now daily lessons. The Professor assigns names: he cynically tells them: "You must have names . . . because it will keep you from having to remember who you *really* are as you grow older" (238). Of the nine children, Charlie and Lily begin to surface as leaders. Having a marvelous time, though he would deny it, the professor teaches elementary concrete words—*food, knife,* and *sleep.* Academic lessons completed, he then begins vocational training in ceramics and pottery. Of all the children, Charlie is the first to grasp more abstract concepts—*work* and *use.*

By scene 3, all the children are clothed in foliage or animal skins, but only Lily still wears long hair. (Here Hansberry has cleverly reversed the costume technique of Eugene O'Neill's *Emperor Jones:* the children's clothes and groomed hair signify their return to civilized society.) A strict but loving teacher, the Hermit threatens to cane them if they do not hasten to their lessons: Now pupils of "the humanities," the children try to understand the concept of beauty. At the climax of the play, the Hermit responds to their questions: "What *use* are flowers? Ah, but the uses of flowers are infinite! One may smell them—One may touch their petals and feel heaven—Or one may write quite charming verses about them—" (244). Horribly off-key, the Hermit sings a verse of "Greensleeves" which makes the children giggle. Charlie comes to his aid with a primitive reed flute, which he has made to surprise the other children. "Surprise" is another concept the Hermit has taught them. The children sit in silence and refuse to join in. But the music itself, not the pleading of the Hermit, finally induces them to sing along. The Hermit then declares: "Tomorrow—Beethoven's Ninth!" (246).

In the darkness of scene 4, Charlie's flute haltingly, then firmly, plays the first notes of Beethoven's Ninth, the ennobling Choral. The lights come up on the children arranged in the semicircle of a chorus, as Lily beats time on a great clay drum, as the Hermit conducts Charlie and the singers:

> Joy, thou souce of light immortal!
> Daughter of Elysium!
> Touched with fire, to the portal
> Of thy radiant shrine we come.
> Thy pure magic frees all others
> Held in Custom's rigid rings;
> Men throughout the world are brothers
> In the haven of thy wings. . . . (249)

They have ascended from savagery to humanity: love has surpassed sheer survival. As the group disperses, the Hermit calls Charlie into his lean-to. He describes "socializing": "We sit and we look at one another and eventually begin to tell one another perfectly outlandish stories. . . . It was kind of a ritual." The Hermit then tries to explain jokes: "A chicken crosses the road to get to the other side" (250). Charlie is not amused, just perplexed. Cocktail parties, he adds, were "where most really important matters were generally decided" (250). But the Hermit has a serious underlying purpose: somehow he must convey to this ten-year-old boy that he must perpetuate the human race (he lamely speaks of Lily's long hair). Meanwhile, the children outside suffer a drastic setback. Jealous of another boy's superior pottery, one boy yanks away his pot, bashes his head bloody, smashes a lean-to into scraps: they are savages fighting to maim, to destroy. Failing to quell the fight, the Hermit yells: "YOU DO NOT DESERVE TO SURVIVE!"—and collapses (251).

Blue lights rise a few hours later on scene 5, as the Hermit lies dying in his lean-to. Standing in a stiff line, the children hand flowers (peace offerings) to Charlie, who gives them to the Hermit. But the Hermit does not want flowers, music, poetry, or even Beethoven. Charlie cannot endure his railings: "I don't like insults . . . " (253). Mellowing as the other children leave, the Hermit tells Charlie: "Only the *absence* of life will seem to you the miracle, the greatest miracle . . ." (254). He will soon die, he will "exude a horrible odor," they must bury him, but they can place a tombstone over his grave: "It won't mean a thing to me, but you will feel better" (255). Grief, he explains, is born of love. Finally breaking through his

Victorian reserve, the Hermit tells Charlie he must take rather good care
of Lily and then blurts out: "Let the race continue" (256). Sensing that
time with his friend is drawing to a close, Charlie must finally explain the
atomic holocaust. (Hansberry saves this incident for the final scene, so that
the audience will focus on the inner growth of the children rather than on
their external obstacles.)

Thomas comes into the lean-to, proudly bearing his invention—a primitive wheel. The hermit praises him. Charlie is so jealous that he hurls the
machine outside. The failing philosopher then says: "To be jealous . . .
means you have placed value on something, and this is fine. But you must
use your jealousy . . . to build another wheel, a bigger wheel" (260).

Charlie's extreme jealousy and consequent destructiveness lead the old
hermit to despair of the children's survival. They cannot raise Egypt and
China, discover the equations of Copernicus and Newton, create the art of
Shakespeare and Einstein; they do not even know about steam. Condemning that "silly sentimental female" whom he learns had saved them, he
says: "Our little adventure among the stars is over!" (260). But as he dies,
the Hermit says: "Charlie, the uses of flowers were infinite . . ." (261).
Unaware that their teacher is no longer with them, the other children
stoop in the dirt, patiently rebuilding the broken wheel.

The Sun Collapsed.   Minutes before the Hermit dies, Charlie feels
the urgency to describe the tragedy which left the children alone and wild.
Hands and body flowing in articulate sign language, he tells the Hermit
that a huge vehicle, rolling like a stone, brought them to this plain, where
great blades of grass grew high and mighty trees stood. Grasping a lily
(lilies are women to Charlie), he says a woman brought them here. She
kissed each child, went back home, and then the circle of his arms falling
down—the sun collapsed. (The atom bomb exploded, spewing orange-red
fire, forming a mushroom cloud.) Anguished by this recital of destruction,
the Hermit declares: "Dear God: what a strange tribe they were! Lunatics
and heroes all" (258).

Bereft of their parents and teacher, stripped of their humanity, these
five-year-olds (they have been in the wilds for nearly five years) were forced
to survive in the bleakest of circumstances: they had no knowledge of
building shelter, cooking food, cultivating gardens, curing illness. The
primal shock of the explosion erased all capacity of speech. Outwardly,
they share none of the innate goodness of Rousseau's "noble savage," but
they also lack the meanness and cruelty of William Golding's schoolboys.
They eat raw meat, for they cannot cook; they push each other about, for

they must survive; they are naked, for they are ignorant of clothes; but they do not torture animals or each other for sport. Most crucially, they have endured.

War, in *What Use Are Flowers?*, is the only real villain. Brecht believes that no one can truly profit from war, but misguided men have sought glory, honor, property, dominion over their fellow men in the gore of battle. The children's naked bodies and frozen speech serve as grim reminders of the spoils of war.

Physically frail but mentally hearty and emotionally tough, the Hermit becomes Hansberry's Godot—who *does* come. While the children do not expect the old man to arrive, they are receptive to his lessons—of food, pottery, work, beauty, and grief. They giggle at his scratchy version of "Greensleeves," the laughter of delight, not the lifeless hysteria of Vladimir, Estragon, and the servant. Unlike the two tramps' empty charade of exchanging hats, the children's games are related to survival, to life, even in their bitter struggle over poverty. Much of the tragedy of *Waiting for Godot* lies in the men's inability to feel, to care; when the children have offended the Hermit, they feel grief and beg his forgiveness with flowers.

Lorraine Hansberry knew *What Use Are Flowers?* had its flaws. There was the practical problem of sustaining the performances of the "wild" children—one solution she considered was having modern dancers portray the children on stage.[29] As the play now stands—and her death prevented revision—*Flowers* is overly sentimental, lacks sound character motivation and development, and has a glib treatment of war. The Hermit, a former college professor, elects to spend his final days with a group of unruly children for no clearly discernible reason. Teaching, for that matter, may have driven him into solitude. However loveable and crotchety the old man may be, he does not seem fully convincing as a leader who virtually overnight can transform wild children from eaters of raw flesh to singers of Beethoven.

While Bertolt Brecht deplores war, he still sets his play very specifically during the Thirty Years' War—the causes of which are well known. Hansberry's war is a vague, offstage "atomic holocaust." War is, of course, one of Hansberry's "evil institutions." But *Les Blancs* explores war and its attendant necessary revolution in modern colonial Africa. Implicitly, *The Drinking Gourd* traces the events leading up to the Civil War. War, in *Flowers,* is amorphous, has no specific locale or time period except "the future." George Orwell in *1984* and Ray Bradbury in *The Martian Chronicles* have frightened and challenged the intellect with their visions of the future, but few American writers have excelled at "futurism." Hansberry is neither an Orwell nor a Bradbury. Her best writing derives from personal observation or careful research.

Hansberry's intention and basic concept in *What Use Are Flowers?* are nonetheless admirable. The play is a simple but moving reply to *Waiting for Godot.* There *is* a Godot, who strips bare the children's savage defenses to find innate goodness, beauty, and love. After twenty years of seclusion, the Hermit has discovered Emersonian "perfect sweetness" in the "midst of the crowd" of children, whom he imbues with humanity and independence. The sun may have collapsed, but the children need not hang themselves from a tree or bash their friends' heads bloody: they have a wheel to rebuild, steam to discover, and flowers to use.

The Cold Wind Blows

A monument to the brilliance of Lorraine Hansberry, *The Collected Last Plays* bridge continents, centuries, and a diverse spectrum of humanity. At first these three plays seem to have few common bonds, but they actually merge to crystallize Hansberry's artistic and political philosophy of the individual and institutions, enslavement and freedom, and despair and hope. Waving throughout the plays is the cold wind of deliberate action. In *Les Blancs,* Madame Neilsen describes the beginnings of the revolt: "Some cold wind blew in over our people here and chilled their hearts to us" (51). The cold wind is revolution—not reform—of people who have passively suffered under tyranny. Cold wind is a fitting image for less sophisticated people in warm, sensual climates. The cold shocks, startles, upsets the balance. The cold wind is then the Mau Mau Revolt in *Les Blancs,* escape from and destruction of slavery in *The Drinking Gourd,* and somewhat more vaguely, the atomic holocaust and the Hermit's restoration of humanity to the wild children in *What Use Are Flowers?* A devotee of Brecht, Hansberry detested senseless war, but she understood the necessity of passive resistance, direct confrontation, and at the most extreme, violence when corrupt societies repressed the vital right of the individual—freedom.

All three *Collected Last Plays* are framed by the archetypal rhythm of the seasons: late summer signifies harvest of the old crops (the reigning order); winter becomes death (revolution); and spring signals rebirth (the new order). Each of the three plays opens in the late summer months. *Les Blancs* opens to stifling summer heat, as Marta stores medicine in banana leaves for refrigeration; the rainy season (the tropical equivalent of winter) seems far away. In *The Drinking Gourd,* cotton-picking season (always in late summer) is at its peak; hogs are being fattened for their winter slaughter. Late summer parallels a stagnant society twice in *What Use Are Flowers?:* five years before the main action of the play, the children were abandoned in lush summer grasses, going to seed, before the cold wind of the atomic explosion; and, the Hermit waits nearly a month before clothing the children in autumn leaves. In the still air of summer, a distressing status quo pervades each play: the white Europeans dominate the peaceful, democratic Kwis; aristocratic white masters own black slaves, descended from African royalty; perhaps greedy materialists wage senseless war, deserting their small children, who are found five years later leading a dehumanized existence. Moreover, the society of each play is dominated by paternalistic rule: the Kwis are "children" to Reverend Neilsen, Major DeKoven, and other Britons, while the slaves in *The Drinking Gourd* are "children" to their masters. In *Flowers,* all but one of the characters *are* children, rescued once by a woman teacher, redeemed five years later by an elderly, moral, and ethical man.

When the cold wind of winter blows, the oppressed freeze their smiles and silence their voices, except to insist on personal freedom. (War is immoral in *Mother Courage,* since Brecht feels the soldiers had little personal interest in the Protestant-Catholic conflict of the Thirty Years' War; war is villainous in *Flowers.*) Having pleaded for freedom with petitions, delegations, and discussions, the Kwis are forced into the cold wind of deliberate action in resistance. Denied the basic human needs of marriage, family stability, and education, some slaves rebelled violently, as did Nat Turner in 1831, but, more typically, Hannibal learns to read, and Rissa rejects her master after her son's mutilation. In the futuristic *Flowers,* the wild children have lost the ability to laugh or speak.

Fanning the cold wind, a generally mature leader emerges, at first resisting his or her role, having a touch of the cynic, but finally knowing what must be done. Dr. Amos Kumalo presses the Kwis onward to freedom. Despite her usual compliance, Rissa steals her master's gun and bids the three young people to follow the North Star to freedom. Placing the children's welfare above her own, a thoughtful teacher delivers them from destruction; five years later, the Hermit teaches the youngsters the uses of flowers, poetry, and beauty. The cold wind cannot spare some innocent victims—Madame Neilsen, Hiram Sweet (though he is master, he questions the morality of slavery), and the brave woman teacher.

The fresh breeze of spring—the creation of a new, free world—does not rush freely until after the action of each play is ended. But the new society will emerge: the demise of young Abioseh and Reverend Neilsen signals

the collapse of European rule and the rise of African rule; the declaration of
the Civil War marks the end of the old order of slavery and freedom for all
peoples—black and white; the sun may have exploded, but the children
speak, sing, and reconstruct the wheel—the renaissance of civilization.
The new orders reaffirm Hansberry's romantic realism, her conviction, in
part, that the human race will survive. In 1959, she wrote:

I wish to live because life has within it that which is good, that which is beautiful,
and that which is love. Therefore, since I have known all these things . . . I wish
to live. (224)

Revolution is not without its price. Hannibal is blinded in *The Drinking
Gourd*. Brother kills brother—a tragedy as old as Abel and Cain—in *Les
Blancs*. The revolution is offstage in *What Use Are Flowers?* We grieve that
Hiram Sweet must die, that Madame Neilsen must die—even though they
are part of the white institution—with whom Hansberry has less patience
than with the black institution. Hansberry was a solid researcher, and history does not seem to suggest better means of ending slavery in the South
than civil war or more effective methods of securing black control in Africa
than outright revolution. One yearns, however simplistically, for reform
rather than revolution. Reform becomes possible when people can accept
or are not threatened by those who are different from themselves, when
men and women so fully believe in themselves that they can believe in
others. Reform requires communication and compassion—neither of
which really exists in *Les Blancs* or *The Drinking Gourd*. Perhaps the most
subtle tragedy in these plays, rife at the end with dead and mutilated bodies, is that reform was not possible.

Chapter Seven

The Human Race Concerns Me:
To Be Young, Gifted and Black

To Be Young, Gifted and Black presents many facets and nuances of black life—black nationalism, cocktail parties, slavery, financial problems, family squabbles, humor, and universal concerns of man's hope and dreams. At first the play creates a kaleidoscopic effect, as scenes rapidly shift from one intricate pattern to another, seemingly resulting in more chaos than order. But such chaos is necessary in causing us to confront the complexity, beauty, joy, and courage of black life.

After Lorraine Hansberry's death in 1965, Robert Nemiroff began sorting through and painstakingly editing the store of Hansberry work—in over three filing cabinets—at the Hansberry/Nemiroff house in Croton-on-Hudson, New York. By 1969 he had put together a dramatic testament of black life—*To Be Young, Gifted and Black*—from both published and unpublished sources. Enjoying enormous success both at New York's Cherry Lane Theater in 1969 and on its two-year national tour (1970–72), the play derived much of its strength and artistry from Hansberry's increased social consciousness and a strong emphasis on racial pride. Too, the several casts of *Young, Gifted and Black* featured some of the finest performers of the day—Cicely Tyson, Moses Gunn, Roy Scheider, Barbara Baxley, Claudia McNeil, Tina Sattin. Later, in 1973, a television production featured Scheider, McNeil, Ruby Dee, and Blythe Danner.

Given the play's popularity, Nemiroff then expanded it into a book or full-length "informal autobiography," also entitled *To Be Young, Gifted and Black,* which is four times the length of the professional playscript. This later separate and distinct work is for the present "the closest approximation to an autobiography available."[1] In his foreword to the book, Nemiroff calls *Young, Gifted and Black* "the portrait of an individual, the workbook of an artist, and the chronicle of a rebel who celebrated the human spirit."[2] We will, therefore, concentrate on the book, making occasional references to particular scenes and dramatic effects in the play.

Embedded in the pages of *To Be Young, Gifted and Black* are fragments of more than ten separate Hansberry works: portions of the now-published plays, *A Raisin in the Sun, The Sign in Sidney Brustein's Window, Les Blancs, The Drinking Gourd,* and *What Use Are Flowers?*; excerpts from the unpublished fragments of her autobiographical novel, *All the Dark and Beautiful Warriors*; passages from an unfinished play, *Toussaint*; paraphrases from Sean O'Casey; segments of Hansberry's letters, journals, essays, poetry, and interviews; and a few comments by Nemiroff himself. All of these works merge, separate, and merge again into an embodiment of black life.

Despite the rapidly shifting scenes, however, *To Be Young, Gifted and Black* has a definite, though complex, structure, for the personality of Lorraine Hansberry serves as the controlling device for both the book and the play. As the character of Hansberry intones selections from her journals, letters, and interviews, we are introduced to a young woman, brimming with hopes, disappointments, dreams, fears, and laughter. Not only does she become a vital human being, but she reveals—posthumously—the pattern of her entire career as a writer and a thinker.

Art and Propaganda: The Romantic as Realist

In the touring production of *Young, Gifted and Black,* Tina Sattin, the beautiful, vibrant actress who most often portrayed Lorraine Hansberry, intermittently glided onstage, giving us clues to the life and personality of the playwright. Speaking quietly and simply, she revealed the more serious side of Hansberry's life: "I was born on the South Side of Chicago. I was born black and a female" (41). Near the end of the play, she is able to affirm, "My name is Lorraine Hansberry. I am a writer" (228). Yet Hansberry was capable of feisty sarcasm as she told an interviewer, who had suggested *Raisin* was a "play about people," not about Negroes: "I'd always been under the impression that Negroes *are* people" (128). And she sometimes broke into bawdy humor when the occasion called for it: "The white boys in the streets, they look at me and think of sex. . . . Baby, you could be Jesus in drag—but if you're brown they're sure you're selling" (95).

Not only do we learn facts about Hansberry's life, but we also begin to understand her philosophy of life—especially her theory of romantic realism, her conception of art, and her attitude about politics. At the peak of her career, Lorraine Hansberry expressed an essentially romantic view of life at a black writers' conference on March 1, 1959. Transcending the traditional distinctions between romanticism and realism, Hansberry's view of art emphasizes a belief in man's potential. Recoiling at the idea that her plays were naturalistic, Hansberry explained in an interview: "Well, naturalism tends to take the world as it is . . . you simply photograph the garbage can. But in realism . . . the artist who is creating the realistic work imposes on it not only what *is* but what is *possible* . . ." (236).

At the core of Hansberry's romantic realism was the belief in man's possibilities for goodness and greatness. Yet men and women attain their potential by consciously exerting their will on the world around them. As Hansberry explains, "Man is unique in the universe. . . . Man might just do what the apes never will—*impose* the reason for life on life" (40). Then she concludes, "I think that the human race does command its own destiny and that that destiny can eventually embrace the stars. . ." (41).

Yet Hansberry was not naive about the evil side of man's nature or the ills of modern society—"man's very real inhumanity to man." She was well aware of the atom bomb, cancer, lynching, racial hatred, and physical attack. But more than any flaw in man's basic nature, Hansberry blames various institutions of society for twisting and perverting man's basic good, believing that there are no evil people, only evil systems. Marriage, government, racism, and prostitution—all were institutions which separated man from his basic goodness. In this sense, she was thoroughly romantic.

Throughout Hansberry's works, we find numerous examples of characters who became more than even they thought possible. After leading a life of noncommitment and ennui, Sidney Brustein becomes concerned with politics to the point that he must expose the corrupt official Wally O'Hara; in a related instance of realism, he finally sees his wife, Iris, as a total human being rather than as a mediocre actress with beautiful long hair. Walter Lee Younger, working as a chauffeur and living in a crowded apartment, doubts his own self-worth so much that he is tempted to accept the white man's bribe not to move into the white neighborhood. But as his son Travis looks on, Walter Lee proudly announces that he and his family *will* move to their house—the climax of *A Raisin in the Sun*. In *The Drinking Gourd*, Rissa has been a faithful and privileged house servant, loved and respected by her master. But when the new master has Rissa's son's eyes put out for learning to read, Rissa comes to maturity when she refuses to bring the old master his medicine and watches him die in an agony comparable to that of her now blind son, Hannibal.

Closely related to Hansberry's romantic realism was her view of the purposes of art. Unlike most critics today, Hansberry believed that all art is propaganda (used here with no perjorative connotations in the term's sense of the systematic propagation of a doctrine).[3] In "The Negro Writer and

His Roots," she stated: "All art is ultimately social. . . ."[4] In a 1959 letter, she explains, "'Thesis plays' and 'social plays' are supposed to be . . . plays which plead a cause" (133). But she adds, "There are *no* plays which are not social and no plays that do not have a thesis" (133). A "message" in a play becomes offensive when the playwright lacks the skill and sensitivity to render believable his characters, their social problems, their universal dilemmas. Hansberry's personal list of "social" writers includes Arthur Miller, Tennessee Williams, Lillian Hellman, William Inge, Henrik Ibsen, Friedrich Durrenmatt, William Shakespeare, the Italian Commedia dell'Arte playwrights. She concludes, "The fact is—if he really had nothing he wanted to tell us; nothing he wanted to persuade us of; no partisanship he wanted to evoke—well, he wouldn't have written a play" (133).

Robert Nemiroff offers the following view of Hansberry's theory of romantic realism and "social" writing. "Her focus was on . . . circumstances: on the dissection of personality in interrelationship with society, the conflict between our human needs and what society imposes on us, the forces, institutions, ideas that in interaction with our inner needs cause us to act as we do and, as in these plays, so often result in tragedy. . . ." He continues, citing an illustration of her theory from *Romeo and Juliet* that the playwright frequently used in conversation. She said "that Shakespeare . . . was asserting the legitimacy of *love* as a basis for marriage and protesting the consequences of a social order (Elizabethan England no less than Verona) that makes of marriage instead a political/economic compact to cement family alliances and property relationships. . . ."[5]

Nevertheless, Hansberry's theory that all art is "social" occasionally seems flawed. Her analysis of *Romeo and Juliet,* as reported by Nemiroff, would seem to reduce one of literature's great love stories to a Marxist tract, something inconsistent with her theories of art. We may assume, however, that a balance is struck between propaganda and art in Ibsen's or Shaw's pleas for the equality of women, Miller's horror at the persecution of "witches" (really the victims of McCarthyism), and Hansberry's insistence on the dignity and equality of her people. At any rate, we cannot divorce the success of a work of art entirely from its message.

In molding believable characters thrust into extreme predicaments, Hansberry believed that the writer should begin with precise details. In an interview she said, "In order to create the universal, you must pay very great attention to the specific. Universality, I think, emerges from truthful identity of what is" (128). In *A Raisin in the Sun,* she told people "that not only is this a Negro family . . . but it's not even a New York or a southern Negro family. It is specifically South Side Chicago" (128). (In rehearsals for *Raisin,* she found herself wishing that Sidney Poitier could perfect the exact offbeat gait of many South Side black men.)⁶ No doubt her insistence on accuracy stemmed partly from her study of Sean O'Casey. "I love Sean O'Casey . . . the playwright of the twentieth century accepting and using the most obvious instruments of Shakespeare, which is the human personality in its totality. O'Casey never fools you about the Irish . . . the Irish drunkard, the Irish braggart, the Irish liar. . . ." (90). O'Casey's eye for Irish idiosyncrasies probably affected Hansberry's vision of Chicago's South Side and later of African blacks. She once said, "'Negro style' seems broad but is, like the Negro dance, based almost entirely on nuance. It is what Pearl Bailey does *not* say that is so hilarious . . ." (213).

Just as O'Casey caught the Irish drunkard in the midst of his rationalizations and captured the expansive, fierce pride of many Irish people, Hansberry deftly outlines the rhythms and nuances of black life. Rebelling at a common view of the "black intellectual," Hansberry implies that most educated blacks do not want to ignore their black brothers and sisters still in the ghetto or the tarpaper shacks but at the same time are not plagued by the "guilt" of the successful.

Dramatizing differences in life-style between black and white intellectuals, an elegant black woman swishes into a white cocktail party in a scene from *Young, Gifted and Black.* Shifting between standard English and black folk idiom, she parries with a well-dressed white man:

He: If there's one thing I utterly *loathe,* it is to hear the way you colored intellectuals are always affecting the speech and inflections of the Negro masses!

She: Now ain't you somethin' else? Let me inform you—*liebchen*—that we colored intellectuals lovingly use the idiom and inflection of our people for precisely the same reason. We happen to adore and find literary strength in its vitality, its sauciness, and sometimes, sheer poetry. . . . Now why should that confuse you?

He: Now, Negroes *are* different. There's a quality of uh . . . uh . . .

She: I know what you mean. . . . Personally, I go for chitterlings and champagne. . . . (214–16)

The scene ends with the woman swaying back and forth, celebrating black artists:

She: I could see the bridge across the chasm. It was made up of a band of angels of art, hurling off the souls of twenty million. I saw Jimmy Baldwin and Leontyne, and Lena and Harry and Sammy. And then there was Charlie White and Nina Simone and . . . Paul was back! Langston and Julian Mayfield coming on the run. . . .

He: My dear, you are disgustingly emotional— (217–19)

As an artist, Hansberry was fascinated by everyday people. In an interview she said, "The most ordinary human being . . .has within him elements of profundity, of profound anguish. . . . Every human being is in enormous conflict about something, even if it's how to get to work in the morning . . . " (15). Walter Lee Younger, Sidney Brustein, Rissa—all three exemplify her belief that "there are no simple men" (207). Cautioning us not to be deceived by stereotypes of the past, she instead urges writers to follow the examples of Twain, Whitman, Melville, and O'Neill, "to listen and absorb . . . and give back their findings in new art. . ." (207).

At times Hansberry despaired about writing. On September 16, 1962, she wrote, "I sit at this desk for hours and sharpen pencils and smoke cigarettes and switch from play to play . . . and nothing happens. I begin to think more and more of doing something else with my life while I am still young . . . instead of this endless struggle" (179–79). In a January 13, 1962, letter to a Miss Watson, she continued, "I just write—at my own dismally slow (and yes, heartbreaking and maddening) commercially disinterested pace and choice of subject matter" (145). In the middle of a project, though, her fingers would fly across the typewriter: "But I know *what* I am writing now. . . . I was in the kitchen and I wrote fourteen pages in an hour that will hardly need revision . . ." (197).

Delighting in artists who took sharp turns off established roads, Hansberry recalled a memorable lecture from her days at Wisconsin: "I shall never forget when Frank Lloyd Wright came and spoke at the University in the brand new and ever so modernistic Union Building Auditorium. . . . Later, addressing the packed hall, he attacked almost everything—and, foremost among them, the building he was standing in for its violation of the organic principles of architecture: he attacked babbitry and the nature of education . . ." (93). An admirer of other artists of experimental genius, Hansberry hung "the Picasso lady over the couch" and placed Charles White paintings above her bookshelf and tables in her Bleecker Street apartment.[7]

To Be Young, Gifted and Black heavily emphasizes Hansberry's political views, especially her conviction that "Racism is rotten" and must be eliminated. Particularly distresed by stereotyped blacks in white American literature, she cited Mailer and Faulkner among those who had created two-dimensional black characters in unrealistic situations. (Most white American writers have, in fact, created skewed images of blacks—with a few noteworthy exceptions, such as Carson McCullers's Dr. Copeland and Portia in *The Heart Is Lonely Hunter.*) Admiring Mailer for his honesty and "because he seems to encompass the possibilities of the true hero . . . on this unspeakable barren landscape" (208), she nevertheless considered his 1959 essay on "hip" and the existential man, "The White Negro," representative at best of less than 1 percent of the 700,000 people in Harlem.

Stereotypes of black people abound in American literature. Even Faulkner's magnificent Dilsey in *The Sound and the Fury* is too selfless, too controlled to be fully believable. Americans have fantasized about black people—"this image of the unharried, unconcerned, glandulatory, simple, rhythmical, amoral, dark creature who was, above all, a *miracle of sensuality*" (209). White readers find stereotyped blacks a "pressure valve for fanciful longings" (209) and a repository for their repressions and suppressions. Moreover, black women have usually been considered either strong, hardworking, and heroic or sensual, lazy, and promiscuous.[8] Never are they merely human. Black men are "shiftless," "prize bucks," or "upstarts." Not until Hansberry's Walter Lee Younger did the American stage see a dreamer, an ambitious businessman, a family man, a troubled introspective—all facets of the same black character. Lorraine Hansberry may indeed be considered a propagandist in that she sought to erase pale imitations from the stage and replace them with living human beings.

Although Hansberry respected Martin Luther King, Jr., and his "nonviolent resistance," she sometimes advocated revolutionary tactics: "Negroes must concern themselves with every single means of struggle: legal, illegal, passive, active, violent and nonviolent. . . . They must . . . sit-in, lie-down, strike, boycott, sing hymns, pray on steps—and shoot from their windows when the racists come cruising through their communities" (22). A people who published newspapers in 1827 while still in slavery and who had tried petitioning and voting since 1619 had reason to be impatient (246). Yet Hansberry did not automatically distrust whites as do some radical blacks today. An admirer of John Brown, she acknowledged that some of the first and last people to die in the struggle for equal rights were white (247). Basically, however, she remained an "intellectual revolutionary," as we have seen in *Les Blancs*.

Stressing that "we are *one* people . . . the Negro intelligentsia, the Negro middle class, and the Negro this and that," Hansberry stressed that the concept of the "exceptional Negro" was offensive and that "we are represented by the Negroes in the streets of Birmingham!" (229). She also believed that the struggle could not be confined to a traditional or purely religious framework and told an interviewer: "We only revert back to mystical ideas—which includes most contemporary orthodox religious views . . . because we simply are confronted with some things we don't yet understand" (195). As we have seen in *Raisin,* she respected Mama's religious strength, but she believed more fully in self-reliance, in the power of the human spirit. "I rather admire this human quality to make our own crutches as long as we need them. But once we can *walk,* you know, then drop them" (197).

To Hansberry, aggressive political action was necessary to bring about racial equality. Although she knew "shiftless" black men, she knew "*more* men who . . . worked themselves into early graves" (210). The human condition as blacks experienced it concerned her. She anguished over blacks entrapped by poverty and the Ghetto. "In the twentieth century men everywhere like to *breathe;* and the Negro citizen still cannot, you see, *breathe*" (221). She wept for those who were tired. "A Negro says something about 'I'm *tired,* I can't *stand* it no more. I want to hit somebody . . .'" (249). Tired from years of struggle, he might have to strike out to breathe freely.

A romantic realist, an artist fascinated by ordinary people, a political activist—these qualities comprise Lorraine Hansberry, the writer. But the very private personality of Lorraine Hansberry at times surfaces in *To Be Young, Gifted and Black.* A complex and often contradictory woman, she was a powerful, polished speaker, yet sometimes was ashamed of being alone (146). She mourned the death of Ernest Hemingway (143). Especially gracious in answering letters from those who admired her work, she wrote Kenneth Merryman: "I have received . . . I confess, not too many letters from 'a white farm boy living on a rich, fertile farm on the Mason-Dixon line. . . .'" After extensive comments on her work she concludes, "I wish you a happy and rewarding college experience. . . . And—neglect not the arts!" (220–22). In a letter to Madam Chen Jui–Lan, a Chinese woman who had written her, she apologizes for the tardiness of her reply and warmly recognizes the antiquity and richness of Chinese culture (159–60). But in a letter to her own mother, she is tentative and almost childlike: "Mama, it [*Raisin*] is a play that tells the truth about people. Negroes and life. . . . I hope it will make you very proud" (109).

Strongly committed to the idea that her people must be free to breathe freely, she still was consumed by petty fears—of elevators, of hospitals, of bridges, of tunnels. Tearing up twenty pages, sharpening a dozen new pencils, insisting that writing was not a "duty," she took time to train her German shepherd puppy Chaka—named for the great leader of the Zulu peoples. On the most personal level, her love for Robert Nemiroff humanized her theory of romantic realism: "Supposed to get married about September. Spirit: Happy and defiant" (103). And to Nemiroff himself: "I have finally admitted to myself that I *do* love you. . . . YOU ARE NEVER TO FLY AGAIN" (105, 107).

The Published Plays

Embedded in the structure of *To Be Young, Gifted and Black* are excerpts from Hansberry's plays—*A Raisin in the Sun*, *The Sign in Sidney Brustein's Window*, *Les Blancs*, *The Drinking Gourd*, and *What Use Are Flowers?* With few exceptions, Robert Nemiroff chose those scenes and passages that are most dramatic and most closely aligned to black pride. Far from being mere tools of propaganda, they are instruments by which we can examine in some detail the origins and intricacies of black consciousness and black thought.

Ironically enough, *To Be Young, Gifted and Black* contains more passages (twelve in all) from *Sidney Brustein* than from any of the other four published plays. What these passages demonstrate is that her concern is not confined to black people but to modern man and his plight. In the exchanges between Sidney and his wife, Iris, Hansberry examines some of the "evils" of the institution of marriage. They fight about Iris's job, about psychiatry, about ulcers, about Iris's sisters, about money. More important, Sidney is in search of "commitment" and belief. As Hansberry explains, the play deals with "the nature of commitment. It happens to be . . . one of the leading problems before my generation here: what to identify with, what to become involved in; what to take a stand on: what, if you will, even to believe in at all . . ." (168).

Nearly all of the twelve passages from *Brustein* explore modern man's failure to be involved. In a drunken soliloquy Sidney says: "Who am I? Modern man: flat on my back with an oozing intestine, a bit of a tear frozen in the corner of my eye, and not the dimmest notion of what it is all about" (179). But even commitment brings pain as Sidney moans. "I care about it all. It takes too much energy not to care. Yesterday I counted twenty-six gray hairs . . . all from trying not to care." (183). Gloria Parodus, Iris's prostitute sister, poignantly compares her situation to a print of a Goya painting in which a peasant woman is reaching out for the teeth of a man who has just been hanged.

As a young woman of twenty, Lorraine Hansberry had learned an important lesson from Louis Burnham, editor of *Freedom*—that *everything* is political (99). Politics, art, human relationships—all require commitment. In *Raisin*, the struggles of Walter Lee Younger for self-dignity and against racism suggest answers to some of the questions raised by Sidney Brustein.

Of the seven passages from *A Raisin in the Sun*, several deal with Walter Lee Younger's turmoil over his dream of being successful and independent. An early-morning discussion with his wife, Ruth, reveals the warm, loving nature of their marriage as well as the dichotomy between dreams and reality. At the breakfast table, he pokes fun at Ruth: "First thing a man ought to learn in life is not to make love to no colored woman first thing in the morning" (35). As she becomes more preoccupied with eggs, he becomes more serious: "Man say to his woman: I got me a dream. His woman say: eat your eggs. . . . DAMN MY EGGS. . . . DAMN ALL THE EGGS THAT EVER WAS!" (36).

After receiving the $10,000 settlement from his father's life insurance, Walter Lee wants to move his family out of the crowded ghetto, into a white neighborhood with trees and flowers. For a time he is intimidated by the unctuous white Karl Lindner. But finally Walter Lee, standing erect, breaks through to full maturity, to complete manhood, as he refuses Lindner's offer. Representing black heritage and pride in a different way that looks forward to *Les Blancs,* Beneatha dresses in African robes and says to Ruth, "You are looking at what a well-dressed Nigerian woman wears!" (88). She breaks into a frenzied African folk dance and presently Walter Lee, swept up in its spirit, cries out as he leaps upon the table, "AND ETHIOPIA STRETCH FORTH HER ARMS AGAIN! FLAMING SPEAR! HOT DAMN!" (89–91). Ending this lively scene, the black bourgeois George walks in and asks: "Black brother, hell! What is this—a *Mau Mau* meeting?" (93).

Before the Civil War, many southern states had laws that prohibited slaves from learning to read—pernicious policies which Hannibal, in *The Drinking Gourd,* defies. As we have already seen, NBC, which had commissioned the play, never produced it. Some revealing parts of the play, however, found their way into *Young, Gifted and Black*—notably the scene in which Hannibal reveals his newfound knowledge to Sarah:

> *Sarah:*   What you got there? . . . Hannibal . . . Marster find
> you stole that Bible you be in trouble bad!

> *Hannibal*:   Me and you was *born* in trouble with Marster.
>
> *Sarah*:   What you think the Lord think of somebody who would steal the holy book itself?
>
> *Hannibal*:   What you think I would do with a Bible, Sarah? Sarah, I kin read it. I kin. I kin read, Sarah. (55–56)

Later Hannibal simply but forcefully tells Sarah of his bitterness and frustration with the institution of slavery:

> *Sarah*:   We all slaves, Hannibal, but there's some ain't got it so bad, who knows how to bend a little. . . .
>
> *Hannibal*:   Then let'm bend. Me? I am the only kind of slave I could stand to be—a bad one. Every day that come and hour that pass . . . that I can pretend sickness 'stead of health; to be stupid 'stead of smart; lazy 'stead of quick—I aims to do it. And the more pain it give Marster and the more it cost him—the more Hannibal be a *man!* (59)

(At this point in the production of *To Be Young, Gifted and Black* in Tallahassee, Florida, in 1971, the audience rose in a standing ovation.) Unlike stereotypes of the happy slave, eating watermelon, hunting possum, picking banjos on Saturday night, singing on the porch of the cabin, both Sarah and Hannibal reflect the realistic desires of slaves to read, write, think, to be free, to be fully human.

Set in Kenya, *Les Blancs* (The holy ones) is loosely based on the Mau Mau revolution. Of the three scenes from it included in *To Be Young, Gifted and Black,* the most powerful is a discussion between Charlie Morris, the white American journalist, and Tshembe Matoseh, a sophisticated, educated African. Throughout the scene, Charlie has trouble convincing the somewhat cynical Tshembe that he has a genuine, human interest in the African situation. Charlie explains that he is not "one of those obtuse ones who is going to ask you a whole lot of stuff about rituals and lions—" or a pseudointellectual "little magazine type" who wants to discuss "'negritude' and Senghor's poetry" (251).

As their conversation continues, we begin to see Tshembe as a black Sidney Brustein lacking commitment and belief: he has been, in fact, relieved of his duties as commander in the African Liberation Committee for his lack of "passion—for freedom" (254). Despite his seeming apathy, Tshembe says, "I do not hate all white men—but I desperately wish that I did. It would make everything infinitely easier!" (225). In passing, Tshembe mentions the friction between black Africans and black Ameri-

cans, a conflict described by many black writers, including James Baldwin. What surfaces from Tshembe's anger is more basic than lions or
Senghor's poetry: "For a handshake, a grin, a cigarette and half a glass of
whiskey you want three hundred years of oppression to disappear . . ."
(253). He continues to say that "race is a device," as is religion, which
gives one man the excuse to conquer another man. He ends by saying, "A
man who has a sword run through him because he will not become a Mos-
lem or a Christian—or who is lynched in Mississippi or Zatembe because
he is black—is suffering the utter reality of that device of conquest" (256).

Returning to an American setting, Hansberry writes a simple story (almost a parable) in *What Use Are Flowers?* Set during the aftermath of an
atomic holocaust, the play centers on the Hermit and his efforts to imbue
a group of nearly wild children with humane values. The three scenes of
Flowers contained in *Young, Gifted and Black* form an outline of the play as
a whole.

Almost eighty, the Hermit returns to civilization to learn what men
have been doing in the past twenty years, saying, "I am afraid men invent
time*pieces;* they do not invent time" (34). Reminiscent of Thoreau's leaving
Walden because he had "other lives to lead," the Hermit explains: "One of
the reasons I left is because I could no longer stand the dominion of time
in the lives of men and the things they did with it . . ." (33). Knowing
that he will soon die, he is searching for some meaningful last action. By
chance, the Hermit meets the survivors of the holocaust, the children, who
are predictable products of a mechanized age. They have little difficulty
understanding "use" or utility and concrete objects, but they are perplexed
by abstractions and ideals. The climax of the play occurs when one child
asks, "What use are flowers?" The Hermit responds:

> What *use* are flowers? Ah, but the uses of flowers
>   are infinite! one may smell them—
> One may touch their petals and feel heaven—
> Or one may write quite charming verses about them. . . . (173)

When the boy then asks the old man the use of music, the Hermit delight-
edly leads the children in singing and exclaims, "Tomorrow—Beethoven's
Ninth!" (175).

Having completed his mission, the Hermit is prepared to die and must
try to explain the most real of abstractions to them. He says to the young
boy Charlie, "I do not want flowers, music, or poetry. You want to know
why? Well, because you are *human*" (260). Having exposed the children to

the ideal, he must now reeducate them in the real, as he explains that his body "shall begin to exude a horrid odor." But the ideal and real begin to merge as he smiles slightly at Charlie: "Well, put a stone over my head and come and spend hours there pretending to have dialogues with me and you will feel better. It won't mean a thing to me, but you will feel better" (262).

The Unpublished Works

American literature will surely be richer when Robert Nemiroff publishes Lorraine Hansberry's unpublished works. The legacy includes some of her high-school and college work; about twenty sketches and short stories; several hundred pages, in various stages of completion, of the novel *All the Dark and Beautiful Warriors*; twenty or so pages of an unfinished play, *Toussaint*; and various other working notes. Unfortunately, some of the early works—childhood and adolescent writings, high-school and college papers—were lost in a shipping crate when Mamie and her mother moved to California in the early 1960s.[9] Robert Nemiroff includes portions of the novel and the play in *Young, Gifted and Black.*

All the Dark and Beautiful Warriors contains two interlocking plots, one of which is loosely autobiographical. The protagonist of one plot is a young sharecropper, who comes to the South Side of Chicago to seek his fortune, like many blacks from the 1920s to the 1950s. The heroine of the other plot is a young woman, born and reared in Chicago by her affluent family. At one point, she attends a university modeled on the University of Wisconsin. The lives of the two characters intertwine at several points in their youth; eventually they meet in New York and both become involved in the "movement." In various drafts, the heroine has different names—Susan Housefield, Sidney Wallingham, Eve—but finally emerges as Candace Braithewaite.[10] (In one of her scrapbooks, Mamie Hansberry Mitchell has a photo of former Congresswoman Yvonne Braithewaite Burke as a young woman posing with the Hansberry family, but according to Robert Nemiroff, the character is in no way based upon her.) Clearly, though, the heroine of the novel is partly based on Lorraine Hansberry herself. Monasse, an Ethiopian student, is probably based on one of the young African men Hansberry knew at Wisconsin.[11]

In *Young, Gifted and Black,* one dramatized scene opens as Monasse, the African student, is talking on the snowy campus with Candace, a rather liberated young woman. The stage directions explain that Candace is despairing over South Africa and fantasizes that Monasse is an African prince, "one gorgeous black knight-without-armor" (85). Hansberry carefully establishes Monasse's deep devotion to Ethiopian culture and language as he painstakingly pronounces again and again *Netsannet ahun* ("freedom now") for Candace, who distractedly asks, "What are we going to do about South Africa?" Proud and dignified, Monasse is horrified when Candace explains that one of her unmarried friends is pregnant and plans to have the baby. In many ways, the relationship between Candace and Monasse parallels that of Beneatha and Asagai in *A Raisin in the Sun*. Both Monasse and Asagai are serious African students in America fascinated by the liberated young women, Candace and Beneatha.

All the Dark and Beautiful Warriors is probably something of a portrait of the artist as a young woman. *Toussaint,* an unfinished play about the Haitian liberator Toussaint L'Ouverture, is a very different work. Considering *Toussaint* her "epic," Hansberry wrote, "I intend to depart from the traditional canonization of historical heroes, and try . . . to write a man— and yet, at the same time, not to lose the wonder of his magnitude" (138). Dissatisfied with earlier treatments of the liberation of Haiti, which focused on the exoticism of Voodoo rites, the tropical charm of the island, and the compelling powers of Toussaint, Hansberry sought to portray Toussaint as a master of diplomacy and politics, an uneducated but brilliant man, a foe who terrified Napoleon.

Born in 1743 to Gau-Guinou, son of an African king, Toussaint occupied a favored position in his master's household from childhood on because of his superior intellect and talents. Self-disciplined, self-contained, and schooled in a smattering of French, Latin, geometry, and Roman Catholic doctrine, Toussaint became overseer of livestock (a position usually reserved for whites) as a young man, and later an overseer of slaves.

Santo Domingo was a near-paradise, rich in coffee, cotton, and sugar cane. (The French had wrested control of the island from the Spaniards in 1659.) But the wealth of the island was sustained by the hard labor of the black slaves, imported from Africa as early as 1517. Despite the enactment of the Negro Code in 1685 which guaranteed free blacks and mulattoes the rights to property and interracial marriage, the plight of the blacks had become bleak by the mid-1700s.

Toussaint's position gave him special opportunities to be aware of the abuse of the slaves by their French masters. Slaves were forced to work sixteen to eighteen hours per day; they lived in dirty, cramped quarters; they were beaten and sometimes bodily mutilated; families were separated needlessly; most slaves could not read.[12] In 1791 he began to lead bloody slave insurrections, but after four months he decided to try more sophisticated methods. A master diplomat and tactician, he began negotiating with the English for aid, but deserted them in 1793 when they began war with France. Changing his loyalties to the Spanish in 1793, Toussaint switched back to the French Revolutionary government, which abolished slavery in 1794.

Appointed lieutenant governor and major general of Santo Domingo, Toussaint then spent nine of his twelve years in power trying to restructure the government of the country, to educate the ex-slaves, and to restore the agricultural base of the economy. Traveling among the people, he impressed on them the dignity of work, the value of education and religion, and the acceptance and forgiveness of whites. By 1796, Toussaint's word was law. All this time, he was quietly and skillfully urging the French government to grant independence to Santo Domingo. Never completely trusting anyone except his beloved friend Laveaux, he worked tirelessly, sometimes sleeping only two hours a night. Unable to write French correctly, he worked with his white personal advisors to produce masterpieces of diplomatic statements and formulated military policy with his predominantly black generals.

But during the next five years, Toussaint could no longer maintain this double role as friend of the people and diplomat to Europe. Napoleon had become a particular foe of Toussaint. By 1801, Toussaint had lost touch with the common man and Napoleon had come to power in France. In 1802 Napoleon had Toussaint captured and confined to jail, where he died in 1803. Had he lived one year longer, he would have witnessed the independence of Santo Domingo and the emergence of the free country of Haiti.

Taking artistic license, Hansberry sets *Toussaint* in 1780 rather than in the historical 1791, perhaps to avoid having to deal with the French Revolution. But even her fragmentary picture of Toussaint reveals her admiration for the power and personality of the man. A conversation between Bayon, a French plantation manager in Haiti, and Lucie, his Creole mistress, reveals the respect that whites had for Toussaint. In the manner of classic drama, Hansberry introduces the hero by the chatter of minor characters.

Lucie: Who is your Toussaint having punished now?

Bayon: Simon is being whipped.

Lucie: Toussaint is a brute.

Bayon: He is a steward and an excellent one.

Lucie: Do you think he gets pleasure from it?

Bayon: Oh, of course, he does.

Lucie: Personally—I don't think so. I have watched his merciless
           ways with the slaves—and I saw no pleasure in it. (140)

In *Toussaint* no character is stereotyped: Bayon is the most loyal and
unquestioning of Frenchmen; Lucie is an intuitive, humane woman. Yet
even they discuss profound questions.

Lucie: Tell me—what is freedom, Bayon de Bergier?

Bayon: That is an abstraction that no one can answer. Least of all,
           these days, a Frenchman. (143)

In this single scene from *Toussaint* contained in *To Be Young, Gifted and
Black*, Hansberry emphasizes the well-intended triviality of the French rulers in Haiti. As the play opens, Bayon is more distressed at having lost his
garters than at hearing the painful cries of the black slaves. Even the sympathetic Lucie is oblivious at first to the beating as she says to Bayon, "If
you were a true gentleman you would have someone dress you" (140). By
carefully establishing the atmosphere with specific details, Hansberry then
sets the stage for the violent revolution that follows, for the majestic rise
and the tragic fall of Toussaint.

Of the two fragments from the unfinished works, *Toussaint* is more significant and moving than *All the Dark and Beautiful Warriors*, for the *Toussaint* fragment was a more mature work that was apparently intended as a
genuine tragedy. Yet the two reveal the continuity of concerns in her brief
career—above all, an overriding concern with black liberation that does
not preclude sympathy for whites.

Other Voices

Wandering across the campus one day, Lorraine Hansberry strolled into
the theater at the University of Wisconsin. In the darkened auditorium,
she became mesmerized by the play in rehearsal: *Juno and the Paycock* by
Sean O'Casey. In *To Be Young, Gifted and Black*, she writes: "The woman's
voice, the howl, the shriek of misery fitted to a wail of poetry that consumed all my senses and all my awareness of human pain, endurance and
the futility of it—" (87). The one excerpt from *Juno* contained in *Young*,

Gifted and Black provides only a hint of the enormous mark that O'Casey left on her work.

Disdaining the intellectualism of continental drama, Sean O'Casey chose to saturate his plays with local color, religion, politics, and Irish idiom. Written in 1924, *Juno and the Paycock* is set very specifically in 1922 in Dublin and concerns the Boyles, a lower-middle-class family. In much the same manner thirty-nine years later, Hansberry wrote *A Raisin in the Sun* about a South Side Chicago family, in which Mama adhered to traditional Christianity and Walter finally realized the possibilities of self-attainment. Despite the basically serious nature of both plays, both playwrights are careful to include the laughter and joy of their people: perhaps a mark of a minority culture is that everyone laughs at the same jokes.

Robert Nemiroff says that Hansberry loved O'Casey for his ability to tell the awful truth about his characters and still love them.[13] Certainly *Juno and the Paycock* fuses many contradictory aspects of humanity: comedy and tragedy, religion and antireligion, politics (Hansberry would say commitment) and apathy, the petty and the sublime. Almost a manifesto of Irish race and religion, *Juno and the Paycock* served Hansberry well as a model for her own plays about blacks in America and Africa.

As the play opens, Juno Boyle is waiting for her husband, "Captain" Jack Boyle, to return from his morning's visit to the pub and is discussing the death of Robbie Tancred, a fanatic Irish Republican, with her daughter Mary. Captain Jack returns with his ne'er-do-well friend "Joxer" Daly, and the son Johnny Boyle skulks about, disdainful of family trivia. Having been shot in the hip and having lost an arm while fighting against the Free State, he says to Juno, "I'd do it agen, Ma, I'd do it agen; for a principle's a principle."

Act 2 becomes a frightening combination of comedy and tragedy. As Mrs. Madigan, a generous but vulgar and forward neighbor, comes to visit the Boyle family, they begin a midday party with jokes, drinks, and genial lies. At the same time, the funeral procession for the martyr Robbie Tancred is passing on the street below. Urging them to join the mourners, Mrs. Tancred delivers an unrelieved wail of grief: "O Blessed Virgin, where were you when me darlin' son was riddled with bullets. . . . Sacred Heart of the Crucified Jesus, take away our hearts o' stone . . ." (87).

Act 3 signals the downfall of the entire family. Their furniture is repossessed; unknown to Captain Jack, Joxer betrays him; the daughter Mary is deserted by her lover and learns that she is pregnant; Johnny is disgraced and demands that Mary be thrown out of the house. But all these domestic dilemmas fade into nothingness when we learn that Johnny, suspected of betraying the martyr Robbie Tancred, has been killed. Juno then breaks into the same litany that rose to the lips of Mrs. Tancred in act 2.

What was the pain I suffered, Johnny, bringin' you into the world to carry you to your cradle, to the pains I'll suffer carryin' you out o' the world to bring you to your grave! Mother o' God, Mother o' God, have pity on us all! Blessed Virgin, where were you when me darlin' son was riddled with bullets, when me darlin' son was riddled with bullets? Sacred Heart o' Jesus, take away your hearts o' stone, and give us hearts o' flesh. Take away this murdherin' hate, an' give us Thine own eternal love!

But Juno Boyle knows that there is no comfort to be found in her religion, her Catholicism. Leaving home forever, she takes with her Mary, who can bear her child in love and peace. As *Juno* ends, the Captain and Joxer engage in drunken talk and song.

Lorraine Hansberry owed Sean O'Casey a considerable debt. Although only one passage from *Juno and the Paycock* is included in *Young, Gifted and Black,* Juno's wail symbolizes the impotence of religion, the love of family, the brutality and necessity of political involvement, the nature of survival itself.

The form of Hansberry's plays is conventional twentieth-century social drama. In their content, the plays break new ground. Of all the playwrights who might have provided models, O'Casey—chronicler of the Irish struggle for freedom and its costs—most influenced Hansberry's representations of black (and occasionally white) struggles on the American stage. Her permanent debt to O'Casey, like the total pattern of her short career, becomes clear in the book *To Be Young, Gifted and Black*—and the play which is, ironically, more innovative in form than any of the works of the young woman to whom it is both a memorial and an introduction.

Conclusion: Hansberry's Place in American Drama

In the twentieth century, America has produced three major playwrights: Tennessee Williams, Arthur Miller, and Eugene O'Neill. There have also been talented dramatists of the second order: Thornton Wilder, Edward Albee, and Lillian Hellman. Especially since the 1950s, with the advent of television, America has not been notably supportive of drama: the flick of the dial requires less energy than dressing for the theater. Nevertheless, Tennessee Williams has brilliantly probed the southern family—in dramas such as *Cat on a Hot Tin Roof* and *A Streetcar Named Desire*—

with more artistry but no less popular appeal than Lorraine Hansberry's rendering of the black family in *A Raisin in the Sun.*

In 1966 David Littlejohn wrote, "One would not be unfair in dating the emergence of a serious and mature Negro theater in America from 1959, the date of Lorraine Hansberry's *A Raisin in the Sun.*" Littlejohn is correct: Hansberry is our best black playwright. America has also made *Raisin* one of the most popular plays of our time.

The crux of the matter, then, remains Hansberry's ranking as a modern American dramatist. She compared *Raisin* to Miller's *Death of a Salesman*—certainly sensible in terms of character and theme. But the truest test of an exceptional writer is his or her *style* (after all, there are a finite number of plots and characters). There was little of the prosaic in Lorraine Hansberry's style; at its best, it vibrated with poetry (hence, her debt to Langston Hughes). In *Brustein* and *Les Blancs,* however, her "talkiness" fell far short of the exceptional style of Williams and Miller. Nonetheless, in 1959 the New York Drama Critics' Circle deemed *A Raisin in the Sun* superior to Williams's *Sweet Bird of Youth.*

Avoiding facile arguments of what a more timely death would have wrought, Lorraine Hansberry stands firmly in the very respectable ranks of Edward Albee, Lillian Hellman, and Thornton Wilder. The duality of her life—the conflict between upper-middle-class influence and black heritage and revolution—produced creative tension, which led to compelling works. Her literary legacy includes five plays (and one additional posthumous play), which span two continents and three centuries. She told her audiences as she told her sister Mamie, "You're good."

Notes and References

Chapter One

1. Interview with Mamie Hansberry Mitchell (sister of Lorraine Hansberry), Marina del Rey, California, December 30, 1975.

2. *To Be Young, Gifted and Black* (New York, 1970), pp. 46–48.

3. Interview with Mamie Hansberry Mitchell, Marina del Rey, California, January 2, 1976. All subsequent references to Mitchell interviews refer to this date, unless otherwise noted.

4. Robert Nemiroff report, September 1982.

5. Mamie Hansberry Mitchell interview.

6. *Young, Gifted and Black,* pp. 48–49.

7. Ibid., p. 50.

8. Mamie Hansberry Mitchell interview.

9. *Young, Gifted and Black,* pp. 63–65.

10. Ibid., p. 63.

11. Robert Nemiroff report, September 1982.

12. "Talk of the Town," *New Yorker,* May 9, 1959, p. 34.

13. Robert Nemiroff interview, Croton-on-Hudson, New York, June 13, 1978. All subsequent references are to the Nemiroff interview on this date, unless otherwise noted.

14. "Talk of the Town," *New Yorker,* p. 34.

15. In his September 1982 report, Nemiroff writes of the entire "brick through the window" episode: "Who knows which part had the greatest impact on the child—the brick? the mother sitting up nights with a gun? the incidents to and from school? the father away in Washington? the fact that the cops did not defend the home but that blacks had to come from outside to do so? the fact that the family was then evicted by the Supreme Court of Illinois?"

16. *Young, Gifted and Black,* p. 51.

17. Ibid., p. 63.

18. Ibid., p. 61.

19. Ibid., p. 48.

20. Ibid., p. 67.

21. Ibid., p. 69.

22. Mamie Hansberry Mitchell interview.

23. "The Origins of Character," paper read to the American Academy of Psychotherapists, August 5, 1963. Excerpts published as "Playwriting: Creative Constructiveness," *Annals of Psychotherapy* (Monograph 8, *The Creative Use of the Unconscious by the Artist and by the Psychotherapist*) 5, no. 1 (1964):13–17.

24. Faye Hammell, "A Playwright, A Promise," *Cue,* February 28, 1959, p. 20.

25. *New Yorker,* p. 34.

26. Hammell, "A Playwright," p. 20.

27. Robert Nemiroff interview.

28. W. E. B. DuBois, *The Souls of Black Folks* (New York: New American Library, 1969), pp. 79–95.

29. Nathan Irvin Huggins, *Harlem Renaissance* (New York: Oxford University Press, 1971), p. 49.

30. Mamie Hansberry Mitchell interview.

31. Ibid.

32. Huggins, *Harlem Renaissance,* p. 29.

33. Ibid., p. 203.

34. Arna Bontemps, ed., *American Negro Poetry* (New York: Hill & Wang, 1963), pp. 61–67.

35. Philip S. Foner, ed., *Paul Robeson Speaks: Writings, Speeches, Interviews, 1918–1974* (New York: Brunner/Mazel, 1978), p. 34.

36. Robert Nemiroff report, September 1982.

37. All biographical details from "Paul Robeson," *Current Biography* (New York: H. W. Wilson, 1976), pp. 345–47.

38. Mamie Hansberry Mitchell interview.

39. *New Yorker,* p. 34.

40. Mamie Hansberry Mitchell interview.

41. *Young, Gifted and Black,* pp. 50–51.

42. *New Yorker,* p. 34.

43. Ibid.

44. Mamie Hansberry Mitchell interview.

45. Unpublished, undated memoirs (property of Robert Nemiroff).

46. William Leo Hansberry, "Inaugural Address," delivered at the Hansberry College of African Studies of the University of Nigeria, September 22, 1963 (compliments of Viking Press), p. 27.

47. Ibid., pp. 13, 23, 25.

48. *Young, Gifted and Black,* p. 68.

49. Robert Nemiroff said in an interview that Lorraine Hansberry did not want the social life *or* the racial segregation of Howard. He also said she was refused a dormitory room at Wisconsin because she was black. In addition, she entered at an inconvenient time of year, February.

50. Catherine Scheader, *They Found a Way: Lorraine Hansberry* (Chicago, 1978), p. 32.

51. *Young, Gifted and Black,* p. 102.

52. Ibid., p. 72.

53. Scheader, *They Found a Way,* p. 29.

54. "People Are Talking About . . . ," *Vogue,* July 1959, p. 79.

55. *Young, Gifted and Black,* pp. 86–87.

56. Scheader, *They Found a Way,* p. 31.

57. *Young, Gifted and Black,* pp. 73–74.
58. *New Yorker,* pp. 34–35.
59. Ibid., p. 35.
60. Robert Nemiroff interview.
61. *Young, Gifted and Black,* p. 81.
62. Robert Nemiroff, "A Critical Background," in *Lorraine Hansberry: The Collected Last Plays* (New York, 1983), p. 28.
63. Ibid.
64. *Young, Gifted and Black,* p. 75.
65. Mamie Hansberry Mitchell interview.
66. Robert Nemiroff interview.
67. *Young, Gifted and Black,* pp. 76–85.

Chapter Two

1. *Young, Gifted and Black,* pp. 95–96.
2. Philip S. Foner, *Paul Robeson Speaks* (New York: Brunner/Mazel, 1978), p. 39.
3. Robert Nemiroff interview.
4. *Young, Gifted and Black,* p. 97.
5. Robert Nemiroff interview.
6. Robert Nemiroff report, September 1982.
7. *Freedom,* June 1953, pp. 6–7.
8. *Freedom,* April 1953, pp. 1, 4.
9. Ibid., p. 4.
10. "McCarthy Bans Books That Honor Negroes," *Freedom,* January 1954, p. 2.
11. Harold Cruse, *The Crisis of the Negro Intellectual* (New York, 1967), pp. 227–38.
12. Obviously, the elephant is the white European; the man is the black African.
13. Hansberry, "Kenya's Kikuyus: A Peaceful People Wage Struggle Against British," *Freedom,* December 1952, p. 3.
14. Robert Nemiroff interview, June 14, 1978.
15. Hansberry, "Gold Coast's Rulers Go, Ghana Moves to Freedom," *Freedom,* December 1951, p. 2.
16. Hansberry and Stan Steiner, "Cry for Colonial Freedom Jostles Phony Youth Meet," *Freedom,* September 1951, p. 6.
17. Hansberry, "Women Voice Demands in Capital Sojourn," *Freedom,* October 1951, p. 6.
18. Hansberry, "Old Timers' Eyes Grow Misty Recalling Florence Mills," *Freedom,* July 1952, p. 7.
19. Hansberry, "Why the Drum-Beaters Fear Roosevelt Ward," *Freedom,* August 1951, p. 2.

20. Hansberry, "Noted Lawyer Goes to Jail: Says Negroes' Fight for Rights Menaced," *Freedom,* May 1952, p. 3.

21. Robert Nemiroff interview, June 14, 1978.

22. Hansberry, "NLC Rights Job Bias in N.Y. Hotels," *Freedom,* March 1953, pp. 1, 9.

23. Hansberry, "Harlem Children Face Mass Ignorance in Old, Overcrowded, Understaffed Schools," *Freedom,* November 1952, p. 3.

24. Hansberry, "Life Challenges Negro Youth," *Freedom,* March 1955, p. 7.

25. Hansberry, "Child Labor is Society's Crime against Youth," *Freedom,* February 1955, p. 2.

26. Robert Nemiroff considers this trip a key event in her life.

27. Hansberry, "Illegal Conference Shows Peace is Key to Freedom," *Freedom,* April 1952, p. 3.

28. Robert Nemiroff interview, June 15, 1978.

29. Hansberry, "No More Hiroshimas," *Freedom,* May–June 1955, p. 7.

30. "Frederick Douglass School Opens Its Doors in Harlem," *Freedom,* March 1952, p. 2.

31. Mamie Hansberry Mitchell interview.

32. Ibid.

33. Robert Nemiroff report, September 1982.

34. Robert Nemiroff interview, June 13, 1978.

35. No one seems to recall who Rick was.

36. Mamie Hansberry Mitchell interview.

37. Robert Nemiroff recalls that, had the families not made such elaborate preparations, he and Hansberry would have postponed the wedding. They had spent the preceding day, June 19, picketing the Chicago Federal Building in protest of the execution of Julius and Ethyl Rosenberg which took place that night— despite considerable public outcry. Nevertheless, Hansberry and Nemiroff went ahead with the wedding as planned. They spent the night of June 20 at a family friend's home and then drove back to New York where their jobs awaited. Several weeks later, they were able to go on a honeymoon (Robert Nemiroff report, September 1982).

38. Mamie Hansberry Mitchell interview.

39. Robert Nemiroff interview, June 13, 1978.

40. Ibid.

41. Mamie Hansberry Mitchell interview.

42. Robert Nemiroff interview, June 13, 1978.

43. Ted Poston, "We Have So Much to Say," *New York Post,* March 22, 1959, p. M2.

44. Mamie Hansberry Mitchell interview.

45. Robert Nemiroff, introduction to *Young, Gifted and Black,* p. xix.

46. Mamie Hansberry Mitchell interview.

47. Ibid.

48. Interview on *Tony Brown's Journal,* February 19, 1978.

49. Mamie Hansberry Mitchell interview.

50. *Current Biography,* pp. 166–67.

51. Robert Nemiroff interview.

52. Robert Nemiroff report, September 1982.

53. Mamie Hansberry Mitchell interview.

54. Robert Nemiroff interview, June 15, 1972.

55. Robert Nemiroff, preface to "The Negro Writer and His Roots: Toward a New Romanticism," unpublished paper (property of Robert Nemiroff).

56. Poston, "We Have So Much to Say," p. M2.

57. Mamie Hansberry Mitchell interview.

58. Robert Nemiroff report, September 1982.

59. Unpublished screenplay, October 1959.

60. Robert Nemiroff report, September 1982.

61. "The New Paternalists," unpublished paper, 1961 (property of Robert Nemiroff).

62. Ibid.

63. "Miss Hansberry Divorced 10 Months Before Death," *New York Times,* February 5, 1965, p. 36.

64. Robert Nemiroff, "A Critical Background," in *Lorraine Hansberry: The Collected Last Plays,* pp. 147, 31–32, 223.

65. Robert Nemiroff believes that Lorraine Hansberry did not know she was dying.

66. Lorraine Hansberry et al., "The Negro in American Culture," in *The Black American Writer: Fiction,* ed. C. W. E. Bigsby (DeLand, Fla.: Everett/Edwards, 1969), p. 81.

67. Mamie Hansberry Mitchell interview.

68. Robert Nemiroff, "The 101 'Final' Performances of *Sidney Brustein*: Portrait of a Play and Its Author," in *Lorraine Hansberry's "A Raisin in the Sun" and "The Sign in Sidney Brustein's Window"* (New York, 1966), pp. 156–61.

69. Ibid., pp. 167–75.

70. Mamie Hansberry Mitchell interview.

71. Robert Nemiroff, "101 Performances," p. 157.

72. Ibid., p. 155.

73. "600 Attend Hansberry Rites; Paul Robeson Delivers Eulogy," *New York Times,* January 17, 1965, p. 88. (Robert Nemiroff finds this account erroneous in part. Wherever possible, I have incorporated his changes.)

74. Robert Nemiroff interview.

75. Robert Nemiroff believes that Lorraine Hansberry sought not merely reforms, but fundamental changes in the socioeconomic system.

Chapter Three

1. Frederick Douglass, *Narrative of the Life of Frederick Douglass, An American Slave* (Boston: Anti-Slavery Office, 1845; reprint, Garden City, N.Y.: Doubleday, 1963), pp. 14–15.

2. Ibid., pp. 26–27, 48–49.

3. Ibid. (1845), pp. 1–2, 5–6, 35, 36.

4. Ibid. (1845), p. 36.

5. Ibid., pp. 33, 37.

6. Ibid., pp. 58–59, 68, 72–74.

7. Philip S. Foner, ed., *The Life and Writings of Frederick Douglass* (New York: International Publishers, 1950), 1:25–26, 59, 67, 82.

8. Ibid., 1:320–21; 2:172–73, 206–09, 284–88, 311, 316, 458–60, 502–17.

9. John W. Blassingame, *Frederick Douglass: The Clarion Voice* (Washington, D.C.: U.S. Department of the Interior, 1976),p. 47.

10. Douglass, *Narrative,* pp. 66–67.

11. Robert Nemiroff report, September 1982.

12. W. E. B. DuBois, *The Autobiography of W. E. B. DuBois: A Soliloquy on Viewing My Life from the Last Decade of Its First Century* (New York: International Publishers, 1968), pp. 61–75, 88–92, 101.

13. Ibid., p. 93.

14. Ibid., p. 75.

15. Ibid., p. 102.

16. Ibid., pp. 107–8.

17. Julius Lester, ed., *The Seventh Son: The Thought and Writings of W. E. B. DuBois* (New York: Random House, 1971), 2:50.

18. DuBois, *Autobiography,* p. 253.

19. Lester, ed., *Seventh Son,* 2:3.

20. Ibid., 2:722.

21. Ibid., 1:385–403.

22. Ibid., 1:391.

23. Ibid., 1:46.

24. W. E. B. DuBois, *Black Folk: Then and Now, An Essay in the History and Sociology of the Negro Race* (New York: Henry Holt, 1939), pp. vii, ix.

25. Ibid., pp. 14, 119, 126–28.

26. Ibid., p. 32.

27. Robert Nemiroff report, September 1982.

28. Saunders Redding, introduction to *The Souls of Black Folk,* by W. E. B. DuBois (Greenwich, Conn.: Fawcett Paperbacks, 1961), p. ix.

29. Robert Nemiroff report, September 1982.

30. Hansberry, "Tributes," *Freedomways,* 5, no. 1 (Winter 1965):17.

31. Paul Robeson, Jr., telephone interview, New York, New York, July 5, 1979.

32. Foner, ed., *Paul Robeson Speaks,* pp. 11–20.

33. Paul Robeson, *Here I Stand* (New York: Othello Press, 1958; reprint, Boston: Beacon Press, 1971), p. 100.

34. Ibid., pp. 6–16.

35. Ibid., pp. 16–20.

36. Ibid., pp. 24–27.
37. Foner, ed., *Paul Robeson Speaks*, pp. 10–11. (*Current Biography* errs in both the date—it cites 1938—and the plot of *Song of Freedom*.)
38. Paul Robeson, Jr., interview.
39. Foner, ed., *Paul Robeson Speaks*, p. 35.
40. Ibid., p. 24.
41. Cruse, "Lorraine Hansberry," p. 295.
42. Robeson, *Here I Stand*, p. 40.
43. Foner, ed., *Paul Robeson Speaks*, p. 37.
44. Ibid., pp. 4, 36–39, 42, 543–45.
45. Ibid., pp. 43–45.
46. Hansberry, "Pulse of the Peoples 1954: A Cultural Salute to Paul Robeson," unpublished script staged in New York City, May 26, 1954.
47. James S. Haskins, *Always Movin' On: The Life of Langston Hughes* (New York: Franklin Watts, 1976), pp. 22–24.
48. Bontemps, ed., *American Negro Poetry*, p. 63.
49. Richard Ellman and Robert O'Clair, eds., *The Norton Anthology of Modern Poetry* (New York: W. W. Norton, 1973), p. 634.
50. Ibid., p. 635.
51. Huggins, *Harlem Renaissance*, pp. 9–10.
52. Haskins, *Always Movin' On*, pp. 1–6, 97.
53. Ibid., pp. 10–17.
54. Ibid., pp. 19–32.
55. Ibid., pp. 52, 59–70.
56. Ibid., pp. 98–99.
57. Ellman and O'Clair, *Norton Anthology*, p. 639.
58. Haskins, *Always Movin' On*, p. 108.
59. *Young, Gifted and Black*, p. 256.
60. Robert Nemiroff report, September 1982.
61. *Young, Gifted and Black*, p. 257.
62. Ibid., p. 236.

Chapter Four

1. *Young, Gifted and Black*, p. 109.
2. Robert Nemiroff, "Lorraine Hansberry Biography," unpublished paper.
3. David Littlejohn, *Black on White: A Critical Survey of Writings by American Negroes* (New York: Grossman Publishers, 1966), p. 79.
4. *A Raisin in the Sun* (New York: Signet, 1966), p. 65; hereafter cited in the text.
5. Cruse, *Crisis*, p. 278.
6. *Young, Gifted and Black*, p. 75.
7. A. Adu Boahen, "Kingdoms of West Africa," in *History of Africa* (New York: McGraw-Hill, 1971), pp. 177–88.

8. Harold Issacs, "Five Writers and their African Ancestors, Part II," *Phylon* 21 (Winter 1960):330.

9. Lorraine Hansberry in interview with Studs Terkel, Chicago, May 2, 1959.

10. Robert Nemiroff interview, Croton-on-Hudson, New York, September 20, 1972.

11. Mamie Hansberry Mitchell interview, Marina del Rey, California, December 31, 1975.

12. *Lorraine Hansberry Speaks Out* (Caedmon Records, 1960), side 1.

13. "Origins of Character."

14. Robert Nemiroff interview, Croton-on-Hudson, New York, June 14, 1978.

15. "Origins of Character."

16. "Letter to the Editor," *Theater,* August 1959, p. 10.

17. Scheader, *They Found a Way,* p. 47.

18. See Terkel interview; Patricia Marx interview; letter to Mrs. Osthoff, February 2, 1962; Lorraine Hansberry, "Willy Loman, Walter Younger, and He Who Must Live," *Village Voice,* August 12, 1959, pp. 7–8.

19. "Willy Loman," pp. 7–8.

20. Eugene D. Genovese, *Roll, Jordan, Roll: The World the Slaves Made* (New York: Random House, 1976), pp. 485–90.

Chapter Five

1. Richard Gilman, review of *The Sign in Sidney Brustein's Window, Newsweek,* October 21, 1964, pp. 101–2.

2. *The Sign in Sidney Brustein's Window* (New York: New American Library, 1966), p. 189; hereafter cited in the text.

3. Robert Nemiroff believes that in Hansberry's view Freudian analysis, as it is customarily practiced, does not sufficiently aspire to *change* the individual but to help him or her *accept* the personality as it is. I do not agree.

4. Robert Nemiroff says that Lorraine Hansberry regarded Iris's Golden Girl job as a failure.

5. Robert Nemiroff interview, June 14, 1978.

6. "Origins of Character."

7. Here, Hansberry also refers to a childhood ritual whereby Mamie would wash her younger sister's "little fishes hands" (Robert Nemirooff interview, Croton-on-Hudson, New York, June 15, 1978).

8. Robert Nemiroff report, September 1982.

9. Max Lerner, "Limbo Plays," *New York Post,* November 2, 1964, p. 53.

10. Rex Reed, "The Curtain Opens," *New York Express,* October 29, 1964, p. 10.

11. Martin Gottfried, *Women's Wear Daily,* October 16, 1964, p. 21.

12. Howard Taubman, *New York Times,* October 16, 1964, p. 32.

13. Robert Nemiroff report, September 1982.

14. Taubman, *New York Times,* p. 32.

15. Robert Nemiroff report, September 1982.

16. Emory Lewis, *Stages: The Fifty-Year Childhood of the American Theatre* (Englewood Cliffs, N.J., 1969), p. xii.

17. Lewis, *Stages,* p. xii.

18. Lionel Mitchell, "Splendid Hansberry Revival at RACCA," *New York Amsterdam News,* February 2, 1980, p. 22.

19. Taubman, *New York Times,* p. 32.

20. Julius Lester, "The Politics of Caring," *Village Voice,* May 28, 1970, p. 46.

21. Mitchell, "Splendid Hansberry Revival," p. 22.

22. Brooks Atkinson, "Of Plays and Novels," *Saturday Review,* December 31, 1966, p. 27.

Chapter Six

1. *Lorraine Hansberry: The Collected Last Plays,* pp. 31–33; hereafter cited in the text.

2. Clive Barnes, *New York Times,* November 16, 1970, p. 48.

3. Donald L. Barnett and Karari Njama, *Man from Within* (New York: Monthly Review Press, 1966), pp. 31–32.

4. Ibid., pp. 36–43.

5. George Shepperson, "Under Colonial Rule," in *The Horizon History of Africa* (New York: McGraw-Hill, 1971), p. 461.

6. Barnett and Njama, *Man From Within,* pp. 37–39.

7. Ibid., pp. 53–55.

8. Shepperson, "Under Colonial Rule," p. 493.

9. John S. Mbiti, *Concepts of God in Africa* (New York: Praeger, 1970), pp. 104–5.

10. Ibid., p. 102.

11. Ibid., p. 101.

12. Ibid.

13. Ibid., p. 98.

14. Robert Nemiroff report, June 1983.

15. Mbiti, *Concepts of God,* p. 106.

16. Ibid., p. 153.

17. Jeremy Murray-Brown, *Kenyatta* (New York: E. P. Dutton, 1973), pp. 209–21.

18. Ibid., pp. 212–14, 246–49.

19. Barnett and Njama, *Man from Within,* pp. 73–75.

20. For an interesting account of the critics' reception of *Les Blancs,* see Nemiroff 's comments in *Les Blancs: The Collected Last Plays of Lorraine Hansberry,* pp. 173–83.

21. Genovese, *Roll, Jordan, Roll*, p. 69.

22. Ibid., pp. 67–68.

23. For a perceptive discussion of Stowe's "Unconscious Impulses" in *Uncle Tom's Cabin,* see Anne Rowe's *The Enchanted Country: Northern Writers in the South, 1865–1910* (Baton Rouge: Louisiana State University Press, 1978), pp. 1–21.

24. Nemiroff, "A Critical Introduction," in *Lorraine Hansberry: The Collected Last Plays,* p. 146.

25. Genovese, *Roll, Jordan, Roll*, pp. 22–25.

26. All pertinent facts and figures tally with those of Eugene D. Genovese in his landmark study of slavery, *Roll, Jordan, Roll.*

27. *Young, Gifted and Black,* p. 163.

28. This version of the lullaby varies slightly from Eric Bentley's first translation of *Mother Courage and Her Children* in 1953.

29. Nemiroff, "A Critical Background," pp. 225–26.

Chapter Seven

1. Robert Nemiroff discusses the origins and histories of both the book (published by New American Library, 1970) and the play (published by Samuel French, 1971) in his postscript to the book, pp. 267–71.

2. *Young, Gifted and Black,* p. xviii; hereafter cited in the text.

3. Robert Nemiroff prefers the term "ultimately social," but the whole point of this section is to place Hansberry's work in the classic tradition of the theater.

4. "The Negro Writer and His Roots," p. 5.

5. Robert Nemiroff report, June 1983.

6. Robert Nemiroff interview, Croton-on-Hudson, New York, July 17, 1974.

7. Ibid.

8. Joyce Carol Oates, review of *Black-Eyed Susans: Classic Stories by and about Black Women,* ed. Mary Ellen Washington, *Ms.,* March 1976, pp. 4, 46.

9. Robert Nemiroff interview; reconfirmed by Mamie Hansberry Mitchell.

10. Robert Nemiroff generously supplied this plot summary (report, June 1983).

11. Robert Nemiroff interview.

12. C. L. R. James, *The Black Jacobins: Toussaint L'Ouverture and the San Domingo Revolution* (New York: Vintage Books, 1963), pp. 1–13.

13. Robert Nemiroff interview, July 17, 1974.

Selected Bibliography

PRIMARY SOURCES

1. Plays

Les Blancs: The Collected Last Plays of Lorraine Hansberry. Edited with critical background by Robert Nemiroff. Introduction by Julius Lester. New York: Random House, 1972. Includes *Les Blancs, The Drinking Gourd,* and *What Use Are Flowers?*

Lorraine Hansberry: The Collected Last Plays (Les Blancs, The Drinking Gourd, What Use Are Flowers?) Edited with critical background by Robert Nemiroff. Introduction by Margaret B. Wilkerson. Foreword and afterword by Julius Lester. New York: New American Library, 1983. This edition restores some sequences cut from the Broadway production of *Les Blancs* and not included in prior editions.

Lorraine Hansberry's "A Raisin in the Sun" and "The Sign in Sidney Brustein's Window." Foreword by John Braine. New York: New American Library, 1966. Includes Robert Nemiroff's "The 101 'Final' Performances of *Sidney Brustein.*" This edition restores a scene and dialogue cut from the Broadway production of *Raisin* and not included in most editions.

A Raisin in the Sun. New York: New American Library, 1961.

To Be Young, Gifted and Black. Adapted by Robert Nemiroff. Acting edition. New York: Samuel French, 1971. The stageplay.

2. Nonfiction—Books

The Movement: Documentary of a Struggle for Equality. Text by Lorraine Hansberry. Photography by Student Nonviolent Co-ordinating Committee. New York: Simon & Schuster, 1964. Reprinted as *A Matter of Colour: Documentary of Struggle for Equality.* London: Penguin Books, 1965.

To Be Young, Gifted and Black: An Informal Autobiography. Adapted with foreword by Robert Nemiroff. Introduction by James Baldwin. New York: New American Library, 1970.

3. Nonfiction—Articles and Speeches

This section was prepared by Robert Nemiroff in 1983.

"An Author's Reflections: Willy Loman, Walter Younger, and He Who Must

Live." *Village Voice,* August 12, 1959, pp. 7–8. Reprinted in *The Village Voice Reader,* edited by Daniel Wolf and Edwin Fancher (New York: Doubleday, 1962); and in *Women in Theatre: Compassion and Hope,* edited by Karen Malpede (New York: Drama Book Publishers, 1983).

"The Black Revolution and the White Backlash." In *Black Protest: History, Documents and Analyses, 1619 to the Present.* Edited by Joanne Grant. New York: Fawcett World Library, 1968, pp. 442–48. Town Hall forum with Ossie Davis, Lorraine Hansberry, Leroi Jones, John O. Killens, Paule Marshall, James Wechsler et al.

"A Challenge to Artists." *Freedomways* 3 (Winter 1963):33–35. Reprinted in *Harlem, USA,* edited by John Henrik Clarke (New York: Macmillan/Collier Books, 1971), pp. 129–35; and in *The Voice of Black America: Major Speeches by Negroes in the U.S. 1797–1971,* edited by Philip S. Foner (New York: Simon & Schuster, 1972), pp. 954–59.

"Congolese Patriot." *New York Times Magazine,* March 26, 1961, p. 4. Letter to the Editor.

"Images and Essences: 1961 Dialogue with an Uncolored Egghead Containing Wholesome Intentions and Some Sass." *Urbanite* May 1961, pp. 10–11, 36.

"The Legacy of W. E. B. Du Bois." *Freedomways* 5 (Winter 1965):19–20. Reprinted in *Black Titan: W. E. B. Du Bois: an Anthology,* edited by the editors of *Freedomways* (Boston: Beacon Press, 1970).

"Letters from Readers: 'My Negro Problem'—11." *Commentary,* May 1963, pp. 430–31.

"A Letter from Lorraine Hansberry on *Porgy and Bess.*" *Theater,* August 1959, p. 10.

"Letter to the Editor." *Negro Digest,* September 1962, p. 98.

"Mailbag: 'O'Casey—Hansberry.'" *New York Times,* June 28, 1959, sec. 2, pt. 1, p. x3.

"Me Tink Me Hear Sounds in De Night." *Theatre Arts,* October 1960, pp. 9–11, 69–70. Reprinted as "The Negro in the American Theater" in *American Playwrights on Drama,* edited by Horst Frenz (New York: Hill & Wang, 1965); and (New York: Drama Book Specialists, 1981), pp. 160–67.

"Miss Hansberry on 'Backlash.'" *Village Voice,* July 23, 1964, pp. 10, 16.

"The Negro in American Culture." in *The New Negro,* edited by Matthew H. Ahmann. Notre Dame: Fides Publishers, 1961, pp. 109–45; and in *The Black American Writer,* Vol. 1, Fiction, edited by C. W. E. Bigsby. Deland, Fla.: Everett/Edwards, 1969, pp. 79–108. Reprint. Baltimore: Penguin Books, 1971, pp. 78–108. Symposium of James Baldwin, Emile Capouya, Nat Hentoff, Lorraine Hansberry, Langston Hughes, Alfred Kazin, WBAI–FM, N.Y.C., January 1, 1961.

"The Negro Writer and His Roots: Towards a New Romanticism." *Black Scholar,* March–April 1981, pp. 2–12. Closing address to the First Conference of Negro Writers, N.Y.C., February 28–March 1, 1959.

"On Arthur Miller, Marilyn Monroe, and 'Guilt.'" In *Women in Theatre: Compassion & Hope,* edited by Karen Malpede. New York: Drama Book Publishers, 1983, pp. 173–76. Also contains "On Strindberg and Sexism."

"On Summer." *Playbill,* June 27, 1960, pp. 3, 25–27. Reprinted in *Short Essays,* edited by Gerald Levin (New York: Harcourt Brace Jovanovich, 1977), pp. 52–56; and in *Journeys: Findings,* edited by Richard J. Smith and Max F. Schulz (New York: Harcourt Brace Jovanovich, 1982), pp. 388–94.

"Original Prospectus for the John Brown Memorial Theatre of Harlem." *Black Scholar,* July–August 1979, pp. 14–15.

"Playwriting: Creative Constructiveness." *Annals of Psychotherapy* (Monograph 8, *The Creative Use of the Unconscious by the Artist and by the Psychotherapist*) 5, no. 1 (1964):13–17. Address (abridged) to Eighth Annual Conference of the American Academy of Psychotherapists, October 5–6, 1963.

"Quo Vadis." *Mademoiselle,* January 1960, p. 34.

"The Scars of the Ghetto," *Monthly Review,* February 1965, pp. 588–91.

"The Shakespearean Experience." *Show,* February 1964, pp. 80–81, 102.

"Stanley Gleason and the Lights That Must Not Die." *New York Times,* January 17, 1960, sec. 10 (Urban League Supplement), pp. 11–14.

"This Complex of Womanhood." *Ebony,* August 1960, p. 40. Reprint. September 1963, p. 88.

"Thoughts on Genet, Mailer and the New Paternalism." *Village Voice,* June 1, 1961, pp. 10, 15.

"Village Intellect Revealed." *New York Times,* October 31, 1964, sec. 2, pp. 1, 3.

"We Are Of the Same Streets. . . ." *Freedomways* 20 (3d Quarter 1980):197–99.

4. Recordings

Lorraine Hansberry In Her Own Words. Los Angeles: Pacifica Tape Library, BB4497.01 (part 1, 3 casettes) and BB5348.02 (part 2, 3 cassettes). Two-part, 7-hour radio tribute by sixty-one leading theater artists performing from Hansberry's published and unpublished works. With Anne Bancroft, Lauren Bacall, Bette Davis, Colleen Dewhurst, Melvyn Douglas, Louis Gossett, Julie Harris, James Earl Jones, Angela Lansbury, Geraldine Page, Sidney Poitier, Cicely Tyson et al, and Hansberry's own recorded speeches and interviews. Narrated by Ossie Davis and Harold Scott. Script and direction by Robert Nemiroff. Produced by Ted Rubin. Broadcast WBAI–FM, New York, January 22 and February 9, 1967.

Lorraine Hansberry Speaks Out: Art and the Black Revolution. New York: Caedmon Records, TC1352, 1972. Interview by Mike Wallace, excerpts from speeches and interviews. Selected and edited with liner notes by Robert Nemiroff.

A Raisin in the Sun. New York; Caedmon, TRS355 (3 records), 1972. Cast album. With Ossie Davis, Ruby Dee, Claudia McNeil, Diana Sands. Directed by Lloyd Richards.

To Be Young, Gifted and Black. New York: Caedmon, TRS342 (3 records), 1971.

Cast album. With James Earl Jones, Barbara Baxley, Claudia McNeil et al. Directed by Gigi Cascio and Robert Nemiroff.

5. Public Interviews

Interview with Patricia Marx. Unpublished. WNYC, New York City, March 30, 1961.
Interview with Studs Terkel. Chicago, Illinois, May 2, 1959. Abridged version in *WMFT Chicago Fine Arts Guide,* April, 1961, pp. 8–14.

6. Unpublished Material

"Memoirs." Undated. About family and childhood.
"The New Paternalists." 1961. Expansion of "Thoughts on Genet, Mailer and the New Paternalism."
"The Origins of Character." Draft and notes for address to American Academy of Psychotherpists, October 5, 1963. Abridged version published as "Playwrighting: Creative Constructiveness."
A Raisin in the Sun. 1959. Original screenplay.

7. Uncollected Material

Articles from *Freedom* magazine, 1951–1955. Housed in Schomburg Center for Research in Black Culture, New York Public Library, 515 Lenox Avenue.

8. Films

The Black Experience in the Creation of Drama. Documentary film. Written and produced by Ralph J. Tangney. Narrated by Lorraine Hansberry and Claudia McNeil. Princeton: Films for the Humanities, FFH-128 (35 min., 16mm. color), 1976. A skillful blending of materials about Hansberry's life and works, with scenes from the plays enacted by Sidney Poitier, Ruby Dee, Diana Sands, and Roy Scheider.
A Raisin in the Sun. Written by Lorraine Hansberry. Directed by Daniel Petrie. Columbia Pictures (128 minutes, 16mm.), 1961. Cast includes Louis Gossett, Diana Sands, Sidney Poitier, Claudia McNeil, and Ruby Dee. A flawed film despite good performances by Poitier and McNeil. The timeliness of the topic probably impressed the Cannes Judges.
To Be Young, Gifted and Black. Directed by Michael A. Schultz. Produced by Robert M. Fresco. WNET, Educational Broadcasting Corporation, 1972. Distributed by Indiana University AV Center, Bloomington (90 minutes, 16 mm. color), RSC–791. Deserving of its popularity on public television, this episodic film is exceptionally well acted. Film based on the book and stageplay. With Ruby Dee, Roy Scheider, Blythe Danner, Al Freeman Jr., Barbara Barrie, Claudia McNeil.

SECONDARY SOURCES

1. Articles and Parts of Books
Atkinson, Brooks. "Of Plays and Novels." *Saturday Review,* December 31, 1966, pp. 26–27. Unequivocally praises *A Raisin in the Sun*; deems Hansberry a "genuine dramatist" of "talent, originality, and vitality"; mixed review of *Brustein.*
Barnes, Clive. Review of *Les Blancs. New York Times,* November 16, 1970, p. 48. Generally enthusiastic about black drama, Barnes pans the play for its shallowness of confrontation, simplistic arguments, and "using Africa as an allegory for America"—hence his questioning of Hansberry's and Nemiroff's knowledge of Africa. Noteworthy because Barnes seems to have wanted to like the play.
Bigsby, C. W. E. *Confrontation and Commitment: A Study of Contemporary American Drama 1959–1966.* London: MacGibbon & Kea, 1967, pp. 156–73 and passim. Reprint. Columbia, Mo.: University of Missouri Press, 1969. Solid analysis of themes, techniques, and irony in *Raisin.* Sees Hansberry as proponent of integration, idealism, and compassion. Considers Asegai as Hansberry's mouthpiece.
Bontemps, Arna. "The New Black Renaissance." *Negro Digest,* November 1961, pp. 52–54. This distinguished Harlem Renaissance writer sees Hansberry as one of the more promising young black writers.
Brown, Lloyd W. "Lorraine Hansberry as Ironist: A Reappraisal of *A Raisin in the Sun.*" *Journal of Black Studies,* March 1974, pp. 237–47. This slightly obtuse article argues that *A Raisin in the Sun* is replete with rich ironies and skillfully fuses technique with "social, or racial significance." Derides Cruse for his "soap opera" comment, Bigsby for unintentional condescension, and Jordan Y. Miller for his "art for art's sake" credo.
Clurman, Harold. Review of *Les Blancs. Nation,* November 30, 1970, pp. 572–73. Positive, though brief review. Says "James Earl Jones . . . is good enough in himself to make the play worth seeing."
———. Review of *Les Blancs,* which Clurman thinks more "mature" than *Raisin.*
Cruse, Harold. "Lorraine Hansberry." In *The Crisis of the Negro Intellectual.* New York: William Morrow, 1967. This chapter, coupled with other references in the book, accuses Lorraine Hansberry of imposing white middle-class values on the black experience. Also derides *Freedom* circle for mindless flirtations with communism and ambivalence on integration/nationalism question. Cruse is not the "enemy" (Julius Lester's term) of Robeson or Hansberry. This lively, intelligent study seeks to keep black (and indirectly white) intellectuals "honest."
Gilman, Richard. Review of *The Sign in Sidney Brustein's Window. Newsweek,* October 26, 1964, pp. 101–2. Gilman, typical of those unsympathetic to the play, writes that Hansberry "hates homosexuals, liberals, abstract artists,

nonrealistic playwrights, white people unwilling to commit suicide," Camus, Sartre, Golding, and "especially, poor, plundered Edward Albee."

Hammel, Faye. "A Playwright, A Promise." *Cue,* February 28, 1959, pp. 20, 43. This lucid, balanced article treats Hansberry's complexities as a black dramatist and a social playwright (compared to Irishmen O'Casey, Shaw, and Joyce). It is valuable for first published references to *Dark of the Moon* and Hansberry's unfinished works (1953–59).

Hentoff, Nat. "They Fought—They Fought." *New York Times,* May 25, 1969, sec. 2, pp. 1, 18. Positive review of *Young, Gifted and Black* with numerous excerpts from the play.

Issacs, Harold. "Five Writers and their African Ancestors, Part II." *Phylon* 21 (Winter 1960): 317–36. Issacs is the first writer to appreciate the importance of the African theme in *A Raisin in the Sun,* seeing the African references as humorous, relaxing interludes. Draws interesting comparisons between the fathers of Hansberry and Hughes, comments on her integrationist and nationalistic beliefs, and mentions that she only heard of Marcus Garvey in 1950.

Kerr, Walter. "Vivid, Stinging, Alive." Review of *Les Blancs. New York Times,* November 29, 1970, sec. 2, p. 3. Considers the play "genuine theatrical work" and "admirably wrought." Performances are "immaculate"—especially James Earl Jones.

Lerner, Max. The Limbo Plays." *New York Post,* November 2, 1964, p. 53. *Brustein* is a "limbo play," full of fine writing and memorable characters, but Hansberry "has not broken through with that touch of finality. . . ."

Lewis, Emory. *Stages: The Fifty-Year Childhood of the American Theatre.* Englewood Cliffs, N.J.: Prentice-Hall, 1969. pp, xii, 150, 155–57. This judicious discussion accurately hails *Raisin* as a Broadway "landmark" with "honestly etched black people." *Brustein* is "flawed" with an "unfinished, wandering" script, but is still a key play for its realistic portrayal of cosmopolitan intellectuals.

"Lorraine Hansberry." *Current Biography.* New York: H. W. Wilson, 1959, pp. 165–67. Solid article, which draws heavily from *Cue* and *New Yorker* articles. Gives concise account of tryouts and subsequent success of *A Raisin in the Sun.* Does not clarify confusing grammar-school attendance and mistakenly says she studied art at Roosevelt University, where she studied German.

Lorraine Hansberry: Art of Thunder, Vision of Light. Edited by Jean Garey Bond. *Freedomways* 19 (4th Quarter, 1979). A retrospective survey by twenty-one writers, playwrights, and scholars, including James Baldwin, Lonne Elder III, Nikki Giovanni, Alex Haley, John O. Killens, Adrienne Rich, Douglas Turner Ward, Margaret B. Wilderson. The 421-item bibliography cites references to such *Freedomways* authors as Ossie Davis, Arthur France, and David E. Ness; dissertations and theses, including those of David E. Ness and E. R. Zietlow; *Crisis* essays by Loyle Hairston and Loftin Mitchell; numerous *Village Voice* and *New York Amsterdam News* articles; parts of book by such writers as Doris Abramson, Loften Mitchell, Jerry Tallmer, and Darwin T. Turner.

"Lorraine Hansberry Left Funds to Rights Cause." *New York Times,* January 29, 1965. An account of her will.

"Miss Hansberry Divorced 10 Months Before Death." *New York Times,* February 5, 1965, p. 36. A valuable report that lacks details.

"People Are Talking About. . . ." *Vogue,* July 1959, pp. 78–79. Short article detailing Lorraine Hansberry's financial success that is primarily important as evidence of her recognition by *Vogue.*

Pittman, Jack. "Lorraine Hansberry Deplores Porgy." *Variety,* May 27, 1959, p. 16. News story about Hansberry's appearance on a Chicago radio program with Otto Preminger, director of *Porgy and Bess* and other distinguished films. She said that stereotypes constitute "bad art" and that Uncle Tom is "the most offensive character in American literature." Preminger called her "a minority of one."

Rich, Frank. "Theater: 'Raisin in the Sun,' Anniversary in Chicago." *New York Times,* October 5, 1983, p. C24. A reevaluation of *Raisin in the Sun,* "a work that portrayed a black family with greater realism and complexity than had ever been previously seen on an American stage," on the twenty-fifth anniversary of its original production.

Robinson, Layhmond. "Robert Kennedy Consults Negroes Here about North." *New York Times,* May 25, 1963, pp. 1, 8. News story about meeting of Hansberry, Baldwin, Lena Horne, nine other blacks, and a few whites with Attorney General Robert Kennedy to discuss civil rights in North and South. (This New York City meeting is covered more fully in Horne's autobiography.) No black leaders of NAACP or SCLC were present.

Scheader, Catherine. *They Found a Way: Lorraine Hansberry.* Chicago: Children's Press, 1978. Juvenile biography. Scheader includes interview material from Mamie Hansberry Mitchell and Robert Nemiroff as well as fairly inaccessible artwork by Lorraine Hansberry. Book lacks, however, an exact grasp of age level of readers. Valuable as first book on Lorraine Hansberry.

Schiff, Ellen. *From Stereotype to Metaphor: The Jew in Contemporary Drama.* Albany: State University of New York Press, 1982, pp. 155–60 and passim. Admires Hansberry's nonstereotypical portrait of Sidney Brustein—"a Jew who is neither wicked, nor crafty, nor even a good businessman."

"600 Attended Hansberry Rites: Paul Robeson Delivers Eulogy." *New York Times,* January 17, 1965, p. 88. Robert Nemiroff finds numerous flaws in this article. He says that Robeson did *not* deliver the eulogy. It does not cite all six speakers, including Leo Nemiroff and Shelley Winters. It does reflect the mood of the service.

"Talk of the Town." *New Yorker,* May 9, 1959, pp. 33–35. Very important source of chronological biographical material. Contains Hansberry's comments on her father's death, "brick through the window" incident, three grade schools she attended, as well as *bons mots* about housework and banana cream pie.

Walker, Alice. "One Child of One's Own." *Ms.*, August 1979, pp. 47–50, 72–
  75. Sidelights on Lorraine Hansberry, Judy Chicago, and white women who
  write about black women. Basic topic, however, is link between childbirth
  and creativity.

2. Interviews

Mitchell, Mamie Hansberry. Sister of Lorraine Hansberry. Marina del Rey, Cal-
  if.: December 30, 1975; January 2, 1976.
Nemiroff, Robert. Former husband and literary executor of Lorraine Hansberry.
  Croton-on-Hudson, N.Y.: June 15, 1972; September 30, 1972. Washing-
  ton, D.C.: June 2, 1973. Croton-on-Hudson, N.Y.: August 4, 1973. New
  York, N.Y.: July 17, 1974; December 27, 1974; December 28, 1976. Cro-
  ton-on-Hudson, N.Y.: June 13, 14, and 15, 1978.
Robeson, Paul, Jr. Son of Paul Robeson. Telephone interview. New York, N.Y.:
  July 3, 1979.

Index